4x 4/13 LY 8/10

Dog Tags Of Courage

Combat Intfantrymen And War Dog Heroes In Vietnam

JOHN C. BURNAM,
MSG (USA RET.)

LOST
COAST
PRESS

Dog Tags of Courage
Combat Infantrymen and War Dog Heroes in Vietnam
Copyright ©2006 by John C. Burnam

Lost Coast Press
155 Cypress Street
Fort Bragg, CA 95437
(800) 773-7782
www.cypresshouse.com

Cover design: Chuck Hathaway/Mendocino Graphics
Book design: Michael Brechner/Cypress House

   Publisher's Cataloging-in Publication Data
Burnam, John C.
   Dog tags of courage : combat infantrymen and war dog heroes in Vietnam / John Burnam. -- 2nd ed. -- Fort Bragg, CA : Lost Coast Press, 2006.
      p. ; cm.
First ed. published in 2000.
   ISBN: 1-882897-88-9
   ISBN-13: 978-1-882897-88-9
   1. Vietnamese Conflict, 1961-1975--United States.
2. Vietnamese Conflict, 1961-1975--Personal narratives, American.
3. Dogs--War use--United States. 4. Burnam, John C. I. Title.
 DS558 .B86 2006
 959.704/3373--dc22 0510   2005931260

Dog Tags of Courage has been revised from its original edition, *Dog Tags of Courage: The Turmoil of War and the Rewards of Companionship* (Lost Coast Press, 2000). New material and new photographs have been added.

Printed in the United States

9 8 7 6 5 4 3 2 1

DEDICATION

To my daughter, Jennifer, and granddaughter, Ariana Vera Barger-Burnam; I document the story of my military service in hopes of giving them a clearer understanding of what I did during the Vietnam War.

Also, I dedicate my story to the exceptionally brave and loyal war dogs and their handlers, of all wars; to all the men and women who lost their lives while serving America during wartime; and to those who were wounded in action but never gave up, because they found the strength and courage to carry on.

Let us never forget our American servicemen still missing in action (MIAs) and our prisoners of war (POWs) of all wars.

FOREWORD

Over the course of our nation's military history, those who have bravely served in battle have been recognized and remembered for their loyalty and sacrifice. In that tradition, one breed of hero has been too often overlooked. Dog Tags of Courage tells the little-known story of some 4,000 soldier dogs who courageously served in the Vietnam Conflict. Because of their loyalty and dedication to the American soldiers who were their handlers, historians believe these trained dogs prevented more than 10,000 American casualties in Vietnam.

Continuing the legacy of war dogs who served our nation's military during WWI, WWII, and the Korean War, the dogs who served in the jungles of Vietnam used their keen sense of smell, hearing, and sight to detect dangers that threatened American lives. The intelligence and adaptability of German shepherds made them ideally qualified to serve as sentry dogs that defended the perimeters of military bases, and scout dogs that led human patrols and searched out enemy traps and ambushes. The acute sense of smell of Labrador retrievers allowed them to excel in their service as tracker dogs, pursuing fleeing ambushers and locating lost soldiers and downed pilots.

As both war dogs and their handlers risked their lives in combat, their bond solidified and grew into a relationship of enduring love and shared loyalty to their mission. John Burnam's captivating account of his experiences as a nineteen-year-old combat infantryman who served as rifleman with the 1stAir Cavalry Division and as scout-dog handler with the 44th Scout Dog Platoon is a testament to the heroism of the war-dog teams who served in Vietnam.

These dog handlers suffered not only the tragedies of warfare, but also the tragedy of losing their K-9 partners when they were ordered to abandon the phenomenal animals, which America classified as "expendable" equipment when they pulled out of Vietnam.

Those of us who have not served in war and who have not been on the frontlines cannot imagine how important the dog handlers and their K-9 comrades were in helping to protect the American soldier. Since meeting John Burnam, however, and agreeing to help dog handlers create a National War Dog Team Memorial in Washington, D.C., I have gained a deep and sincere appreciation for the war-dog team and a compassionate understanding for the dog handler who had to give up his buddy. This book is a thoughtful depiction of the powerful bond of soldier-canine companionship, and a convincing case for the need to recognize the heroic legacy of the war-dog team.

— *United States Congressman Walter B. Jones,*
North Carolina

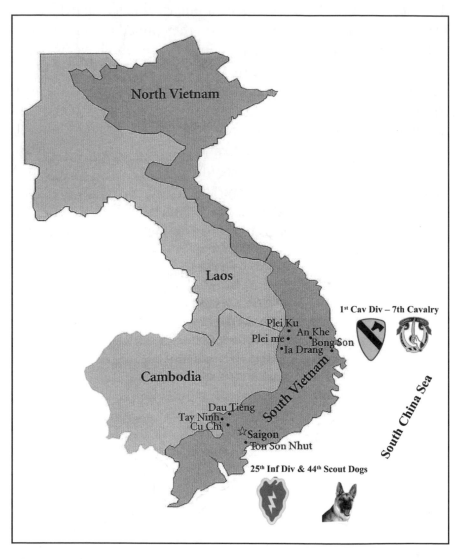

This map depicts the primary locations from 1966–1968, the author, John Burnam, performed combat missions during the Vietnam War as an Infantryman with the 1st Battalion, 7th Cavalry, 1st Cavalry Division, and German Shepherd Scout Dog Handler with the 44th Scout Dog Platoon, 25th Infantry Division.

PREFACE

I am proud to have served America in South Vietnam from March 1966 to March 1968. I was U.S. Army infantry paratrooper assigned to the legendary 7th Cavalry (Gary Owen!), 1st Cavalry Division, and a scout-dog handler with the 44th Scout Dog Platoon, 25th Infantry Division.

In the course of our nation's military history, more than 100,000 dogs of many different breeds faithfully served America during WWI, WWII, Korea, Vietnam, and the Gulf War.

Since the September 11, 2001 terrorist attack on America, the U.S. Department of Defense Military Working Dog Center at Lackland Air Force Base, San Antonio, Texas, is training and deploying more working dog teams in the war on terrorism in Afghanistan, Iraq, and other peacekeeping missions around the globe.

American families have always been there, donating thousands of their loving young dogs to help save American lives in warfare in distant lands. Numerous dogs have been rescued from the death rows of animal shelters throughout the nation and given a chance to live and work again.

At the end of WWII, the surviving war dogs were returned to U.S. soil, hailed as America's canine heroes, and given military service medals, parades, and official discharge certificates. Many were repatriated with the families that donated them, while others were released in the custody of their handlers to live out the rest of their lives in peace.

That was not the case in South Vietnam, however, where all war dogs (approximately 4,000) were classified as expendable military equipment for the duration of the war. That number is very small when compared to the 3½ million American men and women who rotated in and out of Vietnam during the course of that war.

Many war dogs served and survived more than one handler during their brief lives in Vietnam. The American base camps they knew as home had war-dog cemeteries for their fallen comrades, maintained as sacred ground by the surviving war-dog handlers.

BY 1973, when the Vietnam War had ended, and all the American ground troops had abandoned their base camps and withdraw from Vietnam, not one surviving war-dog hero was officially discharged and sent home to the family it once knew, or released to the handler it loved and protected. Instead, all of the surviving dogs (several thousand) were crated and shipped to U.S. military quarantine camps. A few hundred lucky dogs made it out alive and were reassigned to other U.S. military installations in various parts of the world.

Despite the handlers' and veterinarians' pleas to ship the remaining several thousand dogs home, they were instead either given to the South Vietnamese Army as a good-will gesture, or were euthanized by the U.S. military in its haste to evacuate the country. I can only imagine what went on in the minds of those dogs, separated from their handlers and thrust into the hands of an army that spoke a foreign language, or what they must have thought during those final moments before being put to sleep. No one played "Taps"; there was no twenty-one-gun salute or special burial ceremony, and no rows of white crosses etched with their names marked their final resting place.

Vietnam remains the only war in which America has treated its war-dog heroes with such horrifying finality.

United States war dogs have a long, albeit mostly unknown, legacy of heroism and sacrifice on thousands of fields of battle, named and unnamed, around the world. They saved the lives of innumerable Americans and noncombatants, and protected countless billions of dollars' worth of military equipment, structures, and supplies: aircraft and airfields, hospitals, base camps, motor pools of wheeled and tracked vehicles, ammunition dumps, fuel dumps, food and medical supplies, water-storage facilities, strategic communication sites, naval supply vessels, and depots.

America's war dogs are not mascots; they are intelligent, highly trained, and proficient four-footed soldiers, marines, airmen, sailors, and guardians of our coasts. These animals work in every conceivable condition of climate and terrain, successfully performing such dangerous jobs as scout, sentry, tracker, mine & booby-trap detection, trap, water patrol, search & rescue, bomb detection, and drug detection.

They have names like Stubby, Chips, Nemo, Prince, Rolf, Baron, Clipper, Rip, Caesar, Duke, Lucky, Kobuc, Smokey, Flop, Erich, Thea, Rebel, Opal, Tiger, Kelly, Renee, Alex, London, Troubles, Sergeant, Shadow, Paper, Stormy, and Dutch, and they work for food and water and the love of their human companions. In return, their loyalty is unconditional—they never give up on the battlefield and don't know the meaning of the word "retreat."

There is no way the dogs could fully perform their jobs without the professional and healthcare services provided by the military veterinarians and vet technicians. These experts offer the dogs respect, patience, understanding, and loving healthcare. They manage their diets, medicate their diseases, dress their cuts and bruises, mend their combat wounds, and nurse them to health. They attend to the dogs' emotional stress as well, and give them complete physical evaluations every six months. Now that's what I call excellent doggone healthcare at its finest!

In the pages that follow, I describe my experiences in South Vietnam as best I could, not from a strategic command or politically motivated perspective, but from an infantryman's point of view—an ant's-eye view.

My story is as historically accurate as I could make it, and is based on my own memory, tactical military maps and documents, war citations, photographs, and interviews with the men I was privileged to serve with in the 7th Cavalry and 44th Scout Dog Platoon.

Soldiers wear dog tags for identification to make sure they are accounted for on the battlefield and remembered and honored for their service and sacrifice. It is my goal that *Dog Tags of Courage* will help to secure a place in U.S. military canine history for the Vietnam war dogs who earned their dog tags through wholehearted loyalty, bravery, and sacrifice in the face of war.

All this and more is why I will never give up on a long-overdue National War Dog Team Memorial to honor all dogs and handlers of all wars—past, present, and future.

As a leading free-world nation, America owes its war dogs this memorial, mandated by the U.S. Congress and erected in the nation's capital, Washington, D.C., so the entire world can see and know that they are *not* America's forgotten heroes.

— John C. Burnam, MSG, U.S. Army (RET.)

Acknowledgments

I could not have written this book without the support, information, photographs, advice, and friendship many people have given me. My deepest gratitude goes to Mark Hart and his family for locating my Vietnam War buddy, Kenneth L. Mook, after twenty-five years, and to Kenny Mook, whose reunion with me on Memorial Day in 1991 inspired this book.

Many thanks to Ollie Whetstone, Mike "Mac" McClellan and Dan Barnett, former German shepherd scout-dog handlers with the 44th Scout Dog Platoon; to Kenneth L. Mook, Bob Dunn, Van Wilson, Marlin Dorman, Billy Smith, Donald Clostio, John Engel, and Dennis Blessing of the 2nd Platoon, Company B, 1st Battalion, 7th Cavalry, 1st Cavalry Division. The friendship, insight, and advice of these veterans strengthened my determination to see this project through.

A salute to U.S. Congressman Walter B. Jones of North Carolina for championing the efforts of a group of Vietnam veteran war-dog handlers by submitting a congressional bill to the U.S. House of Representatives and the U.S. Senate to mandate a National War Dog Team Memorial in Washington, D.C.

Special thanks to my editor, Joe Shaw, who helped me become a better writer.

Contents

Book cover: original artwork titled "Scout Dog–On Point" featuring Sgt. John C. Burnam and Clipper, 44th Scout Dog Platoon, Republic of South Vietnam (1967) by Terry Waldron. Artwork is based on authentic photos (www.terryjamesart.com).
Original painting–Author collection

Chapter One

CAMP ALPHA

It was March 1966, a few days before my nineteenth birthday. I had five months of U.S. Army service under my belt, all of it spent training to be an infantryman. I was now aboard a commercial jetliner for the long trip from San Francisco to South Vietnam to fight in a war I knew nothing about.

American soldiers took up every seat on the plane. Sleeping was difficult, so I catnapped most of the way. Finally, the pilot announced our arrival at Tan Son Nhut airport near Saigon. It was daylight outside as I strained my neck and eyes to peer through the small porthole for my first glimpse of the foreign land below. I heaved a sigh of relief at the familiar sound of screeching rubber on pavement. The long ride was over.

Armed military policemen (MPs) boarded the plane and ushered us off into awaiting military buses with bars and thick wire mesh replacing glass windows. For the first time, I saw a beautiful German shepherd sentry dog and his handler in combat gear standing a short distance from the aircraft. I thought, *Wow! I didn't know they had dogs over here.* Little did I know that this quick sighting of a Vietnam war dog was a glimpse into my future.

The driver told us that the wire mesh over the windows was to protect us from grenades that might be hurled at the bus while we traveled through the crowded city of Saigon. I smelled the hot, sticky air with its peculiar odor of stale fish. Raised in the Denver suburb of Littleton, Colorado, I'd never experienced a climate or permeating smell like this. Where I came from the air was dry, fresh, and clear, the land a mile above sea level.

As the bus slowly maneuvered through the crowded streets, I stared at the foreign cars, bicycle riders, and pedestrians. Most of the people wore black or white pajamas, straw hats, and flip-flop sandals. During the ride I didn't hear any shooting, witness any explosions, or see any buildings on fire. In fact, I didn't see anything in Saigon but Vietnamese civilians and soldiers going about their business in peace.

Where is the war? I thought.

The bus finally stopped at the front gate where a sign read CAMP ALPHA. It was a U.S. Army replacement center. Armed MPs quickly herded us into a large wooden building to be in-processed. After handing over our assignment orders, personnel files, finance, and medical records, we were moved into another part of the building. No one talked much. I felt like a robot following orders: "Stop! Wait here! Follow me! That's far enough!"

The camp commander arrived wearing a clean, starched khaki uniform with polished brass, and shined shoes, the silver leaves on his collar designating the rank of a lieutenant colonel (LTC). He greeted our group with a smile and gave a "Welcome to Vietnam" orientation. He briefed us on the Vietnamese culture and why we were sent to help stop the spread of communism from North to South Vietnam. Our military presence was stated as no more than a "police action," because the United States had not declared war on North Vietnam.

I whispered to the soldier next to me, "What the hell's the difference between a *declared war* and a *police action* if both sides are killing each other?" Getting no response, I shut up and continued to listen. Fresh out of high school, with only a few months of military service and training, I wasn't sure what to expect next.

Camp Alpha consisted of long rows of tin-roofed wooden buildings with screens for windows. It reminded me of the infantry training centers I had stayed in at Fort Leonardwood, Missouri; Fort Ord, California; and Fort Benning, Georgia. I was housed in a numbered wooden building with a concrete-slab floor and several rows of metal bunk beds lining the walls. Each building accommodated about fifty men and had electric lights but no air conditioning. I doubted I would ever adjust to Vietnam's heat, humidity, or the persistent smell of stale fish.

John Burnam – Littleton High School Graduation Picture, Littleton, Colorado – 1965. (Author collection)

John Burnam – U.S. Army Basic Training, Company A, 3rd Batallion, 3rd Brigade, Fort Leonardwood, Missouri – 1965. (Author collection)

Like me, most of the replacements were bewildered teenagers, fresh out of training, with a quarter inch of hair on their heads, wearing new fatigue uniforms and army-issue baseball hats. A tall barbed-wire fence surrounded the camp, and armed guards were stationed in towers. I felt like I was living in a small prison.

Camp Alpha had a small store where one could buy soft drinks, candy, cigarettes, toothpaste, and other sundries. A small service club featured live music sung by a Vietnamese rock-and-roll band. I thought it was hilarious that the musicians couldn't speak English and butchered the words to Rolling Stones and Beatles songs. The club was always crowded, sticky-hot, and filled with cigarette smoke. There was nowhere else to unwind except a small chapel with posted notices for religious services.

Being a gregarious person by nature, I usually started conversations by asking a soldier where he was from or what his job or MOS (military occupational specialty) was. I met guys from almost every state in the Union. There were truck drivers, medics, helicopter and vehicle mechanics, personnel and supply clerks, military police, cooks, and construction engineers. Most of them had trained for jobs other than the infantry.

During my stay at Camp Alpha, I met Kenny Mook, a twenty-one-year-old draftee from the farmlands of northern Pennsylvania. I had no idea at the time that we would soon be fighting for our lives in a place called Bong Son, an experience that would bond us for life.

Both Kenny and I were in excellent health and physical condition. Before joining the army, I had played varsity football and baseball at Littleton High School. I had also placed first in several conference and invitational wrestling tournaments in the 122-pound class. Kenny wasn't an athlete, but he was strong from farming in northern Pennsylvania.

We felt a kind of chemistry between us and quickly became friends. And we were both infantrymen, destined to fight in the jungle, defend a base camp, and protect supply roads, airfields, motor pools, and hospitals. Although our mission was a little scary, we liked to talk about how important our jobs were. Kenny was what paratroopers call a *leg*—a nickname for an infantryman who was not trained as a paratrooper to jump out of airplanes at 1200 feet. To become a paratrooper, a soldier had to be a volunteer and pass a three-week training course that was physically and mentally taxing and had a high dropout rate.

I said, "I didn't go to three weeks of jump-school hell to be assigned to an infantry leg unit. I'm sure the army will assign me to an elite paratrooper outfit."

Kenny replied, "The only things that fall out of the sky are bird-shit and fools. Besides, once you land, *you're* a leg too."

Throughout our infantry marksmanship training, Kenny and I had both trained on the M14 rifle. We didn't know what standard-issue M-16 rifles looked like until we saw camp guards carrying them. I asked one of the sergeants who ran the camp if I would be issued one. He looked at me with a smile on his face and said no. He told me Camp Alpha was well protected, and that I'd get an M-16 when I arrived at my combat unit.

As replacements, we were all unarmed and vulnerable if the enemy attacked Camp Alpha. I worried that by the time I was issued a weapon and ammunition during an attack—provided there were enough to go around—I'd be dead. Many frightening thoughts like that ran through my mind while I waited for an assignment to an infantry combat unit.

Less than a week after my arrival, my name was called over the loudspeaker, and I was told to report to the personnel office. Kenny's name was also called. By a stroke of good luck, we were both assigned to the 1st Air Cavalry Division, located in the central highlands about 250 miles northwest of Saigon.

Kenny and I were sick of replacement centers, both stateside and in-country, and we were always happy to leave them. We knew their routine all too well: "Hurry up and wait." I'd been waiting six months to get assigned to an active unit that wasn't a training or replacement center. Now, late March 1966, my training was over, the travel had ended, and replacement centers were about to be history. I relished the prospect of fighting in real combat as an elite paratrooper.

There would be some life-and-death experiences before my adventures with German shepherd war dogs, but now, Kenny and I were at last heading for the mountains of South Vietnam. I wondered how it would feel parachuting out of a plane in a war zone for the first time.

Chapter Two

GARY OWEN

In the early morning light, Kenny and I hauled our duffel bags up the ramp of a C130 military transport plane that quickly filled with troops and supplies. The pilot wasted little time getting airborne. For the first time since arriving in Vietnam, I felt cool air.

It was incredibly noisy riding in that plane, and nearly impossible to carry on a conversation without yelling. The aircraft flew north of Saigon for several hours before the pilot banked left and began his descent. As I peered through the small window, I saw an airstrip and rows and rows of green military tents and equipment below. Camp Radcliff, home of the 1st Cavalry Division, was directly below us. Kenny pointed out a large yellow-and-black 1st Cavalry Division shoulder patch painted on the mountainside above the camp. I thrilled at the thought that we would soon be wearing that patch.

Dense jungle and mountainous terrain surrounded the circular base camp. The small Vietnamese village of An Khe rested near the camp's outer perimeter. Trucks, jeeps, and troops moved along the dirt roads that ran through the camp. Helicopters sat idle in neat rows along the airstrip, which was called "the Golf Course" because it was so enormous. The 1st Cavalry Division, nicknamed "the First Team," had more helicopters than any other division in Vietnam.

From the air, the camp appeared well fortified. The vegetation around its the outer edges was bulldozed, leaving a 360-degree dirt buffer that separated the heavily guarded perimeter from the surrounding jungle and made for clear lanes of fire in all directions. Three or four heavily fortified bunkers were evenly spaced between lookout towers. Strategically positioned artillery pieces and tanks dotted the perimeter.

After the plane landed, we were hustled to the division's personnel and administration building. A clerk collected our individual personnel, finance, and medical records to process us into the division. We had to show our two metal dog tags hanging from chains around our necks. If a soldier were killed, the medic would take one dog tag from the chain, and lodge the other between the dead man's teeth. The first tag went to the unit commander for accountability, and the second to the morgue with the body for identification.

The personnel clerk congratulated us as he handed over a set of orders officially promoting us from private to private first class (PFC). The army's policy at the time was to make such a promotion effective on the soldier's arrival in South Vietnam. That meant a monthly pay increase of at least $50. We also got another $60 per month as combat pay. At the time, I made $300 a month and didn't have to pay taxes. If I were assigned to a paratrooper outfit, I'd get an additional $55 monthly.

An infantry division's organizational structure is layered like a pyramid. At the top is the division commander, a two-star general, who has the ultimate power and authority. The division commander's subordinate commanders, in order of power, are the brigade commander, battalion commander, company commander, and then the platoon leader. These are all command positions occupied by commissioned officers.

There may be three brigades in a division, three battalions in a brigade, and four companies in each battalion. In each company, there may be four platoons made up four squads of enlisted men. There are eleven enlisted men in a squad at full strength. Each squad has two fire teams commanded by a squad leader and two fire-team leaders. A platoon at full strength has a total of forty-four infantrymen.

The enlisted structure is also layered in authority, starting with the division sergeant major, brigade sergeant major, battalion sergeant major, company first sergeant, platoon sergeant, squad leader, fire-team leader, and then the rifleman. Kenny and I were riflemen—peons with no authority.

Dennis Blessing (2nd Platoon) standing in doorway of "Co B 1-7 Orderly Room"—1966 (Photo courtesy of Dennis Blessing)

We were assigned to Company B, 1st Battalion, 7th Cavalry Regiment. General George Armstrong Custer had commanded the 7th Cavalry Regiment in 1876 at the Little Big Horn. Whenever we passed an officer outside the cover of a building, the 7th Cavalry tradition was to say, "Gary Owen" as we saluted. *Gary Owen* was the title of Custer's favorite Irish marching song, which he liked to have the 7th Regiment band play at parades and other festive military functions. I felt a sense of pride that this historical tradition had continued to be observed through the years.

Company B, 7th Cavalry living quarters—1966
(Photo courtesy of James Ertle)

Our new home was a skimpy, old green canvas tent held up by two wooden center poles and wooden tie-down stakes. Several empty canvas cots stood on the packed-dirt floor inside. I couldn't believe that this dark and misty tent would be my home for the next twelve months.

Kenny said, "Well, Johnny, we're finally here."

"Yeah, but I wonder where the hell the platoon is? All I saw when we flew in was mountains and very little civilization."

We're not in Saigon anymore," Kenny said. "We're in a war zone.

The platoon is probably out in the jungle hunting for the enemy."

The dining hall, or "mess hall" as we called it, was a large wooden building not far from our tent. Just outside it were large green canvas bags full of drinking water. We ate from metal trays and sat on picnic tables. Breakfast consisted of powdered eggs, powdered milk, fresh-baked bread, and bitter coffee. Lunch and dinner were nothing to write home about.

After we ate breakfast that morning and were on the way back to our tent, we passed an officer, saluted him, and said, "Gary Owen, sir!"

He returned the salute and replied, "All the way!"

After the officer had passed, Kenny and I looked at each other and chuckled. We thought it was really cool to say, "Gary Owen" instead of "Good morning, sir!"

Kenny and I were introduced to the company supply sergeant, who lived in a tent packed and stacked high with supplies. The supply sergeant told us that he had everything we'd ever need for fighting a war. He issued us backpacks, canteens, ammunition pouches, medical field dressings, a plastic poncho, a nylon poncho liner, a helmet ("steel pot"), a helmet liner, an entrenching tool (field shovel), and a bayonet. He also gave us several division patches like the one we saw on the mountainside when we flew in. The insignia on these cloth patches meant that we were no longer trainees in transit without a unit—we now belonged to a fighting unit.

The supply sergeant told us we'd get weapons, ammunition, grenades, claymores (mines), trip flares, and other goodies after the platoon returned from its mission in the field. He advised us that our new platoon sergeant would decide when we'd be ready to go on S and Ds.

I asked, "What are S and Ds?"

The sergeant smiled and shook his head and said, "Search and destroy missions. That's what we do for a living around here, young trooper!"

Kenny and I wondered what it would be like to meet the other members of the 2nd Platoon, who were due to arrive aboard helicopters within the hour. I was nervous, yet eager to see real combat infantrymen for the first time. *Will the other soldiers accept us?* I wondered. Kenny appeared calm, but his eyes showed that he too was a bit nervous.

The sounds of helicopters filled the air outside the tent. I ran out for a look. Fifteen or twenty ships drifted into view. Fully equipped soldiers clutched their weapons and sat inside the open doors. The door gunners held M-60 machine guns mounted on posts.

Dirt kicked up as the first group of ships touched down about one hundred feet away from us. The wind from the helicopters' rotating blades rippled our fatigues and almost whipped the caps off our heads. Dust swirling all around me, I watched with excitement as the men climbed out and slowly walked in my direction. The door gunners stayed aboard as the empty ships lifted off the road and flew away.

I watched, awestruck, while the men walked past me as if I were invisible. Under their steel helmets, I could see the soldiers' tired faces and eyes. Their dirty fatigues and boots looked as if they hadn't been polished since they were issued. The men carried various types of shoulder weapons, some of which I'd never seen before. They wore backpacks filled with items that I couldn't see. As the men walked by, I noticed that they looked and smelled as if they hadn't taken a bath in a month.

Some of the soldiers entered the tent Kenny lived in. I was too nervous to follow them inside. Finally, I gathered up enough courage, walked in, and sat on my cot like a little kid, silently watching them unpack their gear. Kenny sat on his cot too, quietly observing everyone. It was easy to see that they were happy to be back in base camp.

A short time later, two men walked into the tent and called our names: "PFC Kenneth L. Mook and PFC John C. Burnam."

Kenny and I jumped to our feet and answered, "Here!"

The men approached us, stopped, and looked us over in silence. We remained standing to show respect as we'd been taught during training. The men looked at one another, smiled, and told us to sit down and relax. They were amused at our innocent behavior. One man introduced himself as Sergeant Savage. He was five feet seven inches, about twenty-three years old, huskily built, and had a hardened, darkly tanned face. Sergeant Savage introduced Sergeant Marlin Dorman to us as our new squad leader, then excused himself.

Sergeant Marlin Dorman, 2nd Platoon Squad Leader – 1966 (Photo courtesy of Billy Smith)

Sergeant Dorman smiled and said, "I'm your squad leader. Welcome to the 2nd Platoon and 4th Squad, better known as the 'weapons squad.'"

Sergeant Dorman was a thin twenty-two-year-old, five feet eight inches tall, with bright blue eyes, brown hair, and a deep tan. Even though he hadn't cleaned up yet, Sergeant Dorman had the appearance and presence of a leader who spoke with confidence. He reached into his breast pocket and took out a little green notepad. He asked us for our full names, ranks, ages, service numbers, types of training we'd had, hometowns, next of kin, and the dates we'd arrived in Vietnam. He recorded our answers in his notebook.

Sergeant Dorman explained that a weapons squad had two five-man machine gun teams. Each team had one M-60 machine gun, and consisted of one gunner, an assistant gunner, and three riflemen/ammunition bearers.

He said, "That's an ideal fully manned squad. The problem is that I only have two M-60 machine gunners and one assistant M-60 machine gunner. My squad is critically undermanned. You men are a sight for sore eyes. Forget whatever you were taught in the States about machine gun deployment. Even though my squad is undermanned, it's still the primary firepower of the 2nd platoon. When the shit hits the fan there's nothing better than the M-60. Counting you two, I now have three men on the number-two gun and two men on the number-one gun."

As Sergeant Dorman continued, I gathered that the number-one gun provided firepower to the front of the platoon, and number-two gun provided firepower and security at the rear.

We met number-one M-60 gunner, Specialist Four John Engel, and his assistant gunner, Private Wildman, and number-two M-60 gunner, Specialist Four Bob Dunn. Sergeant Dorman appointed Kenny as Bob's assistant gunner, and I was assigned as Bob's ammo bearer.

Bob Dunn was five feet seven inches tall, weighed about 170 pounds, had blond hair and blue eyes, and wore a crusty mustache. Bob was from New York and spoke in a heavy accent. He had arrived in Vietnam in early January 1966.

I asked Bob where the platoon had been. He said they'd searched the jungle for a week but had made no contact with the gooks.

"You mean the enemy?" I asked.

Bob then translated some new terminology for me. He explained that "VC" meant Vietcong, "NVA" was the North Vietnamese Army, and "PAVN" meant the People's Army of Vietnam. *Gooks, cong, dinks,* and *Charlie* were other terms used to describe the enemy. The NVA, he said, were the toughest of all to fight.

As we started talking about our duties, Bob explained the importance of keeping the M-60 machine gun clean and oiled at all times. Out in the jungle, he told us, the gun got dirty quickly, and rain and humidity caused any part that wasn't oiled to rust and possibly malfunction.

Dunn explained the squad's job: "We get an operations order for a mission. We pack up and leave base camp for a week or so. We hunt and kill some gooks. After that, we come home for a few days to shower, rest, and get some hot food. Then it starts all over again. Believe me, you guys will get your share of the action and then some."

When Bob gave me my first M-16 rifle, I acted like a little kid with a new Christmas toy. Kenny and I test fired our weapons at a safe location on the camp's perimeter. Bob taught us how to take them apart and reassemble them, and showed us where to put the most oil.

My previous training had taught me how to maintain sight alignment, control my breathing, and squeeze the trigger. I was surprised that the M-16 had little or no kick. As with all military rifles and pistols, the M-16 was designed for right-handed people. When the guns are fired, hot brass casings eject to the right and away from the shooter. Because I was left-handed, the hot casings ejected across my face and body. Not a big problem, but on rare occasions, I'd get a hot casing blown down my collar.

During training in the States, Kenny and I had been awarded Expert Rifle badges for consistently scoring hits in the center of targets with M14 rifles. The different qualification levels of marksmanship were, from lowest to highest ranking, Expert, Sharpshooter, and Marksman. The targets, positioned at various ranges, had been both pop-up and stationary. Shooting positions—standing, prone, kneeling—also varied based on target range. Hitting a target dead center was all in the sight alignment, breathing, and trigger squeeze. Kenny had also scored Expert with the M-60 machine gun. Most soldiers qualified as sharpshooter or marksman, but you were very well respected when you qualified as an expert with two types of weapons. This was probably why Kenny got to be Bob's assistant machine gunner.

As we trained in camp, SP4 Dunn gave us some pointers on how to conserve ammunition. He said, "Never switch to full automatic unless there's no other choice. Always carry your own supply of ammunition. The quicker you use it up, the less you'll have when you need it most." The training sessions boosted my self-confidence. As each day passed, Kenny and I felt more like members of the platoon team. We would need this camaraderie, because we'd soon be meeting Charlie face to face for the first time.

Chapter Three

IA DRANG VALLEY

A few days before my first mission, Sergeant Dorman told Kenny and me a story to fill us in on the history of our new platoon. It was about a mission that took place in the middle of November 1965.

The 1st Battalion, 7th Cavalry had gone looking for a fight and flew into the Ia Drang Valley, a remote area in the northern highlands of South Vietnam, at the base of Chu Pong Mountain, close to the Cambodian border. Lieutenant Colonel Harold "Hal" Moore, the battalion commander, had led the battalion into the valley with the 2nd Platoon, making it one of the first on the ground. Immediately, the landing zone, known as LZ XRAY, was saturated with American artillery.

Sergeant Dorman held us spellbound as he recounted the events of that day. "When our platoon landed, we rushed into the woods, our guns firing. Lieutenant Colonel Moore directed our platoon leader to move the 2nd Platoon about a hundred meters and set up a new position. The platoon fanned out and ran forward toward the base of Chu Pong Mountain. We spotted two or three enemy soldiers moving across our front, and the platoon leader ordered us to chase and capture them. We pursued the enemy for fifty meters and ran into 150 NVA soldiers dressed in khaki uniforms and pith helmets, and coming down off the mountain shooting at us.

"These were hard-core troops from North Vietnam, not your ordinary black-pajama, part-time soldier/farmers. When they attacked, we took casualties before we could hit the dirt and return their fire.

We tried to get behind anything that would provide cover, but we were pinned down by heavy fire and cut off from the rest of the company.

"The platoon spread out. We took cover behind clumps of bushes and trees. Communication was nearly impossible above the noise of blazing machine guns, rifle fire, and grenade explosions. Totally outnumbered, we fought for our lives. We were overwhelmed. Many of our men were already wounded or dead. The gooks screamed at the top of their lungs while they came at us shooting. During one of the enemy's human-wave attacks, our platoon leader, Lieutenant Herrick, was badly wounded; he died bravely, fighting alongside his men.

"The weapons squad suffered so many casualties that the squad leader took over one of the M-60s. He fired it until he was overrun and killed. Then the gooks turned our M-60 machine gun on us. We had several more casualties before we took it back. Low on ammunition and grenades, we gathered what we could from our own dead.

"I don't know how we made it after losing the platoon leader, the platoon sergeant, and the squad leaders. Sergeant Savage was the only sergeant left, so he took over the platoon. He got on the radio and found cover behind a log while he called for artillery strikes. We fought on and off, all day and into the night. Sergeant Savage continued to send periodic situation reports over the radio. We received radio reports that the entire battalion was under heavy ground attack by the NVA. Hundreds of enemy soldiers were storming down from the mountain to join the fight. We were too far out for any immediate rescue attempts. Our orders were to hold our ground until help arrived the next day.

"It was very dark that first night, but none of us slept. We kept quiet and tried to comfort the wounded as we waited to be attacked again. During that night, I heard a bugle call coming from the mountain, and then all hell broke loose again. We withstood several attacks and survived until sky troopers from a sister company rescued us on the afternoon of the second day. The 2nd Platoon became known as the "Lost Platoon" because we'd been the only platoon outside the battalion lines of defense.

"The battle raged for a third day. B-52 bombers dropped tons of bombs on Chu Pong Mountain and the surrounding area. When the fighting was over, our battalion had taken heavy casualties; our company had forty men left out of 115. The North Vietnamese Army had lost over a thousand men. At the time, I was a rifleman in the 2nd Squad of the 2nd Platoon. I don't know how I survived. There were bodies all over the place. The gooks and Americans were lying dead next to each other—that was how close the fighting had gotten.

"Our battered troops were relieved by a sister battalion, 2nd Battalion, 7th Cavalry. We were flown out by helicopter for much-needed rest. The 2nd Battalion, 7th Cavalry moved on foot a mile or so away to LZ Albany. They marched in columns, strung out through the woods. We figured the fight and cleanup was over, but the NVA had other plans. They had fresh battalions in reserve—men who were waiting to join the action and kill Americans. The enemy paralleled the American movement until they were in a position to do the most damage. In a matter of several hours, they cut to ribbons and almost wiped out an entire American battalion of several hundred men.

"Most of our battalion had been in-country for a little over two months before that battle Ia Drang Valley, where hundreds of them were wounded or killed. Afterward, I was promoted to sergeant and became the weapons-squad leader.

"After losing so many men, the replacements we needed in the weapons squad didn't arrive until January. First, SP4 Engel, SP4 Dunn, and PVT Wildman arrived. You and Kenny are the second set of replacements. It's now the first week of April and my weapons squad is still shorthanded.

"I only have to make it a few more months before I go home in August. We haven't been back to Ia Drang since November. I hope I never have to see the place again."

Sergeant Dorman got up, excused himself, and quickly left. I was

wide-eyed, astounded, and speechless. What could I say to someone like him? I felt honored and humbled to know this brave man
who'd had such an extraordinary combat experience. I'd been stateside in Uncle Sam's army for about a month at the time of the Ia
Drang Valley battle. Now I was assigned to a platoon that had almost been wiped out there.

*Will I be brave in the face of the enemy, or too scared to fight? Will
I be killed instantly, severely wounded, or survive like Sergeant Dorman?* I wondered. I found it difficult to sleep the night after Sergeant Dorman told us his story. Instead, I stayed awake, thinking
about the Lost Platoon.

A few days later, Sergeant Dorman came into our tent and said,
"Wake up and listen. After you clean up and get some breakfast,
meet me here for an operations order."

I got out of my cot, grabbed my shaving gear, and slipped on my
"rice-paddy racers"—our nickname for rubber flip-flops. I headed
for the showers, which consisted of several green fifty-gallon drums
welded together, sitting on top of a wood frame with canvas siding.
Flat wooden pallets underneath the showerheads provided a place
to stand above the moldy, wet, mosquito-infested ground beneath.
A trench was dug around the wooden pallets for water drainage.
Towels and clothes hung on nails hammered into the posts holding
the shower frame together. A faucet attached to a pipe controlled
the flow of cold water; there was no hot. We took quick showers to
conserve water for others, and we shaved outside the shower, using
our steel helmets as sinks. When the troops were in from the field,
water tankers filled the shower-water containers daily.

After a shower and shave, it was time for breakfast. Kenny and
I sat at a picnic table with our new team leader, Bob Dunn. He
couldn't tell us anything more about our upcoming mission or operations order. I ate fast and returned to my tent. A few minutes
later, everyone else in the weapons squad was back from breakfast.

Sergeant Dorman arrived and gathered us together. He took out his little green notebook, glanced at his notes, and began to talk in a serious tone.

"We're going back to Ia Drang Valley," he said.

From the story he'd told us only a few days before, Kenny and I knew how Sergeant Dorman must have felt about returning to Ia Drang, but he didn't betray his emotions. Instead, he put his military field map down and pointed to a grid that he knew all too well. The terrain appeared wooded and flat until it reached the base of Chu Pong Mountain. Inside the wooded area, near the base of the mountain, LZ XRAY was clearly marked in grease pencil on the map. The Cambodian border was within marching distance of the LZ. The entire area was completely isolated from any roads or villages.

Sergeant Dorman said, "S2 battalion intelligence reported small concentrations of enemy troops operating in this area. Our mission is to engage the enemy but not pursue them across the Cambodian border. We'll link up with the rest of the company when we get to LZ XRAY, and set up in a company-sized perimeter. Our objective is to check out the area, hike up Chu Pong Mountain, and look for enemy base camps. Then we'll sweep the Ia Drang Valley southeast to LZ Victor, spend the night there, and come back home the next day. We'll be supported by field artillery, gunships, and jet fighters if necessary.

"Pack a basic load and enough food for three days. We'll be resupplied in the field. Be ready to move out to the road for pickup in an hour. Any questions?"

Sergeant Dorman looked at Kenny and me and said, "You two are about to get your cherries busted." He knew, and now we knew, that we were going to lose our innocence on this mission.

Bob Dunn turned to Kenny and said, "Don't forget to pick up the bag of M-60 spare parts from my tent."

The spare-parts bag contained one extra gun barrel, an asbestos glove used to grab and change the barrel when it got too hot, cleaning rods, a metal chamber, bore brushes, small oil cans, and cleaning cloths. The bag had a shoulder strap and weighed about twelve pounds.

I grabbed my pack and filled it with several pairs of socks, underwear, and T-shirts. I checked my shaving kit to make sure I had my toothbrush, shaving cream, soap dish with a new bar of soap, bottle of after-shave lotion, hand towel, and razor. I decided to pack writing paper and envelopes just in case I had time to write letters home. With my small canvas pack already full, Bob directed me to go with Kenny to the supply tent to pick up a basic load of M-16 rifle ammunition (300 rounds), two grenades, two trip flares, one claymore mine, and eight hundred-round belts of machine gun ammunition.

I thought, *Damn! That's a hell of a lot of extra shit to carry.*

When I got back with everything, I had twenty M-16 magazines and twenty boxes of ammo. I loaded each magazine and discarded the empty cartons, inserted several clips in a bandoleer with a shoulder strap, and crammed the rest of the M-16 clips into my pack. I rolled my poncho as small and tight as I could and strapped it underneath the pack.

The M-60 machine gun ammunition was issued in boxes, each holding a hundred-round belt. Every fifth round was a red tracer, which lit up when it left the barrel. Tracers were used to help zero in on a target and for night firing. Each box came with a green cloth bag and a strap so it could be carried slung from the shoulder.

Kenny put two boxes of M-60 machine gun ammunition in the spare-parts bag. He set the other two boxes aside to carry over his shoulder. I brought two hundred-round boxes and Bob attached a hundred-round belt to the feeding mechanism of the M-60. My pistol belt held two canteens of water, two ammunition pouches, two grenades, one bayonet, and a field shovel. We attached adjustable shoulder straps to the backpack and pistol belt to help distribute the weight more evenly between the small of the back and the shoulders. Medical field bandages attached to metal D-rings sewn to the shoulder harness. We placed a plastic bottle of mosquito repellent inside the elastic headband on top of our steel pot.

I lifted the pack onto my back. When I bent over to pick up my M-16 and helmet, the weight shifted forward. I nearly fell on my face. Soaking wet, I might have weighed 130 pounds, but the pack added at least fifty more. My feet pressed heavily into the soles of my boots. I didn't know how I was going to carry all that stuff for any great distance, let alone climb Chu Pong Mountain with it. Kenny looked surprised at the weight of his load as well.

John Burnam—Company B, 2nd Platoon, 1st Battalion, 7th Cavalry.
I was the ammo-bearer for Bob Dunn, M60 Machine-gunner—1966.
(Photo courtesy of Bob Dunn)

When I thought I had everything packed, Bob told me to put my gear down and get three days' C-Rations. Each soldier was issued a case of C-Rations that contained twelve meals. The case was a little larger than a case of beer and about as heavy. When I got back to the tent, there was little time before I had to be at the road for pickup.

I complained, "How am I going to carry nine meals when my pack is full and I have all this other stuff to carry?"

Bob looked at my gear and asked, "What the hell did you pack?"

"Extra clothes, shaving gear, and ammunition," I replied.

Bob laughed. "Take out the extra clothes and use the room to pack essentials. Put cans of food in your long green socks and tie them to your shoulder harness. By the way, John, I know your pack is heavy. Mine is too. Pack only the bare necessities and as much ammunition as you can carry. Also, take only what you think you'll eat for three days, and leave the rest here."

Although I felt like a complete moron, I did everything Bob said. It was my first mission, so what the hell did I know?

Sergeant Dorman spoke in a loud voice, "Saddle up!"

I looked awkward in my new gear. When I walked, it sounded like I was carrying pots and pans. Kenny seemed a little uncomfortable too. The other soldiers in the platoon looked at us like the new recruits we were, but didn't say a word. When we reached the road, we joined the other members of the weapons squad. We sat in the hot morning sun and waited for the choppers.

Sergeant Dorman briefed the squad on the loading plan. We were to split into machine gun teams, one on either side of the road. When a chopper landed, we would board simultaneously from both sides of the ship.

The first group of choppers landed and SP4 Engel and PFC Wildman climbed aboard with members of another squad. The ships quickly took off and another group of slicks landed. Sergeant Dorman ordered our machine gun team to board the nearest ship. When it touched down, I ran a short distance, climbed aboard, and I sat down against the inside wall, away from the open door. I felt a little uncomfortable because the doors remained open during flight.

As the ship lifted off, I felt the metal floor vibrate and rattle. I braced myself, thinking I'd slide across the floor and out the open door. My stomach was full of butterflies; it felt like going down the first steep drop of a roller coaster. As the aircraft gained altitude, it joined a column formation of others. I was still a little tense when the helicopter reached cruising altitude a few thousand feet up. Looking down, I saw the base camp slowly disappear. Several gunships flew escort at a lower altitude—barely above the treetops.

At least thirty ships were in the air. I could see men sitting inside the copters flying alongside us. Despite my nervousness, riding inside a fully armed formation of flying warships was an awesome feeling and afforded an incredible view.

The cool air felt good against my face. Looking around, I noticed that no one spoke. Everyone stared out the open doors. The door gunners had their machine guns loaded and tilted down. They wore green flight-crew helmets with intercoms so they could communicate with the two pilots. The formation traveled for about an hour before descending; then the treetops got closer and closer.

Green smoke swirled up from the ground of LZ XRAY in the Ia Drang Valley, indicating that the LZ was cleared for landing. The gunships buzzed around the zone as the choppers approached the landing area. In the near distance, Chu Pong Mountain stuck out like a pyramid covered with tropical vegetation. When our chopper got ready to land, I noticed the other soldiers scooting closer to the open doors. As soon as the landing gear touched the earth, everyone quickly jumped out. Kenny and I followed Bob, and we created a small perimeter around the ship until it lifted away.

Sergeant Dorman barked, "Bob, get your gun over to those trees and cover our asses."

Bob ran. Kenny and I followed to a tree line about fifty yards out. My adrenaline spiked. My eyes were wide open, scanning for anything unusual. Bob put the gun down on its bipod and loaded the chamber for firing. He told me to move to my left and link up with the next man in the platoon. I reacted without a word. About twenty yards away, I spotted another member of the platoon. After we made eye contact, I dropped down on one knee and faced outward into the surrounding trees.

Helicopters kept landing with more troops. Bob and Kenny manned the M-60 machine gun about forty yards from the landing zone and about five yards to the left of my position. Knee-high grass, dried by the hot sun, surrounded the trees. I nervously tapped the bottom of the magazine inserted into my M-16 rifle. I jacked a round into the chamber and made sure the selector switch was on "Safe." Everyone lay quietly in a prone position on the hard, dry grass. I scanned my front, trying to see and listen for anything resembling enemy movement. Minutes passed. Nothing happened. Sergeant Dorman was busy going from man to man, checking that each of us was present and in correct position.

The sergeant ordered Bob to follow him to a better location. Kenny and I briskly moved behind them in a crouch. As I walked, my helmet felt loose on my head and kept moving in front of my eyes. When we finally stopped, Sergeant Dorman pointed to where he wanted the M-60 machine gun set up. The position he picked faced Chu Pong Mountain.

He instructed Bob, "Before you dig in, check in front of your position about thirty yards to make sure you know there's nothing out there."

Bob took Kenny with him but ordered me to stay back to cover them. After slowly walking around with the machine gun at the ready, they returned with nothing to report.

Over a hundred men were on the ground by then. The gunships still buzzed around but weren't firing. Gunships didn't have door gunners but were heavily armed with machine guns and aerial rocket artillery controlled by the pilots. I felt safe, but still wasn't confident about what I was doing or what to expect.

The order was given to dig in. Bob stood guard behind the M-60, while Kenny and I dug a three-man foxhole. Sergeant Dorman said he normally didn't put three men in one position, but since we were new, he wanted Bob to teach us how to set up a machine gun position.

After we dug the foxhole, Bob showed Kenny and me how to set up a claymore mine. He said, "The first thing to remember is that the claymore has FRONT printed in large letters on one side. Be sure to point that side in the direction of the enemy. Claymores are real easy to set up, but if you don't do it right, Charlie will turn the mines around and put them closer to your foxhole, and when it's time to squeeze the trigger, you'll blow up your own ass. Remember: surprise is important, so camouflage the mine without disturbing the natural look of the surrounding vegetation. A claymore has a fifty-foot wire. One end has the blasting cap attached. It screws inside a well in the mine. The other end has the trigger mechanism; also, there's a circuit tester to make sure it's armed.

"Don't set out trip flares during the day, do it right before dark. Trip flares are a little touchy, but you want them that way. When the enemy trips the wire, the pin should pop out easily and ignite the flair. To keep Charlie from tampering, attach a second tripwire to the bottom of the claymore. Charlie will be caught by surprise like a deer in headlights. Then we'll kill him."

Patrols were scheduled for the next morning to search the area and climb Chu Pong Mountain. The sun was setting. I went out with Bob to assemble the claymores and trip flares, while Kenny watched from behind the machine gun. When we got back, I boasted to Kenny with a big smile, saying, "It's a cinch!"

Kenny replied, "Good, then you can do it all the time."

Bob laughed and said, "Kenny, tomorrow it's your turn."

Sergeant Dorman came by to remind us to keep alert and make sure someone manned the M-60 machine gun at all times. He also gave us the password for the night. We would use the password, which changed daily, to get back through friendly lines if people got split up during a nighttime firefight.

Bob scheduled two-hour guard shifts. Everyone ate supper before the first watch. I used a tiny can opener called a P38 to open a warm can of beefsteak and potatoes. It tasted terrible, but I ate every bit.

Each box of C-Rations had a dark-brown plastic bag full of goodies—a plastic spoon, a tiny roll of toilet paper, a sample-size box of four cigarettes, little packets of sugar, creamer, salt, and pepper, one book of matches, and a packet of instant coffee.

To cover our exposed skin, we used mosquito repellent. It was powerful enough to keep the bugs from biting us at night. Each man carried a green plastic poncho to sleep on. By then, I'd concluded that sleeping in a foxhole was like sleeping in a grave.

Everyone awoke at first light. We used water from canteens to brush our teeth, wash up, and mix powdered coffee. We were required to have clean-shaven faces, even though no one but the army cared what we looked like. When I finished shaving, I slapped on some Mennen Skin Bracer.

To my surprise, Bob blurted, "Who the hell has the after-shave lotion on?"

I confessed, and Bob ripped into me. "You can't go on patrol smelling like a whore. Charlie will smell you a mile away. Charlie has instincts like a fucking animal. He lives out here, for crying out loud. What the hell's wrong with you? You don't need to fucking help him out!"

I was stunned and so embarrassed that I didn't say a word. I also knew the smell would take time to wear off. I quietly dug a hole and buried that bottle of Skin Bracer and wiped my face with dirt, trying to get rid of the smell. When Sergeant Dorman found out what I'd done, he couldn't stop howling. Before long, I was the topic of conversation throughout the platoon. They called me "the Mennen Boy."

What a way to start my first full day in the field with a bunch of veterans!

Bob and Kenny went to retrieve the trip flares and claymores. Our orders were to hike to Chu Pong Mountain and scout for enemy base camps. Sergeant Dorman directed the number-two machine gun to bring up the rear of the platoon. He ordered the number-one machine gun team to get behind the point man. The platoon spread out and traveled in column formation. Flank guards were placed about twenty-five yards out on each side of the column. With the flat terrain, visibility was good. We walked slowly and cautiously through the trees and knee-high brown grass while avoiding large termite mounds.

I was close to the last man in the formation. We traveled at a slow pace through a clearing. I stepped over a branch and crushed two huge millipedes crawling near my boot. Red ants, called fire ants, covered the trees. When they bit, it stung like hell, so I quickly learned to avoid them.

The patrol halted before reaching the base of the mountain. I spotted a helmet on the ground a short distance away. I picked it up. It had a large bullet hole in the front. I examined the inside and saw a piece of dried scalp stuck to the back of the helmet liner. The name on the headband read, "Sgt. Bernard." I put it down and wondered about the man who had worn it, feeling sorry that an American had been killed out here in the middle of nowhere. I looked around and noticed that other soldiers were finding remnants of a battle that had taken place there.

Shallow foxholes overgrown with grass appeared everywhere. Military web gear from a backpack stuck out from a mound of dirt. Tarnished brass from all types of spent shells littered the area around the foxholes. The positions of everything indicated that the fighting had been fierce — possibly hand-to-hand combat.

Kenny located a splintered human jawbone and a skull with a bullet hole in it. Near me, the rains had partly washed away the dirt and exposed what appeared to be human bones. Bob told me that these weren't American remains, because we don't leave our dead behind. I wondered how all this had happened. Never in my nineteen young years had I seen this kind of devastation.

The patrol moved out again; eventually, we reached the base of the mountain, which was rugged, dense with vegetation, and dark. The point man used a machete to cut a path. The sunlight barely penetrated to the jungle floor as we started to climb at a snail's pace. My pack snagged on vines every step of the way.

We hadn't traveled far before someone at the head of the platoon spotted a huge enemy base camp built in a large bamboo forest. A few soldiers checked for booby traps before we entered the camp, the entire platoon slowly moving inside. Sunlight reflected off the bamboo, creating a yellow glow. We were warned to watch out for snakes, especially bamboo vipers. I shuddered because I'd always hated the sight of snakes.

We set up a defensive position inside the enemy base camp. Half the platoon spread out and searched, but the camp was empty. We did, however, uncover a huge cache of ammunition, mortars, and rockets, hidden in camouflaged holes in the ground. We found cooking utensils, a meeting area, and a small hospital with a few medical supplies. Bunkers and tiny one-man foxholes dotted the area. Small piles of grenades, with wooden handles and strings dangling from them, were scattered throughout the camp, which looked as if it could have held several hundred North Vietnamese soldiers.

I thought, *This had to be one of the base camps that the enemy used to launch attacks on our company.*

Sergeant Dorman couldn't believe the B-52 bombers had missed this place, although it couldn't be seen from the air. There wasn't a crater anywhere inside the base camp. The platoon leader got on the radio to speak with the company commander. They decided to set charges and blow up the enemy munitions.

When we returned to our foxholes that evening, we were dirty and tired. I had to take a shit real bad, so I asked Kenny, "Where do you think I should go?"

"Out in the woods, I guess. I haven't had to go yet."

Overhearing us, Bob said, "We'll cover your ass!"

He and Kenny broke into laughter. It would have been terrible for the enemy to catch me by surprise with my pants down, so I put up with the sarcasm and accepted their protection.

That night, we set up an ambush at a creek beside the mountain, about 150 yards from my foxhole. Sergeant Dorman teamed me with "Ranger Mac," as he was called, a black veteran soldier and a survivor of the battle of Ia Drang. He spoke in a tense, nervous voice about not being very happy to be in this place again. After we talked for a few minutes, he set up the trip flares and claymores in front of our foxhole.

While on guard duty in the foxhole, I heard rifle and machine gun fire coming from the direction of the creek. Ranger Mac woke up and jumped in the foxhole with me. We pointed our weapons into the darkness and listened, waiting to be attacked.

Ranger Mac blurted out, "I hope them gooks trip the flair, so I can blow their asses to hell with the claymore."

He instructed me to put my ammunition in front of me so I could reload as fast as possible. The firing in the distance lasted about half a minute, then total silence. Nothing else happened the rest of the night.

The next morning, Sergeant Dorman told us that the 1st Platoon had killed two enemy soldiers at the creek. He said that the company commander was pissed because someone had sprung the ambush too soon, and the main element had gotten away. The two kills were NVA soldiers who'd been armed with AK-47 rifles.

Later that morning, the entire company swept the valley to LZ Victor, a few miles southeast of LZ XRAY. Our route followed the east side of Chu Pong Mountain, parallel to the Cambodian border. I walked next to Kenny. It seemed to get hotter and hotter as we pushed in the direction of LZ Victor. The water in my canteen was so hot from the sun that it was unbearable to drink. I forced it down anyway. The temperature must have been over 115 degrees. My fatigue jacket was soaked with sweat.

Almost out of water, my legs weakening under the heavy load on my back, I kept walking as Kenny pointed out nearby bomb craters. Helicopters flew above to cover our advance through the lightly wooded area. After the platoon stopped for a break, Kenny saw that I was slowing down. Determined not to give in to the heat, I wanted to make it to LZ Victor on my own.

When the platoon stopped again, I drank the last of my water, but was unable to stand. I felt dizzy and went down on one knee. I stayed in that position for a moment. Then, struggling to stand, I felt a hand on my shoulder and heard a voice ask, "Are you okay, trooper?"

Without looking up, I replied, "I feel a little dizzy and weak."

"How long have you been in-country?"

I finally looked up and recognized Lieutenant Colonel Moore, the battalion commander who had led the ill-fated battle of Ia Drang Valley that Sergeant Dorman had told us about.

I tried to steady my legs, but fell against the tree. LTC Moore grabbed me under the arm and held me up. I thanked him and confessed that this was my first mission.

He gave me some water from his canteen and said, "Where are you from, trooper?"

"Littleton, Colorado, sir."

"It's going to take you a while to get used to this type of heat and humidity, but it's an unusually hot day."

LTC Moore didn't have a pack on, only a belt with a .45-caliber pistol and two canteens of water. He looked fresh, as if he'd just arrived, and he'd hardly broken a sweat. He instructed me to take off the pack.

"Now you'll cool down faster. Grab your rifle and follow me."

LTC Moore picked up my pack and carried it. We walked at a brisk pace, and I finally cooled down. When we got to LZ Victor, I followed my commander to the command post. He gave me my pack and ordered one of his men to fill my canteens and have the medic check me.

LTC Moore turned and began to walk away, so I said, "Gary Owen, sir!"

He turned and smiled, "All the way, sky trooper!"

I made it back to my platoon and didn't see LTC Moore again, but I knew that I'd be forever grateful for that act of kindness from my commander.

Our mission to Ia Drang Valley was over. The helicopters lifted us off LZ Victor and we headed home to An Khe. Even though I never fired a single shot, my first mission had taught me valuable lessons about packing gear, riding in troop-assault helicopters, moving in a tactical formation, and setting up a defensive position. My thoughts of not getting an assignment to an elite paratrooper unit didn't seem to matter anymore. I felt lucky to be with the men of the 2nd Platoon.

Later on, I'd learn the value of relying on a German shepherd scout dog to lead me through more treacherous enemy territory in South Vietnam. But my next mission would teach me the reality of combat, which was something I could never have imagined.

Chapter Four

BONG SON

During the month of April 1966, we had been running patrols in Ia Drang and around the Plei Me Special Forces Camp, and guarding Highway 19, a major supply road to An Khe. Though Kenny and I made no enemy contact, we continued learning and gaining valuable experience.

Living in a tent was now a luxury compared to how I had to live, eat, sleep, and hunt in the heat, rain, and mud of the Vietnamese countryside. But that luxury didn't include companionship with my tentmates. It wasn't easy for me to make friends. Other than Kenny and Bob, I hardly knew the guys who shared my tent. When we moved in tactical formation, each man maintained a comfortable distance from the next, and we remained silent for the most part. Riding in loud helicopters made it difficult to talk. At night, platoon members teamed up in foxholes strategically spaced apart, and visiting was not a good idea, so the only men we really got to know were the ones with whom we shared a foxhole. I began to realize that getting to know others and making lots of friends wasn't encouraged in a combat zone. The men we befriended one day might be killed in the next day's battle, so friendships often ended in pain and loss.

Although I didn't think of him as my friend, I looked up to Sergeant Dorman for his leadership. He commanded the respect of every member of the platoon and his fellow squad leaders. Sergeant Dorman always smiled and asked how Kenny and I were getting along. He teased me for being a "cherry jumper"—a paratrooper who'd recently graduated from jump school and hadn't made a parachute jump since then. I'd earned my parachute wings by going through a physically rigorous three-week course at Fort Benning, Georgia, where the dropout rate was traditionally high. There were three levels of paratrooper qualification: basic, senior, and master jumper.

I was proud to wear my basic paratrooper wings, even though I wasn't working in a paratrooper outfit. My aspirations of getting assigned to an elite paratrooper unit had diminished since joining the 7th Cavalry. The 2nd platoon was my new home and I was going to make the best of it.

Sergeant Dorman advised Kenny and me that we'd soon be eligible to earn a Combat Infantry Badge (CIB), which was awarded only to infantrymen. To qualify for a CIB, a soldier had to have been officially schooled as an infantryman and awarded an 11B Military Occupational Specialty. Ultimately, a soldier had to serve in a combat infantry unit for at least thirty days during wartime. The CIB was considered the badge of courage. Only a small percentage of soldiers in the entire army were authorized to wear one. When a soldier earned a CIB, he wore it with pride.

The CIB, about three inches long and an inch wide, was designed with a long silver rifle inlaid in a small, rectangular, blue-enameled background. An oval silver wreath surrounded the inlaid rifle. The badge was worn above the left breast pocket and above all other service medals, ribbons, and badges. Sergeant Dorman once said, "A CIB is only for men with enough guts to be infantrymen and the balls to hunt Charlie for a living." The sergeant had earned his CIB in the battle of Ia Drang Valley in November 1965. His combat awards included a Purple Heart for combat wounds, Bronze Star for valor, and an Air Medal for making combat air assaults from Huey helicopters into enemy-held territory while under enemy fire.

Sergeant Dorman was a man you wanted by your side in battle, but there were other soldiers in the platoon who were also toughened by combat experience, their stature like that of Sergeant Dorman. When you needed them, you could count on soldiers like Billy Smith, Lewis Rodrigues, Dennis Blessing, Sergeant Savage, Tom Bible, Knutson, Bob Dunn, John Engel, Donald "Frenchie" Clostio, and others. All of them had already earned the coveted CIB; some had Purple Hearts for combat wounds, and scars they'd wear for the rest of their lives. I was just the new guy most of them knew little about, so I tried to fit in as best I could.

A young Texan, Donald "Frenchie" Clostio, rifleman, 2nd Platoon, participated in the battle of the Ia Drang Valley as one of the reinforcements that landed on November 18, 1965. Under attack as soon as he hit the ground he fought for his life, and witnessed the brutal slaughter on both sides.

Donald "Frenchie" Clostio
(2nd Platoon)
Wounded in Action—1966.
(Photo courtesy of Donald Clostio)

Before I met Frenchie, he had already received two Purple Hearts for bullet wounds in his right elbow and thigh during combat action against the North Vietnamese Army in the central highlands. I served with him on a separate combat mission, when he was critically wounded a third time and nearly died. The 2nd Platoon had set up a defensive perimeter not far from base camp. Knowing right where we had dug our foxholes, an enemy sniper fired a few shots at us but injured no one. Foot patrols were immediately dispatched to locate and silence the shooter.

Van Wilson, M-60 machine gunner, recalls returning with his patrol and crossing Frenchie's foxhole position as he headed to the command post for a debriefing. Wilson had no idea that an enemy patrol of several Vietcong in black pajamas had been quietly trailing him. When the VC snuck up to Frenchie's foxhole, they caught him by surprise. Frenchie took a point-blank burst from a VC AK-47 rifle; seven bullets made mincemeat of his right hip and leg. As if this weren't enough, the VC tossed a grenade, and the rest of

Frenchie's body became a pincushion of fragments. A firefight instantly erupted, driving the VC patrol back into the jungle where they disappeared.

Frenchie was immediately evacuated by helicopter. His wounds were so severe that he was transported from South Vietnam to Fort Sam Houston, Texas. He spent fifteen months in a military hospital and was subsequently medically discharged from the U.S. Army.

It was strange how the army threw young men together and hoped for the best. Kenny and I got to know Rodrigues ("Rod") the day he showed us how to mix and spice up C-Rations. A large man of Hispanic decent, Rod was a jovial man by nature and well liked by everyone. He carried himself with

Lewis Rodriguez, Rifleman, 2nd Platoon and Bong Son survivor – 1966. (Photo Courtesy of Van Wilson)

a sense of confidence, toughness, and experience. Rod was being considered for the next available promotion to squad leader.

Doc Bell, platoon medic, was not an infantryman, but was highly respected by everyone in the platoon. A stocky black man with the biggest of smiles, Doc was a trained combat medical specialist. His job was to take care of casualties, save lives, and issue survival basics such as malaria tablets and salt tablets. Doc Bell's field gear consisted of a large green shoulder bag containing field medical supplies, and he wore a .45 caliber pistol on the belt of his combat gear. During combat missions, Doc was positioned near the platoon leader and radiotelephone operator (RTO). He wasn't eligible for a CIB. Instead, he had earned a CMB (Combat Medical Badge), which very few soldiers in the medical field were eligible to receive. Like the CIB, the CMB could only be earned while serving in combat. When in base camp, Doc Bell's quarters were with the medical staff at the battalion aid station. Doc had already experienced combat

with the platoon and would soon see more of the same in a place called Bong Son.

There was Dennis Blessing, a tough, no nonsense man soldier when he was on a mission. He was a seasoned veteran of many combat missions and skirmishes with the enemy. You could always count on Blessing to do his job under fire and be there to help you when you were in trouble. Dennis was well liked and respected by the rest of the 2nd Platoon.

Dennis Blessing, 2nd Platoon, firing at a sniper during a combat mission – 1966. Dennis had been to Bong Son and was going again. (Photo courtesy of Blessing).

During the first week of May 1966, we'd been back in base camp only a few days when Sergeant Dorman gathered the squad to brief us on a new operations order. He told us we were going to Bong Son. On that mission, dubbed "Operation Davy Crockett," our entire battalion was to sweep Bong Son from the mountains to the South China Sea.

Sergeant Dorman put his map down on a cot and pointed out the location of Bong Son. The map showed hundreds of rice paddies dotted with hamlets. Our 2nd Platoon would be settling in for the night on top of the mountain range bordering Bong Son. Choppers would pick us up early in the morning and fly us into the valley.

S-2, battalion intelligence, reported that Bong Son was a major North Vietnamese Army stronghold. For years, Charlie had used its heavily populated villages as safe havens. Several thousand heavily armed NVA regulars were reported to have been operating in small groups throughout the area of our operation. We were told it was *hot,* meaning that some firefights were already underway between the enemy and our battalion's advance units.

The entire 1st Battalion, 7th Cavalry, was to air assault Bong Son and eradicate the enemy forces. A convoy of troop trucks would be used to transport the battalion from An Khe to Bong Son before loading onto choppers for our air assault into the valley. Everyone had to pack three days' supplies and ammunition. Sergeant Dorman informed us that when we reached the beach of the South China Sea, we'd be rewarded with a day off to swim in the ocean and eat hot food.

After the sergeant left the tent, I turned to Kenny and asked, "Did you hear him say fighting is already going on?"

"Yes, I did."

"Well, I guess this is it, Kenny. We're finally going to see combat."

For a few seconds, Kenny and I stared at one another, neither of us saying a word.

Then I said, "Kenny, if anything happens to me, please write my family and tell them how it happened. I want them to know from you."

"Johnny," he replied, "if anything happens to me, you write my folks."

At that moment we exchanged addresses and stuffed them into our pockets.

Shortly afterward, I asked Kenny, "Hey, buddy, how do you feel?"

Kenny turned to me with a smile and simply replied, "Fine!"

Having never experienced combat, I hoped that all the missions leading to this one had prepared me to be brave in the face of the enemy.

Billy "Smitty" Smith, M-60 machine gunner and rifleman, had arrived in the 2nd Platoon in December 1965, a month after the battle of Ia Drang. Smitty had three Purple Hearts—all from being wounded by punji stakes (bamboo spears). He had lost his best friend, John Paul Travis, in Bong Son on January 26, 1966, so he wasn't too excited about our mission to go back there. I remember walking with Smitty to the battalion aid station to get a bleeding punji wound on his lower right calf redressed. He had torn several stitches, and I could hear the blood squishing inside his boot with each step he took. It didn't seem to bother him, and he didn't need me to lean on, either. Smitty was a pretty tough young soldier from Mississippi, who never complained about the pain of those three punji-stake wounds.

Billy Smith, M60 Machine-gunner and rifleman, 2nd Platoon. Billy was wounded in combat three separate times—1966.

(Photo courtesy of Billy Smith)

While I packed my basic load, Bob Dunn came by and asked me how many more belts of M-60 ammunition I could carry. Bob, Kenny, and I had ten belts among us, a total of 1000 rounds. I told Bob I'd add two more hundred-round belts to my load. I also packed several hand grenades. When I finished packing, my total load weighed at least sixty pounds. I decided not to lighten the load and risk being sorry about the decision later. I was learning to simply deal with the weight and the pain of carrying it, without complaining.

John Engel, M60 Machine-Gunner, 2nd Squad—1966.
John was key to our survival in Bong Son.
(Photo courtesy of Billy Smith).

A few more new men had been assigned to the 2nd Platoon since our return from our last mission guarding Route 19. I figured that the new guys probably felt the same way Kenny and I had when we prepared for our first mission. They were probably wondering if the veterans would accept them. With our platoon pumped up to about twenty men, morale was high. We talked and joked while waiting for orders to move to the pickup point on the road.

A loud voice sounded, "Saddle up!"

We lifted gear onto our shoulders and headed toward a long column of troop trucks lining the road, bumper to bumper, as far as the eye could see. Each two-and-a-half-ton truck was stripped of its canvas top, except for the cab area. The drivers stood behind the dropped tailgates of their trucks. The smell of diesel fuel was thick in the air. One by one, soldiers climbed into the beds of the trucks and sat on foldout wooden benches, resting their feet on a sheet of solid steel flooring. Each squad leader accounted for his men and then he and the driver climbed into the cab.

Company B, 7th Cavalrymen riding in a long convoy of troop trucks to help fight the enemy in Bong Son, May 4, 1966. (Photo courtesy of Dennis Blessing).

Each truck slowly rolled down the dirt road. As the convoy moved, more trucks linked up from other roads leading out of An Khe. The distance between the trucks increased as they drove out of the gate.

An M-60 manned by a gunner was positioned on the top of each truck's cab. The rest of the troops sat or stood, weapons ready. Overhead, gunships and helicopters flew escort. If Charlie were to attack, the battalion could respond with troops, gunships, artillery, and fighter jets. Seeing so much military firepower assembled for this mission was quite an impressive sight.

The convoy motored ahead, winding through the mountains and thick vegetation on each side of the road. Several men catnapped, while others watched the trees and road for signs of danger. Riding in the back of an open truck made us easy targets. If Charlie wanted to snipe or spring an ambush, he could easily cause a lot of casualties and bring the convoy to a confused halt.

The ride was long. As day turned into night, the drivers turned on tiny night-lights that limited the enemy's ability to see the vehicles at a distance. The tiny lights gave the drivers enough visibility to see the vehicle in front and behind, as long as they slowed the pace and tightened the distance between vehicles.

Kenny kept poking the weary driver of our truck, who would veer left and then right. I wondered if these drivers, unlike us infantrymen, weren't used to working many hours without sleep.

Early the next morning, the vehicles stopped on a huge mountain plateau covered with short vegetation and dense jungle. We dismounted and moved away from the convoy. My platoon secured an edge of the mountain high above Bong Son.

The sun shone early that morning as we looked into the rice paddies below. The steep cliff, thick with vegetation, made the mountain appear impossible to climb. I could see no path or man-made road leading down into Bong Son. What I saw below my position in the dirt was the water in the paddies reflecting the sunlight like tiny rectangular mirrors. Bong Son looked like a giant checkerboard of colorful rice paddies dotted with palm trees and small straw-hut villages all the way to the South China Sea. It was a beautiful sight from high above the valley.

A steep ravine between the mountains separated us from another company of the 1st Battalion, 7th Cavalry, occupying the ridge on the other side. After we settled in, I accompanied a patrol to check out the ravine. It was another breathtaking view: the ravine was meticulously terraced with rice paddies and dikes all the way down to a rushing river that wound its way into the mouth of the valley. It must have taken hundreds of years to carve this mountainside into giant terraced rice paddies. No Vietnamese farmers were working anywhere in sight. Kenny quipped, "It looks like a picture straight out of *National Geographic.*"

Despite all that beauty, a war raged in the valley below. I spotted several navy warships in the waters off the coast of the South China Sea. From my vantagepoint, the tiny vessels appeared to be firing their deck guns inland. Puffs of smoke blew from the stationary ships. Seconds later, flashes of light and billowing smoke from the exploding rounds appeared on the ground below. The sound was muffled, like a distant echo.

To the right, air force jets dropped bombs and fired their twenty-millimeter cannons, which can only fire on full automatic, expending 2000 rounds per minute. When the pilot presses the trigger, the air is filled with a burping sound that lasts several seconds. A twenty-millimeter round, from casing to tip, is about five inches long and as thick as a fat cigar. I could only imagine what happened when those huge bullets hit their targets.

Above the valley floor, I could hear helicopter gunships firing M-60 machine guns and launching rockets into the trees and rice paddies. On and off during that night, I could see bright flares in the sky above the valley and flashes of fire from explosions. The whole situation was unlike anything I'd seen in my two months in Vietnam. I commented to no one in particular, "There must be a hell of a lot of enemy troops down there to get the navy, the air force, and the cavalry involved."

Bob replied, "The reason for all the fireworks is to prepare the valley for our air assault tomorrow morning."

Kenny and I didn't get much sleep that night, knowing that in the morning we'd be flying into that valley of death.

Everyone stirred as the sun rose in a sky that was bright blue and clear of rainclouds. I wiped the morning dew from my weapon, gave it a quick mechanical check, and oiled the exposed metal parts. Breakfast was C-Rations and water. In minutes, everyone in the 2nd Platoon was prepared to move at a moment's notice.

Soon, a long stream of choppers flew in and landed not far behind our positions. Each chopper was empty except for two pilots and two door gunners. With doors locked in the open position, the rotors turned at idle speed. The first load of infantrymen from another platoon climbed into the slicks, lifted off, and headed down into the valley.

A familiar voice called, "Saddle up!" The 2nd Platoon scrambled to their feet. A few minutes later, a bunch of choppers roared to a landing. Following Bob and Kenny, I ran to our designated slick. As soon as everyone was aboard, it swiftly lifted off, flying fifteen feet off the ground. When the chopper reached the ravine, the pilot banked sharply to the right and down we went. The ground looked like it was parallel to the chopper, and I thought I was going to fall out through the open door. When the pilot leveled us out, he dove down the ravine at breakneck speed. The air escaped from my lungs as I held on for dear life. The chopper swooped so close to the treetops, I could almost reach out and touch the leaves.

We flew into the valley like a swarm of bees. This was the fastest helicopter ride I'd ever had. The chopper suddenly slowed, and then landed in a huge, dry rice paddy a mile or so from the mountain we'd left behind.

A stream of red smoke, signaling that enemy contact was imminent, marked the landing zone for the pilots. As the choppers prepared to land in the hot LZ, they lifted the noses of their ships slightly and touched down briefly. Lickety-split, everyone was out and rushing for cover. I looked around and saw more and more choppers dropping troops into the dry paddies. Eventually, the entire battalion, several hundred combat infantrymen, would join in the tactical sweep to the South China Sea.

7th Cavalry Sky Trooper Air-Assault into Bong Son on May 5, 1966. (Photo courtesy of Dennis Blessing).

Not far ahead of me, Bob and Kenny lay prone on the ground behind their M-60. Suddenly, a voice bellowed, "Move out!"

I rose to my feet and felt the extra-heavy weight of my pack pulling me down and cutting into my shoulders. Rice paddies surrounded us in every direction. We all spread out, about fifteen to twenty feet apart, as the platoon began cautiously stepping forward. I kept my eyes on the uneven ground in front of me and tried to keep my footing.

American soldiers on the left and right of our platoon slowly faded into the distance. After a while, my platoon was moving as a single unit. The valley seemed a lot bigger and very different from how it had looked from the mountaintop. I couldn't see the ocean or the navy ships anymore. The mountain we'd left was a long way behind us now.

Suddenly, a shot rang out overhead, breaking the silence. We hit the ground at once. The shot sounded as though it had come from a wall of trees to our front. We waited a minute, but nothing more happened, and then we were ordered to move out again. One by one, we got up, then, crouching, we carefully advanced toward the tree line from where the shot had come.

As the 2nd Platoon continued its sweep, I was positioned close to the rear. Someone spotted two enemy soldiers in the distance, running across our front. The platoon leader ordered us not to shoot or pursue because they were too far out of range and because other Americans, whom we couldn't see, were operating in the area. He didn't want a repeat of the situation that had trapped the 2nd Platoon in the Ia Drang Valley, where, after chasing a few fleeing enemy soldiers, they ran into a buzz saw.

We encountered no resistance as the platoon continued moving closer to the wall of trees. By late afternoon, my platoon had pushed deep into Bong Son. We halted inside a lightly forested area surrounded by rice paddies. The platoon leader decided to set up a perimeter around it, partly encompassing a nearby dry paddy. Bob found a good spot to set up the M-60.

After the platoon sergeant was satisfied with each platoon's defensive position, he ordered us to dig foxholes for the evening. I had excellent visibility to the front of my position, and clear lanes of fire on flat ground. I could easily see and communicate with adjacent fighting positions.

Before dark, I was about twenty-five yards away from my position, setting up the claymore mines and trip flares, when a loud explosion rocked the air no more than a hundred feet behind me. My immediate instinctive reaction was to sprawl facedown in the dirt and look in the direction of the sound. Then I saw a small billow of white smoke.

Someone yelled, "Incoming!"

Moments later, a second explosion ripped through the same spot.

I quickly crawled on my belly back to the foxhole. Kenny and Bob were already inside and preparing for the worst. From the direction of the explosions, I heard men repeatedly crying, "Medic!" In total silence, we waited for the enemy to attack. Several minutes passed; nothing happened—not one bullet was fired. Except for the commotion behind us, where someone had been hit, an eerie quiet hung in the air.

Bob said that the first explosion was white phosphorus, commonly called "Willy Peter." The second was high explosive or "H.E." Bob explained that Charlie didn't use Willy Peter; Americans did as spotter rounds to mark targets with smoke before unleashing a volley of H.E.

The mortars had been launched accidentally by an American mortar squad from another company; they hadn't known that friendly troops were operating in their target area. Our platoon leader, platoon sergeant, a squad leader, and two riflemen had been meeting at the command post (CP) when the two mortar rounds exploded. They all suffered severe torso and leg wounds, but no one had been killed. A medical evacuation chopper landed and lifted them to a field hospital. Though the 2nd Platoon was reduced in manpower, Sergeant Dorman reassured us that we could continue the mission and reminded us to stay sharp.

Early the next morning, May 6, 1966, I went out to disarm and retrieve our claymore mines and trip flares. The day was heating up as I packed my gear and buried the trash from the food I'd eaten. It was time to saddle up and continue the mission, sweeping on foot to the South China Sea. As the platoon moved out, the men began to put some distance between one another. I positioned myself with Bob and Kenny's M-60 at the rear.

As the last man in the platoon formation, my job was to keep an eye on the rear. As we moved across the rice paddies, I spotted the flank guards about fifty yards to the left and right of the column. Searching my surroundings, I saw no other friendly units.

The platoon crossed several large rice paddies before pausing at a dike. I knelt on one knee and heard aircraft in the distance. Soon the jets were flying about 200 feet directly overhead. Their engines screamed as they flashed by and headed toward the trees in front of us. Bombs released from their wings exploded with tremendous force in the woods ahead. If they'd dropped a hundred yards closer, the bombs would have exploded on top of us. Someone had called in the air strike, but I didn't know who it was.

Suddenly, gunships appeared and began firing aerial rocket artillery into the trees. After the air strikes, I scanned for signs of the enemy, but saw nothing.

The platoon sergeant positioned the platoon in a circular defensive perimeter. We were told to keep looking for the enemy. Each rice paddy was surrounded on all four sides by dikes roughly two feet high; these held water for the Vietnamese, who watered their crops using manual irrigation. Because they rotated crops, there were dry areas, and our platoon happened to be set up in a dry rice paddy, although there were many wet ones nearby. The dikes presented excellent cover from the shrapnel of exploding bombs.

In the distance, other American troops halted and took cover from the air strikes. Our front was clear of obstacles all the way to the tree line, about a hundred yards away. The platoon held tight until the air force and the 1st Air Cavalry gunships ceased their strafing runs.

Kenny and Bob positioned the M-60 on the corner of the dike and aimed it at the trees ahead. I set up a short distance to their right and, without thinking, pointed my M-16 toward the inside of the perimeter, my finger on the trigger. Several hundred feet above us, an air force jet screamed in from behind and dropped two bombs simultaneously. They fell into the trees, and an earth-shattering explosion followed. The ground beneath my feet shook violently and, at that instant, I flinched and jerked the trigger of my rifle. It was on full automatic, and fired a long burst into the center of the perimeter. I watched in fear as bullets kicked up clumps of dirt, and my fellow soldiers scrambled for cover. I realized instantly what I'd done; my finger released the trigger, but it was too late—everything had happened in seconds.

Sergeant Dorman rushed over in a crouched position and asked where the shots had come from. Kenny and Bob looked at him and said nothing. I confessed that it was my fault and tried to explain. The sergeant interrupted, screaming, "Are you fucking nuts? Do you have any fucking idea what you just did? You just about fucking killed me and the other squad leaders!"

I froze, rigid with nervousness, while looking into the rage in Sergeant Dorman's eyes.

"Next time you check your fucking weapon and always keep it pointed out and away from anyone. Do I make myself clear?"

Yes, Sergeant!"

He turned and stomped away, cussing and shaking his head. I had almost killed someone by mistake. I'd never felt so humiliated in all my life. I told Kenny and Bob that I must have left the selector switch on the AUTO setting after oiling my M-16 that morning. Kenny saw that I was completely dejected. He put his arm around my shoulder and said, "Hey, buddy, it's okay. This could have happened to anyone. Shake it off—you didn't kill anyone!"

I recalled the after-shave incident in the Ia Drang Valley and thought, "Man, am I prone to make mistakes or what?"

After the bombing stopped, the platoon ended up not going in the direction of the air strikes. Instead, we headed back the way we'd come, and circled to the left toward what appeared to be a distant village. We spread out and patrolled very cautiously, looking into the trees and on the ground in front of us. My load kept shifting, which made walking on the uneven ground difficult.

I kept watching the ground and thinking about what had happened back at the rice paddy. I felt something blunt hit my helmet, and a voice said, "Keep your head and eyes up; Charlie's not in the dirt."

Looking up, I recognized that it was Dennis Blessing. It really was an art to learn to walk on uneven soil with a heavy load, keeping your head up and your eyes constantly scanning all around for signs of danger. I was beginning to realize that my months of intensive stateside infantry training had not prepared me for Vietnam. I was learning to be a combat soldier on the job, and my mistakes didn't make it any easier to gain the confidence of the soldiers in my platoon.

Our platoon, now somewhere in the middle of Bong Son, rearward mountains dwarfing us, was about to enter a Vietnamese village. The lead element stopped and everyone dropped to one knee. A squad of men was signaled to enter the village first. They separated from the platoon and went forward, their weapons at the ready. Bob lay behind his M-60 machine gun with Kenny at his side. I held my position at the tail end of the platoon and faced the rear.

The squad entered the village and checked out the straw huts as the rest of the platoon waited nearby. From a distance, the village appeared deserted. Not long into the search, however, someone uncovered several Vietnamese hiding inside bunkers and spider holes. These holes were very narrow and just deep enough to hide and protect one person. Usually covered with a lid of vegetation, they were difficult to spot. The rest of our platoon quickly moved into the village to support the search and provide security.

Training our weapons on the Vietnamese, we ordered them to move into a group as we rounded up ten elderly unarmed women and some young children. They squatted and huddled nervously in a group. It was easy to see the fear in their eyes and on their faces. An older woman cradled her crying infant. All wore black pajamas and no shoes; the babies didn't have a stitch of clothing covering them.

An American soldier spoke in Vietnamese, saying that we wouldn't harm them. He asked where the Vietcong were hiding. An elderly woman kept crying out, "No VC! No VC!" Several men continued the search but uncovered nothing else.

We stayed in the village to eat lunch. The occupants appeared to be simple peasant farmers, and the village was entirely surrounded by rice paddies. I was impressed with how clean the area was, and how beautiful the palm trees, coconut trees, and several fruit-bearing banana trees. I wondered where all the men and boys had gone. I speculated that maybe our captives were the families of Vietcong soldiers. Bob surmised that we hadn't found young men, women, and boys, because the Vietnamese thought we'd take the young men as prisoners, rape the women, and kill the boys. He went on to say that the men and boys were probably hiding somewhere nearby, and that when the platoon left, they'd return to their families—a typical reaction when American troops invaded the privacy of a village.

Eventually, we released the Vietnamese to carry on with their daily routines. Several women showed their hospitality by offering us fresh coconuts and bananas. The soldiers accepted the gifts with gratitude. I felt safe, and thought Charlie was nowhere near the village as we relaxed in the shade of the trees.

Some of the guys started to horse around, chasing chickens through the village. The Vietnamese children laughed at the crazy Americans. After we ate and rested, it was time to move again. When we departed, an older Vietnamese woman bowed as each soldier passed. I was truly impressed by her respect and hospitality.

Continuing our tactical sweep to the South China Sea, the platoon headed across another rice paddy. I spotted helicopter gunships overhead firing rockets and machine guns into a forested area just ahead of us. As we neared another village, I heard a machine gun that didn't sound like an M-60 or anything else I'd heard before. It had a slower, thudding, firing rhythm. Bob quickly pointed out that this was the sound of an NVA heavy machine gun exchanging fire with our gunships.

Because Bob had been in other firefights with Charlie, I valued his knowledge and combat experience. This was his second mission in Bong Son. The first had been in February 1966, a month before Kenny and I arrived in Vietnam.

While we marched, my mind filled with crazy thoughts of how I could sneak up with a hand grenade and knock out that enemy machine gun nest. I wanted to make up for my earlier mistakes and regain the respect of Dorman, Blessing, and the other members of my squad and the platoon. My fantasy quickly disappeared when we were ordered to move to the right and away from the enemy machine gun.

Yet another village lay ahead in our path. The platoon entered it much the same way as we had the previous one. The lead squad approached and nothing happened. The rest of the platoon followed in three-man fire teams. One team crouched, rushed about fifty feet, and knelt down; the other team moved in the same manner. The advance alternated until we were all inside the cover of the village. Specialist Four Engel manned the number-one machine gun for the platoon. He was positioned to provide firepower for the few men who searched the straw huts for enemy hiding places.

As the platoon poked around outside, they were completely surprised when several Vietnamese men, hands held high over their heads, came running out of an underground hideaway. Some of them wore black pajamas; others were dressed in khaki shirts and trousers. American weapons quickly trained on the unarmed men. One of the Vietnamese repeated loudly, "Chieu hoi! Chieu hoi!" He was referring to the "open arms" program, promising clemency and financial aid to Vietcong and North Vietnamese soldiers who stopped fighting and returned to live under South Vietnamese authority. In short, *Chieu hoi* meant, "I surrender."

The one man in our platoon who could speak some Vietnamese made the men lie facedown on the ground so they could be searched. The soldiers found no weapons or documents. The hands of each prisoner were immobilized, and a rope linked them together for security. Bob, Kenny, and I were given responsibility for guarding the prisoners. After a short while, the platoon captured several more Vietnamese men who'd been hiding in the village. We now had a bunch of Vietnamese prisoners, who, after a short interrogation, confessed to being deserters from a battalion of North Vietnamese Army regulars operating in that area.

For the first time, Kenny and I faced the enemy up close. I wasn't afraid to guard them, and they didn't appear to be afraid of me, either. They actually stared at me, probably wondering what I was going to do with them. The platoon stayed in the village for about an hour but didn't find anything else. With all the prisoners roped together, a squad leader positioned them near the center of our formation.

I asked, "What if they try to escape?"

Sergeant Dorman replied, "Shoot first and ask questions later."

The platoon headed out of the village to the edge of a clearing, our prisoners in tow. They had to be evacuated as soon as possible. The platoon sergeant used the radio to call for a chopper and to make contact with the company commander. At the center of the platoon, I could hear what was going on over the radio and could see the point man leading the formation. When we spotted a chopper nearby, Sergeant Dorman popped green smoke in the air to mark a landing site. The chopper, already crammed with gear, took all but two of our prisoners.

I was given sole responsibility for watching over the remaining two. I walked behind them as they followed Kenny and Bob. Not long into the journey, from across a clearing, a sniper fired several shots at the platoon. We hit the ground and got into prone position. The front of the platoon quickly returned fire. Engel's M-60 let go several short bursts. I didn't fire my weapon. Instead, I watched the prisoners to make sure they remained tied up and didn't try to escape. I wasn't going to make another mistake—if they ran, I'd shoot them, as ordered.

The sniper had shot our point man. Doc Bell assisted the wounded man while we radioed for a Medevac (medical evacuation helicopter). With the platoon still in the middle of a rice paddy, we crawled on our bellies to form a hasty perimeter. A few minutes later, the Medevac hovered overhead. We popped red smoke and the copter, its nose up, descended close to the ground. An enemy machine gun fired at it, and the chopper appeared to have been hit, because it took off before the wounded man could be loaded. As soon as it was airborne, the enemy stopped firing. I thought that the platoon's counter fire had silenced the enemy machine gun, but it hadn't.

It was quiet for a while, and the Medevac was radioed to return. As soon as it started to touch down, the enemy opened fire again. I couldn't believe what I was witnessing. Here was an unarmed Medevac with visible bright-red crosses painted on its nose and doors, and Charlie was determined to knock it out, totally disregarding the rules of the Geneva Convention. The Medevac took off again, leaving our wounded comrade behind.

The front of the platoon opened fire in an attempt to silence the enemy in the trees once and for all. A short time later, two air force jets appeared directly overhead. I checked my M-16 to make sure I had secured the safety and pointed my weapon away downrange. One jet dived down to just a few hundred feet above our heads—so close that I could see the pilot in the cockpit—and released two silver-colored canisters.

Kenny and I watched in amazement as those canisters tumbled over our heads. When they hit the trees, they exploded into a huge wall of orange and red flames. Bob told me that this was napalm, a jelly-like mixture of fatty acids and gasoline that incinerated everything it touched. I could feel the intense heat fifty yards away. A few seconds later, a second jet zoomed over and fired its twenty-millimeter cannons, shattering tree limbs and kicking up dirt everywhere. I thought nothing could have survived the barrage. The tress and village were ablaze and smoking. This village wasn't far from the one where we had captured the prisoners.

After the blaze had died down, we advanced across the clearing and into the burning hamlet without a shot being fired. Our wounded point man had his arm in a sling; for maximum protection, he was positioned in the center of the formation, Doc Bell beside him. Smoke billowed everywhere as small fires burned all around us. I kept my weapon trained on the two prisoners, who looked emotionally shaken and remained silent as they moved forward.

As I passed a burning hut, a dark figure stumbled out of a haze of smoke directly in front of me. I froze in my tracks and yelled, "Oh, my God, it's a woman!" Her clothes had been burned off, and her charred body was smoking. Her face was badly burned and bleeding as she raised her hands, cupping them to her mouth as if asking for water or for help. She stood in front of me and spoke softly in Vietnamese. There was nothing I could do; I actually thought of shooting the woman to put her out of her misery. She took a few more steps and fell facedown on the ground. I stared at her motionless body.

The incident caused me to lose my concentration, but I soon realized where I was and quickly composed myself. The prisoners hadn't moved and were still securely tied. The other members of my platoon weren't far ahead, so I moved the prisoners at a quick pace away from the scene and didn't look back.

When I caught up with Kenny and Bob, Kenny asked me if I'd shot the woman. I told him I'd thought about it but hadn't. He asked what had happened to her, and I told him that she'd fallen down and died. Kenny said there was nothing anyone could have done for her.

A deep, wide ditch filled with muddy water halted the platoon's advance. The only way across it was a rotting board that connected to the other side. One man at a time, the platoon carefully walked on the board and crossed to the other bank. The weight of our bodies and our loaded packs bowed the plank to its limits.

When Rodrigues stepped onto the plank and got about halfway across, his 200-pound body and heavy pack cracked the rotted wood. He plunged straight down into the muddy water five feet below and sank up to his chest, keeping his rifle above his head. He couldn't move anything but his arms and head, and cursed up a storm as the rest of us laughed hysterically, breaking the silence of our movement.

After Rod was pulled out and the rest of the men made it across the ditch, we continued our trek to the South China Sea. From where we were on the ground, I had no idea how far away it was. As the platoon spread out into a tactical sweeping formation, we entered another village that was still smoking from the napalm drop. The air was filled with the smell of fuel and burning debris. My throat and lungs burned from inhaling smoke, so I drank some water and washed my eyes.

Suddenly, the front of the platoon came under attack by automatic weapons. We hit the dirt and returned fire. Being close to the rear with the prisoners, I wasn't in a position to fire my weapon. Bob and Kenny covered the rear of the platoon with the M-60 machine gun. Enemy bullets whizzed over our heads. We continued firing, and, after a brief exchange, maneuvered to the right and away from the attack.

Several VC tried to flank the platoon on the left front as each squad moved right. We had little protection, and it was a miracle that none of us was hit. A small clearing on the right led to a group of trees and a straw hut on the other side of them. Crouching, we ran in that direction, but stopped short of entering the clearing.

Rod led the first assault squad. He directed a team of three riflemen to provide a base of fire while he and two others crouched and darted into the clearing, stopped, got down, and fired as the next three men charged in behind them for support. The maneuver was a textbook leapfrog technique commonly used by the infantry to advance on an enemy position.

Charlie kept up the pressure on our left side. As the first squad entered and secured the other side of the clearing, the rest of us quickly moved across in groups of four or five. Bullets sliced the air very close to me. I figured that Charlie had spotted the prisoners. Kenny pointed out a water buffalo frantically exiting a dried-up waterhole near where Rod stood. Its horns appeared to scrape against Rod as he desperately tried to get out of its path. The huge beast ran through the middle of the platoon and into the clearing behind us.

When I reached the trees, I saw a fellow soldier lying on his back in the open, his helmet off. His face was covered in dirt and sweat, and blood spurted from his throat, a continuous stream of it running down the side of his mouth. His eyes bulged as he bled and gasped for air. I stopped and knelt beside him to see what I could do, but Sergeant Dorman screamed, "Get your ass and those prisoners under cover before you get shot."

Doc Bell came out of nowhere and began to assist the wounded man. Holding the rope that tied the prisoners, I pulled them along behind me as I rushed into the trees and jumped into the same dry hole the buffalo had left moments before. About chest deep, this pit lay at the edge of a row of banana and palm trees. About ten feet to my right, Kenny and Bob lay behind a banana tree, savagely firing the machine gun.

From a hastily formed defensive perimeter around a small clump of trees with a straw hut in its center, the platoon made a stand and fought off Charlie's onslaught. The heaviest action was on my left flank. From the left, Engel yelled to me, "There they are! There they are!" as he fired his M-60. VC, clad in khaki uniforms, fired back, darting from place to place across our front. Some enemy soldiers fell dead from our hail of bullets and grenades.

For the first time since arriving in Vietnam, I aimed my M-16 at enemy solders and fired. The VC bobbed up and down and fired back from behind a dike about fifty yards away. I carefully aimed and fired a slew of magazines above the dike, trying to hit the VC as they stood up to fire back. I thought I'd silenced some of them, but others held their positions and fought back hard.

On my right, Kenny loaded another hundred-round belt of ammunition into the M-60 while Bob maintained his aim behind the gun. Their machine gun kicked up dirt and debris all over the area, and the lifeless bodies of several VC littered the ground in front of us.

American voices called for a medic; the platoon had taken some casualties. Deadly enemy machine gun fire had raked our small perimeter. Everyone kept reloading and firing back. I noticed that less shooting and fewer explosions came from the right side of the perimeter.

Someone screamed, "There they are on the left! The left!" This was the direction of the village the platoon had vacated minutes earlier.

Gunships swarmed overhead, firing rockets that exploded almost on top of our platoon. I flinched as shrapnel whizzed through the air, splintering trees and making dirt fly up around me. The noise was intense. Charlie fought from well-fortified defensive positions in the rice paddies' dikes, shooting back fast and furiously after each rocket exploded. We were all in reaction mode and I wasn't thinking about what could happen to us.

The extra ammunition I'd decided to carry now came in handy, as I'd already expended about 150 rounds by firing my M-16 rifle on semiautomatic.

Kenny's machine gun jammed with a bullet still in its chamber. If it cooked off, that bullet would explode inside the chamber and damage the firing mechanism, which could make the weapon useless. Kenny had little time to fix the problem. He reached back to pull his bayonet out of his pistol belt to pry the jammed cartridge out of the chamber. Almost immediately, his arm smacked him in the chest; he fell over onto his side and curled up on the ground beside his gun. Kenny's helmet rolled away from his head.

"I'm hit!"

Bob yelled for a medic and then called, "Johnny, Kenny's hit!"

I looked in Bob's direction and saw Kenny lying still in a curled-up position. Afraid he was dead, I quickly crawled over to him, leaving my prisoners unattended.

Kenny's first words were, "You're white as a ghost!"

It was a shock to see my best friend lying there, moaning in severe pain, with open wounds that made him look like he was bleeding to death. All I could think was *Please don't let him die. Please don't. This is my best friend. You can't take him away from me like this!*

The medic arrived, but he couldn't work on Kenny in the open with all the lead flying around. Incoming bullets whizzed around us. We dragged Kenny a few yards into the dry waterhole. I thought, *Thank God he's still alive!*

Kenny had been hit by a VC .30 caliber machine gun blast. He was suffering and complained of sharp stomach pains. With one sleeve of his blood-soaked fatigue shirt ripped completely off, I could see that a large part of his forearm muscle was missing, the white of the bone exposed. His wounds bled heavily. There were several bullet holes in his stomach, but no exit wounds in his back. I carefully removed Kenny's shoulder harness and backpack to make him more comfortable. After I got his gear off, he doubled up in pain. Doc Bell placed Kenny's good arm under his armpit to try to slow the bleeding. He then dressed the wounds and gave him a shot of morphine to ease the pain. The two prisoners looked scared but remained tied together, lying where I'd left them, in the dirt at the bottom of the hole.

Doc Bell grabbed my shirt and pulled me down into the hole. He told me that if I didn't keep my head down, I'd be killed. As he dressed Kenny's wounds, I rejoined the fighting, while trying to keep an eye on Kenny and the prisoners. Bob was still on the right; he had changed the barrel and continued firing short bursts at enemy targets. I tossed him a fresh hundred-round belt of ammunition from Kenny's pack.

Above all the shooting and explosions, Sergeant Dorman yelled, "Grab the wounded and dead and get ready to move out!"

The enemy had surrounded our platoon on three sides and was closing in fast. We were about to be overrun and captured or killed. As fast as I could, I untied Kenny's poncho from his pack, rolled it out, and put it under him. Charlie continued pouring it on with AK-47 rifles, machine gun fire, and grenades. The grenades all fell short and exploded outside our perimeter.

Sergeant Dorman yelled, "Hurry up! We got to go!"

I couldn't lift and carry Kenny by myself. Bob was loaded down with equipment, the M-60 machine gun, and ammunition. Bob and I grabbed the corners of the poncho, lifted Kenny a few inches off the ground, and rushed in a crouched position to the far right of the perimeter—the side away from the enemy. Our platoon carried out all of our wounded and dead. No one was left behind.

Sergeant Dorman took a quick count of his men and said, "The rest of our company is waiting for us in the graveyard on the other side of this rice paddy. We have to move about one hundred yards in the open and we'll be exposed to enemy fire. Stay crouched and close to the dike on the left of the paddy for cover."

From the time the sergeant gave the order, it took us only minutes to grab up the wounded and dead and move into position to cross the rice paddy. The next thing I heard was, "Let's go!"

Almost at once, we started running in a crouched position as fast as our legs could go. Firing continued in front and behind us. I don't remember anyone stopping for even a short breather. As our ragged platoon came closer to the other side of the rice paddy, soldiers from our parent company waved us on while covering our advance with a base of fire. When we finally reached the American lines, we were exhausted and breathing heavily. A couple of American soldiers hurried the two prisoners away at gunpoint.

Inside the American lines, other soldiers helped us move the 2nd Platoon's wounded and dead comrades to a collection point inside the Vietnamese graveyard. The Vietnamese build their graveyards on dry ground above the water levels of the rice paddies. Each grave is a mound of dirt about three feet high, and the graves are lined up in rows as in any cemetery. The mounded graves provided a great defensive position and security for our wounded and dead.

Medics began to assist the wounded soldiers who lay on ponchos scattered on the ground. Not far from the wounded, the lifeless bodies of Robert Engberson and Earl Shelton, two young men from our platoon, were completely covered in green plastic ponchos, only their boots exposed. Staring at them, I thought how sad it was to see these men, lying side by side in the hot sun, in the dirt, beneath pieces of plastic.

When I saw Kenny again, I looked at him and said, "We made it! How do you feel?"

It was difficult for Kenny to talk, but he said he was fine and that the morphine was helping relieve much of his pain. Straining to speak, Kenny said, "Thanks for helping me, Johnny. Don't forget to tell my folks that I'm okay." I assured him I'd keep my word and write to his folks to tell them what had happened to their son.

The fighting seemed to have stopped. Apparaently, Charlie had broken contact or else had been wiped out by our reinforcements. Sergeant Dorman, Rod, Dunn, Engel, Blessing, Smitty, and the other survivors of the 2nd Platoon came by to pay their respects to the dead and wounded. I stayed with Kenny until the medics assisted my friend onto a stretcher and carried him to the designated liftoff area.

Several Medevac helicopters landed, and the wounded were loaded aboard. As Kenny and the others lifted off safely into the sky, I watched until the chopper disappeared. After Kenny was gone, I felt relieved that he'd be okay, but desolate at the thought of not having his company.

Will I ever see my friend again? I wondered as I walked along the perimeter.

Specialist Four Bob Dunn, Weapons Squad, 2nd Platoon, Company B. Bob manning his M60 Machinegun – 1966. I became his assistant gunner after Kenny Mook was wounded. (Photo courtesy of Bob Dunn).

I found Bob sitting behind his M-60, staring vigilantly across the rice paddy. I took Kenny's place as Bob's assistant gunner. It was quiet except for the Medevacs and supply ships flying in and out of the graveyard.

It was getting late, and darkness began settling in. Bob and I talked about how the events of the day had unfolded. Sergeant Dorman informed us that our sister company had made a sweep of the area and reported that a lot dead enemy soldiers were found around the positions our platoon had defended. The sergeant told us how proud he was of us for being brave and fighting like hell. After he left, it started raining.

I felt empty and alone for the first time since arriving in Vietnam. I felt I had lost my brother. I didn't know whether Kenny was going to live, or if he'd die before they got him to a hospital. What would I say to Kenny's family? What does anyone say to the families of men who were wounded or who had died for their country? I realized how quickly death can come. Tears streamed down my face; trying to hold them back was useless. Bob put his arm around me and assured me that it was okay to cry.

I pulled my poncho over my head and stared into the dark, feeling sad and angry. I couldn't stop thinking about every detail of what had happened that day, but the memories only pushed me deeper into depression. I promised myself that I'd never forget the men who had lost their lives. I hadn't known most of them, but they were Americans, and that was all I cared about. I wanted to kill every VC for what they'd done to Kenny and the others.

Later, the rain stopped and the clouds cleared. Bob and I stayed alert all night, waiting for a counterattack that never came. We took turns catnapping. The fighting appeared to have ended — my first combat experience was finally over.

The next morning I ate my C-Rations, shaved, and prepared to move out. I felt better, but I was ready to get the hell out of that place. The platoon was re-supplied with ammunition, water, and food for the rest of our journey to the South China Sea. Because we'd been reduced to about a squad and a half, we were attached to a sister platoon.

No one talked much as we joined the other platoon. My squad, led by Sergeant Dorman, was positioned as rear guard for the lead platoon. Two radios supported us as we passed through a few more burned-out villages that showed no signs of habitation. We didn't even see a chicken, a dog, or a water buffalo. Bomb and rocket craters pitted the ground. Charlie was nowhere in sight, and the quiet was spooky.

To my amazement, we were within a mile of the ocean. I figured that the platoon must have covered several miles since we'd started moving a few days earlier. Finally, I could see the ocean straight ahead.

Bridge over Bong Son and looking towards Shower Point—1966. A lot 7th Cavalrymen were wounded and killed in this beckoning place of beauty. (Photo courtesy of Dennis Blessing).

When the platoon arrived at the beach, some American soldiers were already in the water. Men spread out and relaxed in the sand all along the shoreline. I appreciated the peaceful setting even though I wasn't in the best of spirits. It was great to see my fellow soldiers splashing in the water and having fun. I stopped for a moment and stood on the white sand, listening to the waves splash against the shore. In the distance, I spotted large, gray navy ships. I wondered if they were the ones I'd seen from the mountain, firing into the valley.

The platoon stopped in an area where there was room to spread out and set up positions. After Bob and I put our equipment down, Sergeant Dorman came by and told us to enjoy ourselves for the rest of the day. As he promised, we had hot food, relaxation, and time to go swimming.

I kept thinking about Kenny, knowing that he'd have enjoyed this beach time. Starting to feel much better, I propped my back against a palm tree, rested in the shade, and wrote a letter to Kenny's parents, explaining what had happened to their second son.

Another battalion pulled perimeter security guard while I slept on the beach beneath that palm tree. I awoke the next morning to the sounds of sea gulls and ocean waves.

A bunch of choppers landed on a nearby road to take us back to An Khe. I climbed aboard one and lifted off into the cool high-altitude air and headed home. I sat on the floor of the slick, peering out the open doors. I tried to locate the positions where we'd fought with Charlie, but everything below looked the same. The Bong Son plains appeared peaceful from 1000 feet up. I don't remember how long it took us to fly home, but it was a very long ride over the mountain range.

When the base camp became visible in the distance, the choppers began their descent. As we flew closer to the huge perimeter of Camp Radcliff, I could see the road we'd traveled in the backs of the trucks going to Bong Son. The choppers made a sharp left turn and landed single file on the road behind the green canvas tents of our company's living quarters.

I slowly walked to my tent. When I got to my cot, I took my gear off and unpacked all the ammunition, claymore mines, grenades, trip flares, and empty magazines. The first priority was to check over everything for serviceability and possible replacement. Second priority was to clean and oil my weapon, which was full of carbon buildup and sand.

Sergeant Dorman walked in. He asked me to pack Kenny's gear and take it to the company supply tent, so I stuffed all of Kenny's belongings into his duffel bag, which was lying on his cot. Kenny had spent only a handful of nights sleeping in that cot. His wounds were so severe that he wouldn't be reporting back for duty. Neither would Earl Shelton and Robert Engberson, both killed in action.

The soldiers we lost in Bong Son were the real heroes of our platoon. They'd lived a tough life: marching long distances through hot jungles and rice paddies, hunting for a fight, eating canned C-Rations with plastic spoons, digging foxholes after a long day's patrol, carrying sixty-pound packs, pulling guard duty every night, and catnapping in the dirt, rain, and mud. I was beginning to learn and understand what Dorman, Blessing, Dunn, Smitty, Engel, and the other surviving veterans already knew. As darkness fell, I lay on my cot and prayed for the fallen and the safety of the survivors.

My next lesson in Vietnam would involve learning how an ordinary bamboo stick could be turned into a deadly weapon.

Chapter Five

WOUNDED IN ACTION

I got a liberty pass to go to "Sin City"—An Khe, the dusty little Vietnamese town outside base camp. I went with Sergeant Dorman and Bob Dunn. We had a great time. I bought a small mirror with a frame that was handmade from a beer can. The back of the mirror was part of a cardboard C-ration box. The Vietnamese always seemed to find use for Americans' trash, and sold back to us what we'd originally gotten for free.

FIRST CAVALRY DIVISION (AIRMOBILE)
LIBERTY PASS

This pass in only valid for visits to the town of An Khe and vicinity, between the hours of 0900 and 1800 daily.

BURNAM JOHN C   RA-17229988   E-3
NAME   ASN   GRADE

Co B. 1/9 Cav.   Camp Radcliff
ORGANIZATION   INSTALLATION

APRIL-16-66
DATE ISSUED

John C. Burnam   (signature)
SIGNATURE   SIGNATURE OF
                                 COMMANDING OFFICER
AVC Form 7
(26 Mar 66)

Private First Class John Burnam's first Liberty Pass to An Khe's "Sin City"–April 16, 1966. (Author collection).

After a morning shower and shave using my new mirror, I grabbed a quick breakfast at the mess hall and returned to the platoon area for an operations order. Sergeant Dorman had directed the platoon to pack a one-day basic load of ammunition and food. He showed us his field map and pointed to several mountains for a combat mission he called "hill jumping."

After studying the map, it was determined that several mountaintops had clearings large enough to land a few helicopters where S-2 (Battalion Intelligence) had reported enemy sightings. Charlie had been operating in small, highly mobile strike squads equipped with mortars and shoulder-mounted rocket launchers. They had been harassing our airfield, trying to destroy our aircraft on the runways, our ammunition dumps, and our communications towers and bunkers. Retaliatory artillery strikes weren't solving the problem, so our platoon was given the order to search on foot and destroy Charlie's hit-and-run squads.

My platoon was to assault onto each hilltop LZ by helicopter, and probe the surrounding woods and jungle in an effort to make contact with the enemy and take him out. If the LZ was hot, we were to secure it and radio for gunships and field-artillery support. If we didn't make contact with the enemy, we were to radio for liftoff and air assault into the next LZ marked on the map. The operation was to continue until dark or until all selected targets were checked out. Each team leader was assigned a radiotelephone operator.

I was assigned to Van Wilson's M-60 as assistant gunner. Van had provided security for the 3rd Brigade commander, Colonel Hal Moore, before joining the 2nd Platoon. Van was from Arkansas and six feet tall—much bigger than I. He had joined the army in May 1965. After he had completed basic training and advanced infantry training, and graduated from paratrooper school, he arrived in Vietnam in December 1965, four months before I did.

Van told me that the reason he had joined the army was because a North Vietnamese soldier had shot his brother in the ass. "I couldn't let the enemy get away with shooting a Wilson in the ass, so I joined up." Van had a cheerful personality and we got along great.

Specialist Four Van Wilson, M60 Machine-gunner,
2nd Platoon—1966. Van enjoying some leisure time fishing in a
Vietnam lake. (Photo courtesy of Van Wilson)

One day, in an idle moment while we were in defensive posture on a mission, Van challenged me to a wrestling match. It didn't last long: I took Van down to the dirt and pinned him in seconds. He couldn't understand how a little guy like me could have done it so easily.

I joined the service in September 1965, right after graduating from Littleton High School and taking the summer off. I wasn't ready for college, even though I had a potential wrestling scholarship to attend Trinidad Junior College in Colorado. I was more interested in leaving home and being on my own than in pursuing a college education.

I saw a large poster of a soldier wearing a green beret in the window of the U.S. Army recruiting station. I got excited and decided to inquire about joining the Special Forces. Next thing I knew, a sergeant in a snappy army dress uniform had my complete attention. That recruiter told me that the army offered a great way to travel to foreign lands and visit exotic cities and cultures that I'd otherwise have to pay a lot of money to experience on vacation. I was young, trusting, had no money, no job, no girlfriend, and was eager to make a positive change in my life, so I signed on the dotted line.

The army shipped me by train from Denver to Fort Leonard, Missouri, for basic training, then to Fort Ord, California, for advanced infantry training, and finally to Fort Benning, Georgia, for paratrooper training. After graduating from paratrooper school in February 1966, I was ordered to Vietnam with no specific unit of assignment listed on my paperwork. I was shocked, as I'd had no idea there was a war going on in Vietnam or where on Earth that country was located. I asked lots of questions, but learned little to satisfy my curiosity. I wouldn't have enlisted had I known I'd be sent off to fight in a war, but it was too late—I was now a soldier and I belonged to Uncle Sam.

In preparation for the mission, Van prepared his M-60 and packed several hundred-round ammunition belts, while I checked the spare-parts bag for the M-60 and packed it with two hundred-round belts. I also packed 200 rounds of M-16 ammunition into magazines and slipped them into the pockets of my shoulder-sling bandoleers. I hung several grenades on the webbing of my shoulder harness.

This, one day's worth of supplies, was the lightest load I had ever packed for a mission.

Three ten-man squads were alerted, packed, and ready to go in under an hour. Each squad consisted of a grenadier with an M79 grenade launcher, a man armed with a twelve-gauge shotgun, four M-16 riflemen, a medic, and an M-60 machine gunner and assistant gunner. Each squad had enough diversified firepower to handle any small group of VC they might run into.

Sergeant Dorman led one of the three squads. The time came to saddle up and assemble at the pickup point on the road not far from our living quarters. This would be another mission without Kenny Mook, who'd been like a brother to me. We'd been inseparable from the day we first met at the replacement center in Saigon, and it felt strange not to have him at my side. I didn't trust anyone as much as I trusted Kenny. I missed him terribly and wondered, now that my best friend was gone, who would protect me the way he had?

While we waited for the choppers, I sat on the ground, leaning against my backpack like the other seasoned combat veterans. Now I knew what to do and how to fight when I made contact with the enemy. I didn't simply fear the possibility of seeing combat—I now expected it.

The noisy choppers threw dust in our faces as we made our way to their open doors and climbed aboard. I was positioned in the first chopper with Van and several other soldiers. When we lifted off, I noticed that only three troopships were required to cart my entire squad. As we flew over the perimeter of our base camp, a gunship joined the group at low altitude.

2nd Platoon Sky Troopers Air Assault
into enemy territory—1966 (Author collection).

The morning sun felt good, and so did the fresh air circulating inside the ship. The lush jungle canopy blanketing the ground below looked peaceful. The choppers climbed toward a small range of hills. Before long, they began their descent into a clearing on the first hilltop. As my ship got closer to touchdown, I scooted to the open door and prepared to jump out. The choppers didn't land in the clearing; instead, they hovered a few feet off the ground just long enough for us to jump.

I dropped to the ground, ran a few feet, and crouched on one knee, facing the trees ahead. I didn't look back but could hear the sound of choppers drifting away. When I finally turned around, they were gone. Our entire squad was alone, and it was quiet on the ground. The drop-off had taken place in less than a minute. The squad leader lifted his arm and pointed in the direction he wanted us to move. I heard birds chirping in the trees as we cautiously moved forward in crouched positions, weapons at the ready. The noise of a nearby chopper broke the silence, but I didn't look up, I focused on looking for signs of danger.

When we got inside the vegetation beyond the skirt of the small clearing, Sergeant Dorman sent two riflemen to probe deeper into the surrounding area. When they returned and reported seeing nothing suspicious, the sergeant moved the squad clockwise to a different spot and repeated the probing tactic around that entire LZ until we were back to where we'd started. We found no indication that Charlie had set up mortars or rocket positions near that hilltop.

After an hour of reconnoitering, Sergeant Dorman reported our squad's situation by radio. Minutes later, three choppers landed. The door gunners on each side pointed their M-60s at the trees, ready to fire. Without incident, we quickly boarded and flew off to another hilltop.

A gunship escorted our squadron of choppers to our next drop-off point on Sergeant Dorman's map. During the short ride, I scooted on my butt to the open doors to get ready for my second jump. Tall elephant grass covered the entire clearing below. Suddenly, bullets zipped through the air and hit the metal skin of the ship. The door gunner immediately returned fire with his M-60 machine gun. I quickly moved into the open door and saw that I was just above the weaving grass below. I lowered my feet onto the landing skid and stood up. With my right hand, I held onto the side of the ship. With its nose up, the ship moved forward slowly, but didn't land. I was fully exposed and not feeling safe. Bullets kept slamming into the chopper's side as I hung on, preparing to jump out.

The door gunner tapped my hand and pointed his hand down as my signal to go. I jumped into the elephant grass and hit the ground hard. A sudden sharp pain ripped through my right knee and I fell, twisting onto my belly. I tried to get up, but the pain in my knee drove the idea out of my head. Looking down, I saw a yellow bamboo punji stake sticking right through my knee. It had entered under the kneecap and exited the other side. The rest of the stake splintered below my leg. I tried again to move, but was in severe pain and anchored to the ground.

I knew that the VC carved small bamboo spears and planted them among the natural vegetation, placing them in the ground at forty-five-degree angles, with their sharp points at about thigh level. Anyone who walked into or fell onto one of the spears was immediately incapacitated. Worse yet, the VC dipped the sharp end of the spear into human waste to add infection to the wound. Charlie also placed those sharp sticks in man-sized holes covered with vegetation, and along the sides of well-traveled footpaths, so if you took cover by diving off the path and into the brush, punji stakes were waiting for you. Charlie was a very clever warrior who made good use of his natural surroundings.

I couldn't believe I'd been wounded by one of those primitive, yet debilitating, bamboo spears—I'd always thought I'd be shot. Despite being in pain, I prepared to defend myself. With a round in the chamber of my M-16, my finger rested on the trigger, the safety off and the selector on FULL AUTO.

A lot of shooting and tremendous explosions shook the ground all around me. The tall elephant grass surrounding me blocked my ability to see anything but the sky above. Over the noise, I heard Van's M-60 firing. He was close, but I wasn't able to move in his direction.

As I tried to prop myself into a better position to shoot, I heard American voices screaming for a medic. Immobile, I lay in agony and tried to remain calm. Soon, I heard movement in the grass nearby. Not knowing the source of the sound, I decided not to take any chances by calling out. I remained silent, my heart pounding a fast and steady rhythm. The noise in the grass moved closer and the adrenaline started to rush through me. I pointed my M-16 nervously toward the sound, finger on the trigger. A voice cried out, "Are you okay?" An American helmet broke through the grass near my feet. It was Doc Bell. He crawled to me on his belly as the intensity of the shooting and explosions increased around us. I sighed in relief as I eased my finger off the trigger and dropped the rifle barrel to the ground beside me.

I felt safe with Doc. He encouraged me to lie still as he checked me over, then he gave me a shot of painkiller and a drink of water. When Doc Bell moved my knee and snipped away the splintered pieces of bamboo around my wound, I gnashed my teeth and my eyes squirted tears of agony as the blood gushed. With one hand, Doc quickly pulled the large piece of bamboo from under my kneecap. I cried out in excruciating pain. It was hard to lie still while he bandaged the wound. I grew very dizzy, hot, and weak all at once.

Doc Bell talked to me the whole time, telling me that Van had pointed to where I was and that was how he'd located me. He told me to stay calm while he went to help the others. I watched him crawl into the grass and out of sight.

The whole time I lay there, I could hear VC voices through the grass but couldn't see anyone. An hour must have passed, but I didn't fire a single shot. I still couldn't believe I'd been stuck by a damn punji stake. I didn't fear being captured or overrun, but I wondered if I'd ever be able to use my right leg. All sorts of thoughts passed through my mind: *Hell, I was the first-string linebacker on the varsity football team and won all those wrestling championship medals at Littleton High. How could this happen to my leg now? Am I ever going to walk right again?"*

Eventually, the firing and explosions trickled to a stop, and a long period of silence followed. I began to hear other Americans moving through the grass, saying, "Watch out for those punji stakes." Then Van Wilson was standing over me, asking if I was okay. Van said he'd seen me go down before he jumped, and that he was lucky not to get stuck too. He said freshly planted punji stakes were all over the place.

Helicopters soon flew overhead like a swarm of bees. The enemy was gone. God only knew how many of them had died during the firefight. Van helped me take off my heavy pack and stand on one foot, but I felt lightheaded. I grabbed Van's shoulder as he pulled me up by my belt. I hobbled on one leg to the waiting helicopter.

Van fetched my gear and put it beside me in the chopper, which held two other wounded soldiers. Before long, we were airborne and on our way to a field hospital in Qui Nhom. After being examined there, I was evacuated to a hospital that had better facilities for reconstructive knee surgery.

My only recurring thought was *Will I survive this wound and walk normally again?*

Specialist Four Van Wilson, M60 Machine-gunner, 2nd Platoon—1966. I can never thank Van enough for helping me get on that chopper and safely out of harms way. (Photos courtesy of Van Wilson)

Chapter Six

106 GENERAL HOSPITAL

Feeling relieved to be in a country that wasn't at war, I arrived at the 106 U.S. Army General Hospital in Kashini Barracks, Yokohama, Japan. The hospital was situated in a former WWII Japanese Army installation. Tall barbed-wire fence surrounded the entire compound. Armed U.S. Army military policemen dressed in heavily starched khaki uniforms, and sporting highly polished black boots, were stationed at the entrance and exit to the base.

I was assigned to Orthopedic Ward D on the second floor of one of the old buildings. At least thirty other young soldiers occupied hospital beds lined up in rows against the beige walls of a large room. The place was clean and tidy, and the air smelled of medicine. Large fans at each end of the ward circulated the warm late-summer air.

Ward D buzzed with indistinguishable chatter: the voices of bedridden soldiers, and nurses moving about with medicine trays. My bed was near the entrance to the nurses' station. The soldier on my left had to lie on his stomach because of a wound in his back. The man on my right had an L-shaped cast that ran from his neck to his fingers. Other men's arms and legs were covered with bandages.

After I got comfortable, a nurse and a doctor came by to give me a complete examination. They introduced themselves as Dr. George Bogumill and Nurse Nancy Jones. Dr. Bogumill had a gentle disposition and a kind bedside manner. He thought I looked younger than nineteen, told me that I was too young to be sent to war, and jokingly asked if my mother had signed the enlistment papers that got me into the army.

Nurse Jones, a pretty woman in her mid-twenties, had a comforting smile and a great figure. I liked the idea that she'd been assigned to take care of me. The medical staff asked many questions about when I was injured, how it had happened, and what type of treatment I'd received before arriving. I appreciated their patience and care, especially when they removed the bandages to examine my wound, then cleaned it and redressed it from upper thigh to ankle. None of them had a clue about what combat was like or the pain of being wounded in action. They could no doubt have filled a small library with short stories of what they learned at the bedsides of the wounded soldiers they nursed to health over the course of their tour in Japan.

As days turned into weeks, I befriended patients in the beds around me. We talked about our Vietnam War experiences. Each man told his story of how he'd been wounded. Almost everyone I spoke to came from a different infantry unit.

The man on my right, Robert Lang, had been shot in the arm while on patrol near the Mekong Delta, 250 miles south of where I'd been wounded. Charlie had waited in ambush for Robert's squad as they moved along a trail. Robert happened to be a flank guard. Charlie spotted him first, and, Robert said, had been a little faster on the trigger than he was. Several rounds from an AK-47 shattered a bone in Robert's forearm and ripped a hole in his biceps. The impact had spun him completely around and onto the ground. He passed out, having never fired one round; the last thing he remembered was seeing the face of the VC who had shot him. Robert said that he often awoke in the night seeing the enemy face that wouldn't let him rest.

Robert had been healing in the hospital for several months. The doctor had told him that he'd soon get his cast off and start physical therapy. Robert was one of the few men on the ward able to get out of bed, eat in the dining hall, and walk around the ward.

Gary Morton was the man on my left. His platoon had been ambushed in the jungle while checking out what appeared to be a deserted VC base camp. As his patrol was leaving, the VC had taken them by surprise. Gary remembered getting down and not being hit by the first volley of small arms fire. He had fired back by emptying an entire twenty-round magazine. While he was changing magazines, an enemy machine gun opened fire in front of him. Something slammed into his upper back and rolled him onto his back. Gary had felt dazed but thought he was okay. When he tried to roll back onto his belly, he realized that he had no feeling in his arms. Then he lost consciousness. By the time Gary regained his senses, he was lying on a cot in an army field hospital.

Since Gary's back was in such bad shape, he could lie only on his stomach. A web of silver metal wires was sewn over his open wound, keeping it from tearing open. The bullets had missed his spine, but had torn a very large chunk of skin and muscle from his back and shoulder. The wound was clean, and I could actually see his left shoulder blade surrounded by raw flesh. Every so often, the nurse and doctor would bring small patches of skin they'd cut from Gary's leg, and graft them onto the hole in his back. During my hospital stay, I watched the progress of those skin grafts. They took hold and grew without much infection, and the size of the hole in Gary's shoulder gradually decreased. I wondered if he would ever have full use of his left shoulder or the muscles on the left side of his back.

Even though the men in my ward had suffered wounds as a result of combat in Vietnam, morale was high. Many of the wounded knew that after they recovered they'd be medically discharged from the army and sent home. Like me, most were young and had been in the army less than a year. Now they'd bear scars for the rest of their lives. Everyone was always talking about home, which made a big difference in how they felt about their health and everything else.

Finally, the day came when I was prepped and wheeled away for a surgery that lasted several hours. When I returned to consciousness, I was in my bed again, feeling dry-mouthed and drowsy. I really needed to take a leak but I couldn't move because of the pain, so I called for Nurse Jones to bring me a bedpan. She placed the bedpan under the covers and stood beside me until I used it. Talk about performance anxiety!

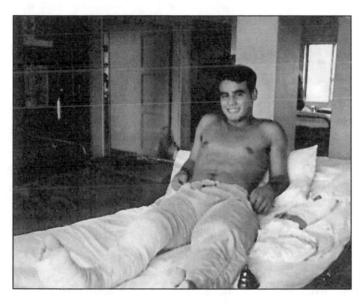

John Burnam–Recovering from punji stick wound at the 106 General Hospital, Kashini Barracks, Yokahama, Japan–1966. I had no pictures of my stay in the hospital until I reunited with Van Wilson in 2003. Van put me on a chopper after I was wounded and gave me this picture I had sent to him in Vietnam with a note on the back and my signature–37 years ago.

The operation was successful. Dr. Bogumill said that I'd be able walk normally again, but would have to work hard at physical therapy. A physical therapist came to my bedside a few days later. He encouraged me to start lifting my leg, and helped me do so. The pain was agonizing. The guys in the beds beside me kept joking and calling me "a pussy." This was typical verbal harassment—a way for us to help each other to persist in whatever we had to do to heal. Despite the pain, I slowly moved my right knee up and down.

After I'd had some success, the therapist draped socks full of sand over my ankles. If I were going to get better, I'd have to ignore the pain and concentrate on strengthening the my leg muscles. As the leg strengthened with the increased repetitions, the therapist added more weight and encouraged me to keep going. The guys in the beds next to me continued chanting, "More weight! More weight!" Eventually, I could sit on the edge of the bed and bend my leg slightly at the knee.

Oh, man! When the blood rushed down my leg, a whole different level of pain brought tears to my eyes. It was the same old thing each time I tried to sit up and hang my legs over the edge of the bed. Eventually, I learned to expect the pain of therapy.

After a month, I was able to use crutches to move around the ward, eat in the dining hall, and pee standing up. I'd gotten cocky a few times and let go of the crutches. After one step, I'd fallen flat on my face, but that didn't keep me from trying to walk on my own. I wasn't going to be a cripple, and that was that!

My wound seemed to be healing faster than Dr. Bogumill had expected. "Maybe," I joked to him, "it's because I'm only nineteen years old." The sixty stitches were removed from the sides of my knee, leaving two ugly ten-inch scars. Sporting tiny stubs of hair, the shaved knee was swollen to twice the size of my left knee, and blood oozed from the puffy holes. My knee looked like the face of Frankenstein's monster—not a pretty sight.

By the end of my hospital stay, I was bored. I watched men in the ward get well and go home, and I thought about going home, too. I missed riding my motorcycle, going on dates, seeing a scary movie at the drive-in, eating a juicy cheeseburger with hot French fries, and hanging around with my family and friends. I craved a cold bottle of Coors. Most of the guys I knew had never heard of the Coors beer slogan, "Brewed with pure Rocky Mountain spring water." I hadn't met any other soldiers from Colorado, so no one understood the special things I missed about my home state.

I had a patient take a photo of me while I was propped up on my elbows in bed. I sent that photo to my friend, Van Wilson, who was still humping the boonies with the 7th Cavalry in Vietnam. He gave it back to me when we reunited in 2003.

As soon as a bed was vacated, it was filled almost immediately with another wounded soldier from Vietnam, like there was a line of wounded men outside the door, waiting for the next available bed. The cycle of men entering and leaving Ward D was neverending. At night, I'd hear the screams of soldiers having nightmares, a constant reminder of the war in Vietnam; I'm sure they heard my nightmares, too. No one ever talked much about what went on at night, unless an emergency occurred. Thank God no one died in Ward D while I was there.

Recovered well enough not to need crutches or a cane, I got a liberty pass to Yokohama, the city right outside our military compound. I had to follow the rules and return to the hospital before dark. Civilian clothes weren't authorized for patients, so I was issued a khaki military uniform, a hat, and a pair of shoes. I signed a partial-pay voucher for fifty dollars and suddenly felt rich.

No patient was authorized to go off the base alone. We had to use the buddy system, so I teamed up with another patient; we caught a cab outside the gate, and off we went. The Japanese cab driver spoke enough English to ask, "Where to?"

"Downtown," we replied.

He nodded, and drove us to what looked like a main street near a pier full of boats and ships; there was a fish market nearby.

The streets of Yokohama were crowded with people going about their usual business. The Japanese women wore colorful kimonos; the men were in street clothes and suits. This contrasted with the attire of the Vietnamese, who wore black pajamas and straw hats. We took our time, slowly walking the sidewalks and resting as much as possible. The Japanese acted as though we weren't there. I guess they were used to seeing American servicemen on their streets. I felt quite comfortable even though we couldn't understand a word they said. There was a sense of freedom all around us—something I hadn't experienced in a long time.

We stopped in a bar, ordered a few Japanese beers, but didn't eat anything. Japanese music played on a radio. We sat, talked, and sipped our brews. After a while, we left that bar and roamed the streets and the marketplace. I wasn't much of a fish eater, so I was repulsed by the awful smell of the fish market we passed. Not long after, we found a cab to take us back to Kashini Barracks.

The day finally came when Dr. Bogumill and Nurse Jones informed me that my prognosis was good enough for me to be discharged from the hospital. My knee didn't hurt much. The muscles in my right thigh were strong again as a result of physical therapy. I'd also strengthened my upper body by using weights and exercising. I could even jog a little now.

Dr. Bogumill told me that I was healthy enough to return to active duty. This wasn't what I wanted to hear.

"How about a one-way trip to Littleton, Colorado, Doc?" I asked, even though my wound wasn't severe enough for a medical discharge.

I sensed from the doctor's manner that he really cared about his patients. He told me to get the hell out of the infantry and find a safer job, and then get out of the army and go to college.

Since I'd joined the army, it seemed that I was always being disappointed. First, I didn't get to go to Special Forces school and was sent to Vietnam instead. When I got there, I nearly killed several of my own squad by accidentally forgetting to secure my rifle's safety. After only two months' service, my best friend, Kenny, had almost been killed. I'd been wounded, and now I couldn't get discharged from Uncle Sam's army because I'd healed too well. I was beginning to think it was my lot in life to be surrounded by tragedy, almost making it to safety, only to get pulled back into the soup again.

While in the hospital, I'd written many letters home, mentioning the possibility that I might be discharged. I'd told people to start planning my homecoming party. Now I had to write and tell everyone to put away the party hats. The army was going to keep me on active duty in the Pacific.

Even if I wasn't going home, the news that I'd soon be leaving the hospital made me extremely happy. I'd soon leave Japan for an assignment in Okinawa. Little did I know that my new assignment would change my life in a totally unexpected way.

I'd soon be meeting my first war dog.

Chapter Seven

SENTRY DOG PLATOON

In January 1967 the U.S. Army released me from the 106 Army General Hospital in Yokohama, Japan, and reassigned me to the island of Okinawa to serve out my remaining tour in Southeast Asia.

Okinawa was a huge military supply depot that serviced the war effort in Vietnam. There were no infantry units there, so I was assigned to the 267th Chemical Company because they needed sentry-dog handlers. I guess the personnel clerk felt that an infantryman could perform the duties of a sentry-dog handler. He must have keyed on the words "infantry" and "sentry" as a close-enough occupational match.

I liked the idea of having a dog of my own, even though it really belonged to Uncle Sam. Training with a sentry dog would involve quite a learning process, but it would prove challenging and exciting. And though they could bark, the dogs wouldn't be barking orders at me like the sergeants did. The idea of having a dog to pal around with sounded too good to be true.

When I reported for work at the 267th Company, I met with the 1st Sergeant in his office. I stood at attention in front of his desk. He looked up and saw that I wore a Combat Infantryman Badge. In a soft voice he said, "At ease, soldier." As I relaxed my position, he commented, "A CIB on such a young boy!" I immediately thought, *Here's that "boy" thing again,* but somehow, coming from a salty old veteran, it didn't upset me, so I didn't snap back. He smiled and then offered me a cup of coffee. "Top," as we commonly called the 1st Sergeant, was an infantry veteran who had fought the Nazis in Europe and the North Koreans and Chinese during the Korean War. Okinawa was probably his last assignment before his retirement.

After trading a few war stories, Top told me that I was the only Vietnam combat infantry veteran in the outfit wearing a CIB and a Purple Heart, which seemed to make him proud to have me aboard. When he briefed me on the mission of the 267th, Top explained that the unit provided security for and managed the contents of the army's ammunition-storage buildings in a controlled area of the island. The job called for a number of sentry-dog teams—German shepherd and handler—to guard the buildings. He explained the sensitive nature of the mission and how important it was not to discuss the work with anyone outside official channels. That restriction included not taking pictures or writing anything about my work in letters home.

Top advised me to be careful around strangers who offered free drinks in downtown bars. "There are spies out there," he said. "They want classified information about what we do. Don't talk or try to figure them out; they're professionals. Report everything immediately to our security officer. Do you understand, soldier?"

I immediately replied, "Yes, sir!"

He barked back, "And don't call me 'sir'—I work for a living!"

It all sounded mysterious, but what the hell did I know about that type of army business? Top instructed me to read and sign an official military document corroborating that our briefing had taken place. I supposed that if I were suspected of talking with a communist, the army would have been able to use that document against me, lock my young ass up, and lose the key.

I thought, *Hell, man! The army doesn't have to worry about me; I'm a true red-white-and blue American who'd never sell out my country to some communist bastard.*

Top got up from behind the desk, shook my hand, and told the clerk sitting outside his office to add my name to the roster of sentry-dog handlers. Sitting beside the company clerk's desk, I filled out a long personal-history form so I could get a security clearance. My next stop was to meet the men of the sentry-dog platoon.

A dog handler named Fred escorted me to my new living quarters on the third floor above the company offices. About my size in height and build, Fred had straight black hair, brown eyes, a square jaw, and a neatly trimmed mustache. His uniform was starched stiff and his boots spit-shined. Fred had joined the army two years before I had, and held the enlisted rank of Specialist Four (SP4), one rank above my Private First Class (PFC).

I picked an empty bunk bed and stored my personals. I was issued a set of white sheets, a blanket, a pillow, and a pillowcase. After having slept in about ten different places since leaving my tent in Vietnam, it was a relief to finally have a new home.

I thought about the members of my old combat platoon. *Is Sergeant Dorman still alive? What about my new friend, Van Wilson, who helped carry me out of harm's way? Van had a November 1966 rotation date and must have gone back to Arkansas,* I thought. I closed my eyes and became lost in thoughts of the men I had left in Vietnam. The sound of Sergeant Dorman yelling, "Saddle up!" and the rat-tat-tat of Van's M-60 machine gun blasting away on that hilltop remained fresh in my memory.

Fred was anxious for me to meet the rest of the members of the sentry-dog platoon, who were out at the kennel or on guard duty. I asked him about the small, one-inch-square patch he wore above his nametag. It had the head of a German shepherd sewn in black against a yellow background. Fred told me that all the army sentry-dog handlers wore that patch. I would have to earn my patch through on-the-job dog training. Fred wanted to know what I knew about sentry dogs. I told him that the only sentry dogs I'd encountered were in Vietnam or behind fences, guarding junkyards back home.

I was the first Vietnam veteran Fred had met. With excitement in his eyes, he questioned me about my combat experiences. I answered him in very general terms, not yet comfortable enough with

Fred or my new surroundings to tell my stories. I felt more comfortable trading stories with the 1st Sergeant: though we were generations apart in age, and occupied different stations in life, that CIB seemed to bond us immediately in unspoken respect.

No one I had met since leaving the hospital had served a day in Vietnam or the infantry. They all had noncombatant jobs in rear-area support, and it wasn't easy to have a one-sided conversation about combat. Most of them told me that they were glad to have been assigned to units not fighting in Vietnam. Staring, they hung on every word I said, treating me like I was something unusual, which made me feel awkward in their company. It felt odd not being around a bunch of grunts carrying weapons. I just wanted to fit in and see those German shepherd sentry dogs everyone was talking about.

Fred informed me that sentry-dog handlers worked night shifts, guarding a highly secured compound. Days off varied, and I'd eventually enter the rotation. Each morning the dog handlers would load up into vehicles and head off to the kennel to work with the dogs.

I had no idea what to expect the first time I arrived at the kennel, greeted by the sounds of a bunch of barking dogs. The dog handlers quickly dismounted the truck and entered the kennels. I lagged behind a little to observe. Inside the kennels, handlers yelled the names of their dogs: Wolf, Mike, Rex, and Lucky.

After the handlers exited the kennel, their dogs attached to leather leashes, I slowly entered. The smell of fresh dog shit and urine on the concrete floor permeated the air. The German shepherds were housed behind thick wire fencing. Each dog's name was written on a piece of plywood attached above his kennel door. A metal choke chain hung on a nail outside each kennel door, along with a leather leash and muzzle. Metal water and food bowls sat inside each dog run.

As I walked by the caged German shepherds, they growled and lunged at me. Had one of those gates accidentally popped open, I'd have been dog meat, literally. It was a horrifying thought. The dogs probably sensed that I was scared shitless. Not one dog allowed me to get close without growling and showing me how big and sharp his teeth were. *Maybe I don't want to be a sentry dog handler after all,* I thought.

At both ends of the kennel were walls lined with wooden bins, each labeled with the name of one of the dogs. Neatly stored in each bin were grooming equipment, long leashes, leather collars, and leather muzzles. Large boxes of dog food were stacked high alongside several large metal lockers. Water hoses were connected to pipes at each end of the kennel. Two dog handlers turned the hoses on and washed the waste on the floor through the back of the fenced runs, laughing as they squirted some of dogs just to piss them off.

Outside, other handlers groomed their dogs on small wooden tables with posts to which the animals were tied. The handlers talked to their dogs while they brushed them, cleaned their teeth, clipped their nails, and checked them for health problems. I watched, impressed at how muscular and fit the animals appeared, not a bit of fat on any of them. The platoon sergeant approached and instructed me to observe and help around the kennels for the next few days.

The sergeant was responsible for matching dogs to new handlers. Usually, a new guy was assigned the healthiest dog that had spent the most time without a handler. Each dog was already trained in basic obedience, but if a dog didn't work on a regular basis, he became lazy. This meant that training with the dogs was an extremely important part of the handlers' routine. Sentry dogs were trained for the primary function of guarding and attacking on command. They learn through repetition, and are taught to react to the commands of only one master. I would soon learn an essential rule for working with sentry dogs: don't befriend any animal other than your assigned dog.

Rex held the distinction of being the most ferocious sentry dog. His handler, SP4 Aldridge, was a tall, husky man with scars on his arms where Rex had bitten him several times.

The platoon sergeant decided to assign me to Hans, the biggest, but not the meanest-looking, German shepherd in the kennel. In fact, none of the dogs was friendly to me; each one charged at me, barking and growling and baring his teeth as I passed by his run. It didn't really matter which dog was assigned to me, because they all wanted to eat me. I think the platoon sergeant figured that if I could handle Hans, I could handle any dog. He was definitely testing my fear-factor level. Right then, I feared every one of those dogs, and they sensed it.

The sergeant said, "Come on, Burnam! Before you know it, you'll have Hans eating out of your hand. The hardest part is overcoming your fear. Besides, this job's a piece of cake compared to what you went through in Vietnam."

I replied, "Yeah, right!"

My first task was to spend quality time with Hans, feeding him, cleaning his cage, and talking to him. During that initial "let's get acquainted" period, I didn't dare go into his run or try to touch Hans through the wire fence. Physical distance was okay with me; I figured I had plenty of time and was in no hurry to put my hands on that big dog. This was so different from what I'd expected. When I arrived in Vietnam, I was eager to fit in and do my job even though I was a "greenhorn," but this dog job was becoming an altogether different kind of challenge.

Someone joked, "Just remember, if Hans bites a chunk out of your ass, you'll be getting a tetanus shot instead of a Purple Heart."

Those who heard the remark burst into laughter. I stood there in silence, realizing that I was going through an acceptance process just as I had in Vietnam.

Every time I visited Hans, he'd growl and try to bite through the wire fence that separated us. The platoon sergeant said Hans' growling was his way of testing my control and my fear. He told me I had to show no fear if I was ever to have a chance at commanding an army sentry dog.

Over time, Hans became accustomed to seeing me and stopped growling. I was getting used to him, too. With each passing day, my fear slowly diminished and the day finally arrived when the platoon sergeant told me to take Hans out of his kennel run.

"Do you think I'm ready, Sarge?"

The sergeant replied, "It's now or never, Burnam! Besides, you survived combat in Vietnam, so handling Hans should be no problem!"

Both the dog and the platoon sergeant were testing me. I had to take Hans out of the kennel and deal with him face to face. I kept thinking, *I can't be chicken-shit about it or let that dog control me. I've got to take control of him and just do it!*

I took a deep breath, cleared my mind, grabbed the leather leash, and connected a choke chain to it. All the while, Hans paced back and forth like a hungry lion in a cage. He knew he was getting out. I tried not to think of what could happen after I opened that door.

The platoon sergeant watched me as I kept delaying the inevitable. I spread the choke chain as far as possible, so that the dog's head could pass through quickly and easily. Then I took another long breath and opened the door. Now there was nothing to keep Hans from eating me alive. To my surprise, he quickly put his nose and head through the loop of the choke chain and charged past me through the open door, pulling me behind him toward the exit and the open area behind the kennel.

Running behind us, the platoon sergeant kept yelling, "Yank back on the leash! Command the dog to heel!" I pulled back as hard as I could on the leash and yelled, "Heel! Heel! Heel!" Hans ignored me and pulled even harder. Finally, he must have gotten tired, because he just stopped pulling and started walking and sniffing the ground. Then he lifted his leg and took a leak on a fence post. After he finished, I pulled on the leash and gave the command to heel. To my surprise, Hans moved to my left side and sat.

The platoon sergeant instructed me to praise Hans by saying, "Good dog! Good dog!" Verbal praise was fine; I just hoped the sergeant wouldn't ask me to give Hans a hug. While we marched around the training yard, Hans stayed at my pace. I had a huge smile on my face, feeling as if I had won the blue ribbon in a basic obedience contest. My fear had been temporarily replaced with joy.

There was a lot more to learn if I was going to become a respected sentry-dog handler. The platoon sergeant told me I'd have to master the commands for basic obedience and learn to control Hans under all circumstances. Hans already knew what to do, but needed a master to make him do it. I had to be consistent in how I handled him. I learned that discipline was extremely important, and could be achieved only by practicing with Hans every day. Through effective training, he could become my companion, and maybe we would make a great team.

Several days passed as Hans and I reached the point that, when I dangled the leash in front of his cage, he would go crazy with excitement. When Hans stood on his hind legs he was taller than I am, one of the biggest German shepherds in the platoon. All the sentry dogs were healthy and lean because of their diet and rigorous daily training. There wasn't one fat dog handler, either; every man was in excellent health and top physical condition.

I was issued a military dog-training manual and was expected to learn and practice what it preached. The manual contained illustrations of tools and procedures for grooming, voice commands, hand and arm signals, deployment, and first aid. The other dog handlers were already versed in the commands and advanced dog-training techniques. Most had graduated from a formal twelve-week military dog-training school in the States, so I watched them work their animals. Everything they did appeared to be simple and smooth, and showed a genuine loving bond between dog and handler, even though each dog was trained to be a lethal weapon.

The platoon sergeant assigned Fred to be my tutor in the finer arts of basic obedience training. Fred's happy-go-lucky personality was quickly rubbing off on me. He always talked about the pretty Okinawa barmaids working at Club Lucky, a downtown bar not far from the base, which the dog handlers frequented and considered their special hangout.

Fred taught me that positive reinforcement was critical throughout the training exercises. My first lesson included the voice commands *sit, heel, come, down, stay,* and *no,* and rules on when to praise the dog. Fred taught me how to use voice inflection when calling out commands to Hans. I practiced for hours each day until I could voice the commands with the precision of a drill sergeant.

At first, Hans was slow to commit to the action when commanded. When I commanded him to sit, he took his time. When I voiced the command "down," Hans would get only partway down and then return to a sit. But after several training sessions, Hans became more responsive, obeying my basic voice commands. The dog that had scared the crap out me before was slowly becoming a loving partner.

Eventually, I was ready to join the rest of the platoon for regular group training sessions. Uniformity was the key. Each dog handler carried the same equipment attached to specific places on his pistol belt. Each pistol belt held a canteen of water, a six-foot leather leash, a leather collar, a choke chain, a twenty-five-foot nylon leash, a leather muzzle, a first-aid bandage, and a .45 caliber pistol in a black leather holster. Of course our green fatigue uniforms had to be clean and starched, our tarnish-free brass belt buckles gleaming, and our black boots spit-shined.

Outside the kennel, the platoon sergeant, positioned several feet away and front and center of the platoon, would assemble the twenty dog handlers with their dogs in a formation of four ranks. When he called the platoon to attention, everyone assumed the standing position of attention—feet together, shoulders back, heads and eyes straight ahead. The position of attention for the dog was a full and proper sitting position at the handler's left side.

Dogs weren't allowed to slouch or sit leaning on one hind leg. Standing little more than an arm's length from his dog, each handler gripped near the end of the choke chain, his left hand close to the dog's neck. That way he could easily control the dog if it decided to attack a nearby dog or handler—after all, these dogs were trained to attack and kill. One of the handlers commented, "When an infiltrator enters my guard post, it's bite, bang, halt!"

We would make our way to the training area, surrounded by a chain link fence, and across the dirt road from the kennel. We'd all assemble in a platoon formation in the center of the training yard and below a tall wooden platform. The platoon sergeant stood on top of the platform to command and dog-drill the platoon.

When the platoon sergeant commanded, "Sit dog command" the dog handlers would simultaneously repeat the command, "Sit!" When all the dogs sat, the sergeant would command, "Down dog command." Again, everyone chorused, "Down!" The sergeant would yell at us if we didn't execute the command in unison. Rhythm and precision were both key to the training exercise.

After calling the platoon to the position of attention, the sergeant would command, "Move to the end of the leash." To carry out this order, the handlers would command his dog "Stay," then march to the end of the leash, turn, and face the dog. Sometimes, the dog would disobey and follow behind the handler. When this happened, the platoon sergeant would get pissed off at the handler and yell at him. I got yelled at a lot during those exercises, because Hans would lie down when I turned my back on him. Once we were all standing at attention at the end of the leash and facing our dogs, the platoon sergeant would bark, "Down dog command!"

We practiced many other basic obedience drills: *sit, stay, right face, left face, about face, down, heel,* and *march.* We weren't allowed to praise our dogs until we successfully completed a movement and the platoon sergeant gave the command "Okay." When the dogs were warmed up, we performed three or four successful movements in sequence and the platoon sergeant would again command, "Okay."

I soon graduated to voice commands with simultaneous hand signals. Hand signals were generally taught with the handler facing the dog at the end of the leash. To get Hans to sit, I'd signal him with my arm and hand and simultaneously voice the command "Sit." We'd practice hand and voice signals for all the movements of advanced basic obedience, including *dead dog, roll over,* and *crawl.*

If there was one command I wore out, it was "No!" But after many weeks of training, Hans would respond with precision when I used hand signals only. It fascinated me that a dog could learn to do so many tricks on command. While training Hans, I often thought that he'd have made a great patrol dog for Vietnam. He was so big that the Vietcong would have run away when they spotted him.

After about a month, I was ready for the next phase of my education: learning how to get Hans to attack and stop on command. This would be the most frightening part of my sentry-dog training. The platoon sergeant marched us into the fenced training yard. He selected one handler and directed him to put on a heavy burlap attack suit. The rest of us removed the choke chains, quickly attached them to our pistol belts, and buckled the leather collars around our dogs' necks. The leather collar was used only when a dog was on official guard duty.

We formed a single line. The platoon sergeant instructed us to turn around and face away from the platform and the man in the burlap suit. Once the leather collars were on our dogs, they knew what was coming next. The handlers had a difficult time keeping their dogs in a sitting position and facing away from the action.

The soldier outfitted in the burlap suit protected his face with a steel mask that looked much like a baseball catcher's mask. The dogs growled but stayed at their masters' sides. Hans sat and stared at the man in burlap. We were instructed to hold our dogs still. Each sentry-dog team would be given the opportunity to perform an attack. There were three commands to the attack phase: "Watch him," "Get him," and "Out." The command "Get Him" meant that the handler wanted his dog to attack the target. "Out" meant that the handler wanted the dog to stop attacking and release from the target.

The platoon sergeant called one of the handlers by name and said, "Attack dog command!" The man in burlap assumed a crouching position about thirty feet in front of the dog. The handler commanded, "Watch him!" The dog watched the target and moved slowly toward the burlap-suited man, who was raising his arms up and down and growling. When the dog was about twenty feet from the target, the handler commanded, "Get him" and let go of the leash, which remained attached to the dog's leather collar. In a flash the dog charged and lunged at the crouching man's throat and then at his groin.

I had never seen a big dog move so fast. Each time the dog lunged, the man in the burlap suit moved backwards from the force of the hit. The dog bit down on the arm of the suit, backed off, and lunged again. At one point, the force of the dog's lunge knocked the man onto his back. Relentlessly attacking the man's throat area, the dog bit down and thrashed his head side to side like a shark in a feeding frenzy.

The platoon sergeant gave the order, "Out dog command." The handler responded, "Out!" Immediately, the dog released his bite and backed off the man lying on the ground. The handler commanded, "Heel!" and the dog returned to his side, where the handler praised his dog with a hug and by saying, "Good boy! Good boy!"

During the attack, the dog is so agitated that it bites down on the burlap hard enough that his teeth sink up to his gums. The dog maintains a strong grip and thrashes his head back and forth, trying to rip out a chunk with his teeth. The friction between the burlap and the dog's teeth and gums causes the gums to bleed.

The man in the burlap suit got up and took a short breather before preparing for the next attack. After four attacks, the platoon sergeant ordered a different man into the burlap suit. After so many dog attacks, the burlap suit was saturated with bloodstains.

When it was my turn, I was nervous, unsure how I'd handle Hans throughout the process. The platoon sergeant gave me the signal. The man in burlap began to kick up dirt and wave his arms. From about twenty feet away, I commanded, "Get him." When Hans reached the end of the leash, the force of his charge pulled it out of my right hand. In a flash, Hans was all over the burlap-clad guy.

I ran behind Hans and grabbed the leash while he had the man on the ground, biting, and twisting his entire body in an effort to tear the man's leg off.

The hair on the back of Hans' neck stood straight up and his teeth dug deep into the burlap. The guy in the suit screamed, "Call him off! Call him off!" I frantically yelled, "Out! Out! Out!" as I pulled back on the leash. Finally, Hans let go. It took every bit of strength I had to keep Hans back and away from the prostrate man. I was exhausted, even though the action had lasted less than a minute. The platoon sergeant told me in what was truly an understatement that I'd have to learn to control my dog better.

After the attack, Hans' gums were bleeding, and the muscles in his shoulders and legs twitched tensely and were hot to the touch. I praised him as he sat, ears pointed high, eyes locked on the man. It was scary to know that Hans was fully capable of killing a man.

Later, the soldier who had worn the attack suit told me that he could feel the powerful jaw pressure of Hans' teeth clamped on his leg, just below the groin. He said Hans had the most crushing bite of all the animals that had attacked him.

Back in the barracks, several of the dog handlers commented on how well my training was coming along. Fred invited me to go to town for drinks at Club Lucky. I didn't make very much money as a Private First Class, but being overseas, I didn't have to pay taxes, either. A few bucks at the Club Lucky went a long way.

Outside the main gate of the base, *skoshi* (small cabs) parked alongside the fence. Fred instructed the driver to take us to Club Lucky. The streets were crowded with people walking, riding bicycles, and driving funny-looking little cars. The signs above the bars were in English: Club BC Night, Club California, Club Chicago, Club Texas, and so on. The streets were crowded with American servicemen — sailors, marines, soldiers, and airmen. Japanese hawkers in black slacks and white shirts stood in the doorways of the bars, trying to entice people inside.

My new friends and I entered Club Lucky as a short, stocky Japanese hawker bowed and opened the door. I was warned not to mess with the hawkers. Although they were little guys, they were also club bouncers, many of them karate and judo experts.

I said to Fred, "You mean these little shits can fight?"

"You bet your ass! he replied. I've seen the little fellows take down some big boys." That was enough to convince me. I'd never been one to pick a fight, though I did enjoy fast one-on-one competition. I still had that wrestling fever I caught in high school. My friends and I referred to wrestling as the fastest six minutes in sports. It required talent, strength, speed, endurance, training, and a driving desire to win. Since I hadn't heard of any wrestlers from Okinawa, I wondered if I could teach these bar hawkers a few tricks. *I'd love to take on one of them in a wrestling match,* I thought.

During my brief tour in Vietnam, I'd learned that, in contrast to wrestling, winning in combat was a team activity with human lives at stake. The prize for winning in that war was to go home in one piece after twelve months. The prize for losing was to get wounded or sent home in a body bag.

The war in Vietnam was a deadly game of cat and mouse, played under severe weather conditions in a giant labyrinth of treacherous terrain. The enemy, unlike a wrestler, wasn't easy to identify, find, or engage. The rules of fighting in Vietnam weren't as clear as they were on the wrestling mats. There was no referee to call a foul in the heat of an exchange, or award a combatant points for a takedown. Body counts seemed to be all that mattered to American military commanders on the battlefields of Vietnam. For a teenage boy, these were harsh reality lessons to learn.

From behind the bar, an older Japanese woman greeted our crowd. She gave us a big friendly smile as if we were all old friends. Everyone called her "Mama San." Small groups of Asian women dressed in long silk flowered dresses sat at the bar and tables, talking and giggling at one another.

Fred ordered a round of Japanese beers and we moved to an empty table to sit down. The jukebox filled the air with the sound of American rock 'n' roll. One of the barmaids came over and asked for money to put in the jukebox. Someone gave her change and off she went. Soon, several other attractive young barmaids came to our table. Everyone but me knew them by name.

When the drinks came, we ordered a round for the girls, too. As I was introduced to them, each one smiled and spoke in broken English. Gradually, I learned that some of the guys considered certain girls their girlfriends, which meant they were off-limits to everyone else. Fred pointed out the women not taken. I wasn't interested in those who were left over, and besides, I was having too much fun watching everyone else.

I quickly learned that if I didn't buy a barmaid a drink, she'd go sit with someone who did. It was their job to rotate to all the customers, which was how they made their tips. The guys all considered the locals poor people who survived on the money we Americans poured into their economy. The bars created big business. Fred told me that none of the women at the Club Lucky were prostitutes; I found that hard to believe.

Meeting decent girls as an American serviceman in a foreign country wasn't as easy as back home. Many of the young women on the island were simply looking for a way to get to the United States, and the best method was to marry an American serviceman, which would assure them a home on a military base, money, medical benefits, and a ticket to the States. Many of the high-ranking soldiers paid for their girlfriends' apartments in town so they'd have a place to shack up after duty and on weekends, a common practice among those who could afford it. As soon as a soldier got reassigned off the island, another was in line to rent his woman and apartment. I never got in line—I couldn't afford it.

Some American servicemen fathered children and then abandoned them when they left the island. It really bothered me to see kids of mixed heritage begging for money on the streets. Most of those kids appeared to be shunned by the people of their own culture.

The Japanese beer gave me a good buzz by half past eleven, as midnight was the curfew set for all military personnel. MPs from all the military services roamed the streets and checked the bars for soldiers who caused problems or violated curfew. The native island police also walked the streets to enforce local law and order. We left the bar, flagged a *skoshi,* and were back on base before midnight. Everyone understood the consequences of missing curfew or being picked up by the MPs. I wasn't one to get into trouble with MPs or to become involved in a court-martial for drunk-and-disorderly conduct. Besides, we all had a great time, and I planned to do it again real soon because there were bars I hadn't had a chance to check out.

By February 1967, my secret clearance had been approved. I could now patrol the classified military sites with Hans. I couldn't wait to work with a sentry dog in a live situation, my first four-hour tour of night shift guard duty. At ten o'clock, I was driven by truck to the kennel. With the barking of dogs in the background, I got my gear together and filled two canteens of water for Hans and one for myself.

Hans had been fed a strict diet of Purina Dog Chow and water. The dogs were not rewarded with treats or table food like family pets. Fred said that the only praise I should give a dog was to hug him and tell him, "Good dog."

I had two seven-round clips of ammunition for my .45 caliber pistol, but I wasn't supposed to insert them until I was at the work site. I attached my poncho to the pistol belt in case it rained. My gear weighed about four pounds, light compared to the sixty I used to carry on my back in Vietnam. I buckled on my pistol belt and strapped the leather collar on Hans.

My right knee was feeling stronger than ever, and I experienced little pain when I jumped down from the back of the truck or stood for extended periods of time. Dr. Bogumill had done a terrific job patching me up. Even the hair around my knee had fully grown back, except along the ugly patches of scar tissue.

There were six sentry-dog teams in back of the troop truck headed for guard duty. Like the rest of the dogs, Hans was muzzled; he sat between my legs for control and protection. I took up the slack in the leash and held Hans by his collar during the entire ride. I had already learned what Hans could do to a man in a burlap suit, so it felt safe seeing him and the other dogs wearing muzzles.

We arrived at the entrance gate of a fully lighted fenced area. The guard checked us over, opened the gate, and waved us into the classified compound. Armed guards patrolled in jeeps between two electric fences that encircled the perimeter. Sentry dogs patrolled the inner fenced perimeter where the munitions buildings were located.

The inner perimeter contained many munitions bunkers, called igloos because of their rounded mound shape. They were well spaced apart and lined up in rows. Each igloo had huge steel double doors surrounded by windowless concrete walls. The entire structure was buried under dirt on which grass grew. The only exposed areas were the steel doors and the air vents on top. From the sky, the area must have appeared to be a flat grassy field with a grid of roads.

My guard post included five igloos. Fred instructed me to check each door to make sure each igloo was secure. When on duty, I was to have my .45 caliber pistol loaded, with a round in the chamber, but holstered until I needed to use it. If a perpetrator entered my guard post area, my orders were to command the dog to attack, after which I would shoot to kill.

I carried two black rubber gas masks, one for me and one for Hans. I asked Fred what was inside the igloos. He told me that that was classified information. I informed him that I had secret clearance and needed to know just what in hell I was responsible for guarding. Giving in, Fred told me that the military stockpiled chemical warfare weapons in the igloos. He warned me that I now had a classified secret to protect and that I was not to discuss it with him again.

There were cages near the vents on top of each igloo. I was to check them frequently, and quietly observe the behavior of the rabbits housed inside. I had to do the same with the goats that would roam freely into my guard post from time to time. I thought, *Holy shit!* It didn't take my young ass but one brain-fart to figure out why the army put animals in there with us: if those chemicals weapons sprung a leak, the rabbits, being right near the vents, would be the first to get the airborne scent. Hans and the goats had no shoes to protect them from contamination if chemicals seeped through the concrete walls and into the soil.

If I smelled or tasted anything foul in the air, I was basically fucked. Whoa! I remembered the tear-gas drill during my infantry training at Fort Leonardwood and Fort Ord. We were escorted into an empty wooden building out in the woods. They closed the doors and forced us to breathe tear gas. I remember coming out of that damn building with my eyes and throat on fire; but it wasn't tear gas stored in those igloos. We were talking about the real killers that no training could ever possibly prepare you for: the horrific effects of nerve gas, choking agents, and blood agents—the type of shit that instantly upset your stomach, burned your eyes out, made you vomit, and caused convulsions, followed by an agonizing death in the fetal position. Even if I were quick enough to get my rubber protective mask on in seconds, I'd still die. What about Hans? He had absolutely no idea that he was a guinea pig too.

I must have practiced putting on my mask ten times that night. Hans was getting annoyed with the exercise, so I stopped when he started growling at me. *Hans, if you only knew!* I thought. *If you only knew!*

By the time my first shift ended, I was thankful that all the rabbits and goats were still alive and not doing the shimmy-shake. As I sat in the back of that troop truck heading back to the kennels, I contemplated how long I'd last doing that job with Hans. I thought I'd rather take my chances fighting the North Vietnamese Army than guard a village of igloos full of rabbits, goats, and killer chemicals.

Hans and I had gotten along fine thus far and I'd come to really love him. For many nights over the course of a month, we guarded those igloos with never an unusual incident to report. Even though my fear never subsided, I was growing bored with the whole routine. During those long night hours on guard, I had plenty of time to become homesick. I missed the majestic Rocky Mountains towering over Denver from the west. I remembered how I'd drive fifty miles to Lookout Point, high above the city, and feel as if I could see forever. I recalled how specially beautiful Denver was, all lit up at night in the crystal-clear air, and how brightly the stars shone in a mountaintop view.

My house in Littleton had been about forty-five minutes from the tranquillity of mountain wilderness. I longed to listen to the whispering aspen leaves, to watch water rapidly rushing over the boulders of a rocky mountain stream, and to breathe fresh, cool air.

During the greater part of 1966 and early 1967, I lived in Vietnam, Japan, and Okinawa, and never got used to the climates. Okinawa was a small island, sixty miles long and twenty wide, and heavily populated by every branch of the United States military. All my friends wore military uniforms; I didn't have one civilian buddy. The local people, culture, food, language, and natural surroundings didn't appeal to me. Even if I'd been a civilian, I wouldn't have wanted to live in Vietnam, Japan, or Okinawa.

I had met a local barmaid, Kiko, who worked at Club Texas. She was the most beautiful Japanese girl I'd ever seen. Kiko looked like a calendar model. It seemed like every time I entered the club, soldiers surrounded Kiko and sat at her table. During my nights off, I'd be at the Club Texas, vying for time with her, but I rarely had to buy her drinks to keep her at my table. It wasn't long before I was taking Kiko to the local Japanese theater and dining at her favorite Japanese restaurants off the main bar strip. We enjoyed each other's company.

Kiko had never been off the island of Okinawa, but had learned to speak and write English from all the American servicemen she had met working in bars. She was eighteen years old, and wanted to have children and make a home with me in the United States. I thought about it many times and even checked into the military administrative procedures. There was a lot of legal paperwork involved, but deep down I knew I wasn't ready for marriage. The only girl I had ever had a crush on before was Tena, who had attended Littleton High School with me. She was *beautiful*. From the letters I had received, Tena was finishing her freshman year at the University of Colorado. I wondered if she'd found a steady boyfriend in college or would ever date me again when I got back home.

The more I thought about marrying a shy, petite Japanese girl, the clearer it became that I didn't want to take home a girl from a totally different culture and have to face prejudice and the problems of a huge cultural transition. Like most guys my age, I was lonely for female companionship, but had concluded that marriage would be too big a step for me at nineteen. That relationship had become way too much for me to deal with, and my need to break it off gave me another reason for trying to leave Okinawa.

The army wasn't going to let me off the island for another year, so I pondered the idea of volunteering to go back to Vietnam. After Vietnam, I could return home to Littleton and attend a state college. That, I thought, was the perfect remedy for my depressing predicament.

I had assumed that being an infantryman was all I was capable of doing at the time, and convinced myself that fighting in Vietnam wasn't such a bad job after all. The idea of leaving Hans troubled me, but I felt that requesting reassignment to Vietnam was my only way out of Okinawa. I thought I might even get to select an assignment with an elite paratrooper outfit. With all that stirring in my mind, I made an appointment with the personnel office to volunteer for a return trip to Vietnam.

My friends thought I'd gone completely out of my mind. Returning to Vietnam as an infantryman was the worst thing any of them could possibly imagine—especially as a way to get off of Okinawa. I was told time and again, "You'll be killed if you go back there."

I tried to defend my reasons, but couldn't convince my friends that I wasn't insane. Their words—*dead, killed, blown away, dying, pine box, body bag, and POW*—failed to trigger any belief that tragedy could befall me. I had confidence in my decisions and in myself, and I didn't fear the dangers they predicted.

I thought about what I needed to buy in Okinawa to add to my standard-issue combat gear in South Vietnam. Something I regretted about my first tour in Vietnam, with the 1st Air Cavalry Division, was that I had not one photo to document my experience. Now I had a chance to go back and record what I would want to remember. I bought my first camera, a Canon 35-millimeter half-frame that was small enough to carry in an ammo pouch. Then I bought a shiny pair of handmade black patent-leather paratrooper boots. I'd wear them in base camp when I wasn't wearing my army-issue green canvas jungle boots. The last item I bought was a bone-handled hunting knife with a six-inch blade. With those items, I started preparing for my planned return trip to Vietnam.

When I went to see the personnel clerk, he told me that I had two options. The first was to fill out a request for transfer to duty in Vietnam. That would get me to Vietnam, and the army would assign me according to its needs after I got there. The paperwork, however, could take several months, which didn't appeal to me in the least. I wanted control over where I was going in Vietnam, and I wanted to get there fast, especially if I was volunteering to return.

The second option was to re-enlist in the army for an additional year and get assigned to the outfit of my choice. The paperwork would only take a week or so, and I could be on my way within a month. I didn't think twice about giving the army another year of my life if it could work that fast for me.

So, I re-enlisted to join the 173rd Airborne Brigade, an elite paratrooper outfit operating in the southern jungles of South Vietnam. A week later, my unit of choice was granted and I received official orders to report to the Republic of South Vietnam in March 1967. My paratrooper jump-school training was about to pay off.

Don Vestal was a good friend at the time, and a former infantry-man. He had a job operating a forklift at the warehouse loading docks. We met while shopping at the Post Exchange (PX). When I saw he was wearing a CIB, I introduced myself. We became friends and started hanging out together after work. Don told me that I had the balls of a real American fighting soldier. He said, "To go back to that hellhole after being wounded is a choice only you can understand. No matter what happens to you in life, John, I will al-ways respect your decision."

Don had been wounded in Vietnam and had received the Army Commendation Medal for valor in combat. He was counting the days until he went home to Texas. I spent my last days in Okinawa hanging around with Don until I boarded a C-130 cargo plane at Kadena Air Force Base and took off for South Vietnam.

I couldn't have foreseen how my sentry-dog training would be a huge factor in why I survived my second combat tour.

Chapter Eight

RETURN TO VIETNAM

I arrived back in South Vietnam in March 1967, a few days after turning twenty years of age. The C-130 cargo plane I flew in on was loaded with new recruits getting their first glimpse of Saigon and Ton Son Nhut Air Force Base. Their innocence and fear of the unknown contrasted with my eagerness to get in-processed and be on my way to the elite 173rd Airborne Brigade.

The airfield was busy with the sounds of equipment moving about and the deafening roar of fighter jets speeding down runways. On the ground, I rode in an olive drab bus with steel mesh over the windows, just like the bus I'd ridden my first time around. The climate was hot and humid, and that familiar smell of stale fish permeated the air.

Officers had been separated from the enlisted troops and rode a separate bus. The vehicles cruised through the airfield, passing armed guards and manned bunkers. I noticed that everything looked much as it had a year earlier. Saigon was still an extremely crowded city, with people, bicycles, rickshaws, strange-looking foreign buses, and tiny cars everywhere. There was no sign of a war going on, but I knew it was a different story outside the city limits and deep in the remote jungles.

Soon I passed through the gates of Camp Alpha. Stepping off the bus, I surveyed my surroundings and realized that the camp hadn't changed, either. In a familiar drill we were quickly shuffled into a large reception building. Personnel clerks greeted us with, "Give me a copy of your orders, soldier. Wait right here and don't move. We'll get you processed as soon as possible." I was accustomed to this hurry-up-and-wait routine. Whatever those folks did was never fast enough for me. My main objective was to get to the 173rd Airborne, and I didn't like the idea of hanging around a deadbeat replacement camp with a bunch of bewildered FNGs (fucking new guys) fresh from the States, sporting bald heads, new fatigues, and farmer tans.

I heard my name called over a loudspeaker, so I reported to a wooden building where a sergeant sat behind a gray metal desk covered with stacks of brown file folders. He asked me to sit while he prepared my assignment. When he finished, he told me I was going to be assigned to the 3rd Brigade, 25th Infantry Division in Dau Tieng.

I couldn't believe what I was hearing. "What do you mean?" I asked. "Didn't you read my orders? There has to be some kind of mistake here, Sarge. Are you sure you have the right guy? I've got orders guaranteeing my assignment to the 173rd Airborne Brigade."

The sergeant looked at me with a complete lack of interest and sternly stated, "Look, soldier, I process hundreds of men through here each day. You're not so special because you were here before or because you have orders to the 173rd. Remember, you're in a combat zone and Uncle Sam reserves the right to change your orders anytime he desires. Got it?"

I replied in anger, "Well, I'm not going to accept this. I was guaranteed an assignment to the 173rd Airborne. That's the only reason I came back to Vietnam."

The personnel sergeant didn't respond. He just sat there with his head down and stuffed my papers back into my brown folder.

I shouted, "Are you listening to me? Look, Sarge, I want to talk to the officer in charge here!"

The sergeant pointed to an officer who was sitting behind a desk and reading documents. I marched over to him, the sergeant right behind me, carrying my personnel file folder.

The army major looked up from his desk and asked, "Can I help you, soldier?"

I blurted out, "Sir, I have a guaranteed assignment to the 173rd Airborne Brigade. This sergeant just changed my orders and I want to know why, sir!"

The sergeant handed him my file. The major asked me to sit down as he dismissed the sergeant. After reading through the papers in my file, he explained that under normal circumstances it would have been no problem to process me for assignment to the 173rd; however, the camp commander had directed that the 3rd Brigade, 25th Infantry Division be given the highest priority for infantry replacements. He indicated that I had just happened to arrive while that order was in full effect. The 3rd Brigade, 25th Infantry had recently suffered numerous casualties, and the major was under orders to process all available infantrymen into that unit.

Again, I couldn't believe what I was hearing. I said, "This is my second tour. I should be given priority since I re-enlisted to come back to Vietnam as an infantryman."

The major listened patiently, but kept telling me that there was nothing he could do to help. Starting to comprehend that I was being screwed out of my promised assignment, I got enraged. I told the major that if I'd known such a thing could happen, I would never have volunteered to come back to Vietnam. He sympathized with me, and told me that I was a brave man for going back into the infantry after having been wounded in action, but there was absolutely no way he could change my assignment. He pointed out that he'd processed only a few soldiers who had returned as infantrymen.

"Sir, is there anyone else I can talk to?"

"No! And seeking counsel with the base camp commander is also out of the question," he barked.

The major assured me that he'd give my new assignment top priority for out-processing. I picked up my orders from his desk and stomped out of the building. There was nowhere I could go and no one else I could talk to. The army had me in a straight-jacket and had completely neutralized my entire plan. I paced around the replacement camp like a wounded tiger, getting more furious by the minute.

After passing the camp chapel for a third time, I decided to step inside. It was quiet and dimly lit with candles. I sat at the end of a pew and stared at the wooden cross above the altar. An older soldier sat nearby. He turned and smiled at me. I immediately recognized that he was an officer wearing the rank of captain, and I saw the small cross sewn to his collar, signifying that he was a chaplain.

Seeing that I was shook up, the chaplain came over, shook my hand, and welcomed me to the place of the Lord. I explained my situation and how unfair I thought it was for the army to treat me that way. The chaplain listened without interruption. Then he told me that he'd talk to the personnel officer and see what he could do.

I waited in the chapel and said a few prayers. When the chaplain returned, he told me that he was sorry, but there was nothing he could do to remedy my situation. Distraught, I thanked him, got up, and walked out of the chapel.

The next morning, my name was again called over the loudspeaker, so I reported to the personnel officer. When I got there, the major told me that my out-processing was complete and a jeep had been dispatched to transport me to the airfield. We shook hands, exchanged salutes, and the major wished me luck. I grabbed my gear and climbed into the jeep for the short ride to the airfield. I still couldn't quite believe I was going to the 3rd Brigade, 4th Infantry Division. My new assignment was located at the U.S. Army base camp of Dau Tieng, sixty miles west of Saigon, not far from the Cambodian border.

When I arrived at the airfield, I didn't have to wait long before boarding a Chinook re-supply helicopter. Flying over the rice paddies, villages, and jungle terrain felt like old times. Not knowing any of the other soldiers riding with me, I sat quietly, my mind drifting back in time. I thought of Kenny Mook and our first copter ride with the 7th Cavalry. It had been almost a year to the day since Kenny and I were brand-spanking-new guys from the States. A few months later, we were in deep shit in Bong Son, and now Kenny was back home in Pennsylvania, recovering from his wounds, and I was back in Vietnam as an infantryman.

I had a lot of concerns and questions on my mind: *What kind of hell did the 3rd Brigade run into to that caused it to lose so many infantrymen and receive high priority for replacements? What will my fellow veteran infantrymen think of my volunteering to return? What platoon and squad will I end up joining? What am I getting myself into this time?*

The second I'd set foot back in this crazy place called Nam, my entire plan had taken a sharp turn off target. Based on what I'd learned and what the army had told me, I had begun to question my ability to make sound decisions. And now I was on my way to a remote outpost west of Saigon and close to the Cambodian border.

I had no idea that this odd twist of fate meant that my involvement with military working dogs was not over. I was about to discover that teaming with a German shepherd scout dog in a combat situation was safer than teaming with any two-legged soldier.

Chapter Nine

DAU TIENG
BASE CAMP

The Chinook began its decent to the dirt runway of a small base camp located in the middle of a huge Michelin rubber plantation. Raised in the inner city and suburbs of Denver, I'd never seen a huge orchard of rubber trees. From the air, the base camp appeared small, remote, dusty, and temporary. The edge of the Vietnamese village of Dau Tieng lay just outside several rings of connected barbed wire, just a stone's throw from the nearest parked chopper. Low mountains within mortar range of the airstrip bordered the north side of the camp.

The two huge rotary blades of the big Chinook kicked up dust as it landed on its four wheels. The airstrip was constructed with interconnecting perforated steel plating (PSP) overlaying the packed dirt. I grabbed my duffel bag and walked down the ramp.

A buck sergeant (three stripes) in dusty jungle fatigues waved us replacements over to him. We handed him copies of our assignment orders and climbed into the back of a small utility truck headed to the replacement facility. Traveling along the camp's main dirt road, we passed by a small field hospital, an armored squadron of tanks, a squadron of armored personnel carriers, a few infantry encampments, and a small motor pool of jeeps and trucks. The truck finally squealed to a stop at the entrance of the replacement center. Barbed-wire fencing enclosed its perimeter.

I asked, "Are they trying to keep the replacements from running away, or what?"

No one answered.

After we jumped out of the truck and grabbed our gear, we moved inside the main wooden building, which was surrounded by sandbags piled waist high. As we sat in a small classroom, the noncommissioned officer in charge, a master sergeant (six stripes), stood before us, a husky, towering figure with the presence of an seasoned drill sergeant.

In a deep, penetrating voice, he welcomed us and emphasized the importance of the 3rd Brigade, 25th Infantry Division's mission. He explained that the base camp was strategically located as a buffer between Cambodia and Saigon. He called the area "III Corps" and "War Zone C" and "the Iron Triangle." "Pick any name you like," he said. "It's all dictated by high-level commanders who decide how this area we operate in will be strategically divided for military operations."

The master sergeant explained that the entire area surrounding Dau Tieng had a high concentration of enemy troops who regularly waged mortar attacks on the airstrip. He said that if the VC tried to overrun our camp, we'd be issued the weapons and ammunition stored in bunkers inside the replacement compound. He also explained that on March 21, the 3rd Brigade's 2nd Battalion, 12th Infantry, had fought a victorious battle with the North Vietnamese Army in a place called LZ Gold, not far from Dau Tieng. The battle was initiated by the NVA in reaction to a "mad minute."

A *mad minute* was an operation designed to discard a unit's old and possibly faulty ammunition by firing it at a predetermined time. At LZ Gold, several hidden enemy regiments were preparing to attack the unsuspecting battalion. When the American infantrymen initiated the mad minute, the enemy, assuming that the Americans were engaging with them, decided to launch their attack, which was a complete surprise to the Americans. In the end, the NVA lost the battle. Bulldozers had to be airlifted into the battle zone to dig mass graves for the hundreds of enemy dead. Although the number of American casualties was low by comparison, the 2nd Battalion, 12th Infantry (Lancers) and the 2nd Battalion, 22nd Infantry (Triple Deuce) were in desperate need of replacements. *That's why my assignment to the 173rd was nixed*, I thought.

The village of Dau Tieng was hostile and off-limits to American soldiers. We were required to carry our weapons at all times when leaving the confines of the base camp and entering any of the surrounding villages within the rubber-tree plantation. At night, MPs patrolled Dau Tieng because of its close proximity to the perimeter of the base camp. Inside the village, the Army of the Republic of Vietnam (ARVN), our allies, occupied a command post that didn't seem to deter enemy presence. That didn't surprise us, since we knew that Americans were doing most of the fighting, and we all felt that the combat capabilities of the ARVN forces had proven less than stellar.

Before my release from the replacement center and my duty assignment to an infantry combat unit, I had to put up with some training. This consisted of orientations, the use and maintenance of the M-16 rifle, hearing the history of the 3rd Brigade, memorizing various simple Vietnamese phrases, and recognizing the different enemy uniforms and equipment and the weaponry they used to maim and kill Americans. It was similar to the indoctrination I got when I joined the 1st Air Cavalry Division up north in the central highlands.

The master sergeant used a pointer and a large military map, thumb-tacked to the wall, to provide a geographical overview. He pointed out the base camp's location in relation to other military camps scattered throughout South Vietnam. The 3rd Brigade's encampment split the district village of Dau Tieng into two parts. A dirt road running straight through the base camp connected the east and west ends of the village.

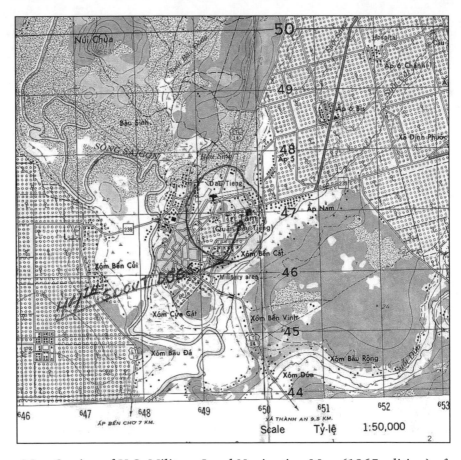

*Map Section of U.S. Military Land Navigation Map (1965 edition) of
Dau Tieng and its surrounding area of jungle, rivers, and the Michelin
and Ben Cui Rubber Tree Plantations, South Vietnam.
(Author collection)*

Dau Tieng was large enough to contain a brigade-sized unit of
three battalions of infantry and an assortment of support and supply units. Each infantry battalion was strategically placed around
the perimeter. Less than a mile west of the perimeter, the Song Saigon River snaked its way north and south. The Ben Cui rubber-tree
plantation was situated west and south of the river.

Tay Ninh, the next largest populated province, was several miles
northwest of Dau Tieng. Southwest lay Cu Chi, home of the U.S.

Army's 25th Infantry Division, nicknamed "Tropical Lightning," with its American home base on the Hawaiian island of Oahu. Cu Chi was big enough to fit five Dau Tiengs inside its perimeter. The three base camps—Dau Tieng, Tay Ninh, and Cu Chi—formed a large triangle on the map, *the Iron Triangle*.

After the briefing, I walked up to the master sergeant and boldly stated, "I've been through all this shit before, so why can't just I skip this bullshit and join an infantry unit right away?"

The master sergeant replied, "You will be treated like everyone else, with no exceptions for past experience. Besides, you can be of value to me by helping the others learn from your combat experience."

I impatiently replied, "I didn't come back to train a bunch of stinking FNGs!"

My remarks really pissed him off' he leaned into my face and shouted, "You, soldier, have a bad attitude. If you don't back the fuck off, I'll put your ass in a sling!"

I got the message and quickly backed off. My only ambition was to get to a unit. Besides, I didn't want any problems or to get on his shit list and be labeled a troublemaker. The master sergeant looked as if he could kick my ass into next week. In those days, it wasn't uncommon for a sergeant like him to take a young trooper like me to the woodshed for a physical eye opener. I had no choice but to go along with the situation.

The next day, everyone formed up for training outside our wooden hooch. The training area had mock booby traps, mines, punji pits, and a huge ball of dried mud with bamboo spikes sticking out all over it, suspended from a large tree branch of a tree by a vine. In real combat, the trap would work like this: The spiked ball, rigged by a tripwire or vine, was camouflaged and suspended above a jungle trail. When tripped by a passing soldier, the ball would swing down with all its momentum and hit the man about chest high. There was little chance of surviving several bamboo spears piercing the torso.

The enemy was very clever at creating all kinds of nasty booby traps for their American foes. I already knew what it felt like to be penetrated by a punji stake. Oddly, I wasn't afraid that I'd be wounded again, and dying was something I didn't think about now that I had a fresh twelve-month tour of duty to deal with. Perhaps the fears I might otherwise have had were pushed aside by my anger at going through this damn training again.

To my surprise, as part of our training, two scout-dog handlers with two leashed German shepherds showed up to give us a presentation on their mission in Vietnam. They were members of the 44th Infantry Platoon Scout Dogs (IPSD), and their presentation was directed at trying to recruit dog handlers. I was excited to hear what they had to say. Oliver Whetstone, a dog handler whom everyone called Ollie, was from Kenosha, Wisconsin. Ollie was a tall, skinny, blond-headed, blue-eyed, friendly guy with a Midwestern accent. He explained the mission of a scout-dog team and how the dog provided an early silent warning for the troops of the 3rd Brigade infantry units.

A scout dog used natural instincts and training to alert its handler of a smell, sight, or sound. It was up to the handler to signal an alert to the rest of the patrol and provide an explanation of the dog's signal. Ollie explained that their dogs alerted on things like booby traps, enemy foxholes, ambushes, and even other animals. I was completely fascinated by his talk about what scout-dog teams could achieve in a combat zone. I immediately started comparing the duty of a scout dog with the experience I'd had with my sentry dog Hans.

The handlers provided a short demonstration of basic obedience. When they gave their dogs the command "Sit," the German shepherds sat and stayed. When commanded to lie down, the dogs obeyed. Each time the handlers gave a command, the dogs obeyed immediately. The discipline between the handlers and their dogs thoroughly impressed me. Each handler demonstrated his dog's ability to attack on command. This reminded me again of Hans.

At the end of their presentation, the scout-dog handlers asked, "Is anyone interested in joining the 44th Scout Dogs?" They assured us that we'd be trained before we had to go out on a mission. All we had to do was to show a genuine interest in working with dogs. Ollie said, "If you don't love animals, then don't consider handling a war dog."

As I listened to the scout-dog handlers describe their job, I knew I'd be joining them. I had dog-handling experience, and I loved animals of all kinds—even Hans, who scared the shit out of me at first. I missed Hans and wanted another chance to work with a German shepherd.

As the handlers talked with the group of replacements, I was getting more anxious to volunteer to work with them. Then someone asked a question that was probably on many minds: "Where is the scout-dog team positioned in a tactical formation?"

The handlers looked at one another as if to say, "We were hoping no one would ask that question, but it's a fair question."

After a short pause, Ollie answered. He told us that the dog and handler always walked point, meaning they led the way. Handlers and scout dogs were first in a combat formation, first in the jungle, first across clearings, first down roads and trails, and, it was hoped, first to find the enemy before the enemy found them. He went on to explain that, after the dog had alerted and contact with the enemy had been made, the dog and handler pulled back inside the safety net of the perimeter.

"Our job is done after we make contact. Remember, we're just the early warning system, but we fight the enemy when we have to."

Ollie explained that dogs must have the best possible conditions to use their senses and instincts. That meant working them up front and on point, where the air is fresh and the scents unobstructed. Ollie concluded that walking point was the most effective way of deploying a scout-dog team, and that they saved lives.

Another replacement asked, "How many dogs and handlers have you guys lost?"

"A few have been wounded," Ollie replied, "but no one has been killed."

Every new replacement in that small training area was quiet. Ollie broke the silence by asking if any of us had experience working with dogs. I stood up and said that I'd had some sentry-dog training in Okinawa. Each dog handler asked me several questions. Apparently, I answered to their satisfaction. Finally, they asked if I wanted to join the 44th.

"Yes!" I said without hesitation.

Of the entire group of replacements, I was the only one who volunteered to join the K-9 platoon, the only one with any experience handling a military dog, and, I guess, the only one who wanted to walk point with a dog. The others thought I was crazy for coming back to Vietnam, and now thought I was doubly crazy for wanting to be a point man. Maybe I was a little different in the head, but I wasn't crazy. I figured I'd rather take my chances with a well-trained dog leading the way than try to survive on my own experience and instincts.

The next day, the master sergeant told me that if I wanted to join the 44th Scout Dog Platoon, he'd let me leave earlier than the others, since I had so much experience with dogs. He called the 44th on the land line to confirm my assignment.

Man, was I glad to get the hell out of that replacement center and back with the dogs—even though I had no idea what was in store.

Chapter Ten

44TH SCOUT DOG PLATOON

The 44th Scout Dog Platoon was the last war-dog platoon to be activated and sent overseas during World War II. They served along with the 811th Military Police Company on the island of Saipan. Japanese soldiers, some in small groups but mostly individuals, hid in the vast number of caves and bunkers throughout the island. The scout dogs helped to locate and eliminate those who resisted capture. The 44th remained on Saipan until the war was over; they returned to the United States on January 6, 1946 and were deactivated.

The 44th Scout Dog Platoon was reactivated in 1966 at Fort Benning, Georgia. The unit was given new life, fresh young soldiers teaming up with spry young German shepherds. Those new dance partners trained and prepared for the war in Vietnam.

The 44th arrived in Vietnam in early January 1967 and built their first home in the Michelin rubber plantation of Dau Tieng.

I walked to the K-9 compound in the company of Ollie Whetstone and his German shepherd scout dog, Erik. As we neared the entrance I could hear the dogs barking in the kennel. Their smell filled the air, reminding me of the sentry-dog kennel on Okinawa.

After stowing my gear in my quarters, I was introduced to the platoon leader, Lieutenant Robert Fenner, a thin man, about five feet seven inches, with short blond hair. He informed me that the entire platoon had graduated together from a twelve-week scout-dog training course at Fort Benning, Georgia. My arrival in March was only three months after they got in-country. There were fifteen scout-dog handlers and twice as many dogs. They were shorthanded for the number of missions they had to support.

Dirt road entrance under the sign of the "44th Scout Dogs" with Kennel in background–1967. (Author collection)

Most of the handlers had attended college, and some were graduates. The majority had failed to finish the U.S. Army Officer Candidate School (OCS) at Fort Benning, and subsequently were reassigned to the local scout dog training center.

Lieutenant Fenner briefed me on their tactical mission and deployment. The dog handlers were assigned to support the scouting needs of the 3rd Brigade, 25th Infantry Division. The combat units of the 3rd Brigade used scout-dog teams extensively; some had participated in the battle for LZ Gold.

A scout-dog team could be assigned to support a squad (ten men), platoon (twenty-five men), company (a hundred men), mechanized armored units, and the local Military Police Detachment. Lieutenant Fenner coordinated the scheduling of assignments when higher headquarters requested support. The assignment policy was simple; one scout-dog team per tactical mission. As a matter of policy, a schedule was developed to ensure equitable rotations, so that no one hander would perform more than his share of missions.

The German shepherd was the only breed assigned to the 44th. The only other breed deployed by the military was the Labrador retriever; they worked exclusively as tracker dogs in CTTs (combat tracker teams). Dau Tieng had no CTTs assigned to support the 3rd Brigade's combat missions.

All the military services—army, air force, navy, and marines—used military working dogs in Vietnam. Several thousand dogs were serving throughout South Vietnam, performing a variety of jobs: scout, sentry, mine and booby-trap detection, patrol, and tracking. The primary breed was the German shepherd.

As I listened to Lieutenant Fenner describe the work I'd be doing, I knew that my new assignment, relying on a dog to save lives in combat, was far beyond what I'd imagined I'd be doing during my second tour in Vietnam. I realized that the sentry-dog training I'd experienced with Hans would prove very useful in preparing me for the job of a scout-dog handler.

Lieutenant Robert Fenner (44th Scout Dogs Platoon leader), Sergeant Walter Shelton, and Sergeant John Burnam in front of sleeping quarters – 1967. (Author collection)

Lieutenant Fenner explained that, over time, an infantryman could acclimate to his surroundings and develop animal-like instincts, but he could never match the natural instincts of a dog. When a scout dog acclimates to working in the jungle, open terrain, woods, and dry and wet weather, his senses and instincts become unbelievably keen.

A dog's eyes can detect movement at greater distances than any foot soldier can, even at night. A dog can hear sounds at much greater distances than a soldier can. A dog's sense of smell and touch is far greater than any human's. A dog's senses, coupled with his loyalty and desire to serve a master, make him invaluable as a scout. The relationship and the bond that develop between a dog and handler is remarkable. The more frequently the handler and dog train, the more experienced they become as a combat scouting team.

A single mission for a scout-dog team in the 44th could last from one day to a week or more. The K-9 platoon had compiled a record of highly successful combat missions on which no one had been killed in action. They had earned the respect of the patrols they supported by performing exceptionally well and saving lives.

The platoon had its own veterinarian technician, Specialist Five Robert Glydon, who lived by himself in a hooch that was fully equipped with medical supplies. Aside from his general medical duties, Doc Glydon was also qualified to perform minor surgery on the animals.

Specialist Four Wade Evans and Robert Glydon, Veterinary Technician, giving scout dog, Buckshot, a shot. Buckshot was Killed in Action after Wade returned home to the States—1967. (Author collection)

During my orientation with Lieutenant Fenner, he noticed my Combat Infantry Badge. He tried to talk with me about my prior Vietnam experiences, but the stories wouldn't come. I didn't feel comfortable discussing the details of what it was like to face the enemy. The lieutenant didn't ask why I'd returned to Vietnam. My new platoon leader was soft spoken, quiet and easygoing. He never pushed his rank around like some of the officers I'd met in the past. I wasn't sure how much I liked him, but he was my new boss, and I had no problem following his orders. I knew that I had to pay attention to everything and learn all I could as I settled into my new job.

The Army Corps of Engineers had built the dog kennels between rows of rubber trees. The floor was a long slab of concrete; wood and metal fence sidings and a tin roof formed the rest of the structure. The engineers had wired the kennel for electricity and installed overhead lights. It had the capacity to house forty dogs. Several empty runs were used for food, supplies, dog crates, and other equipment. A metal fence separated each dog's run from the others. To protect the dogs from deadly shrapnel and small-arms fire, sandbags were filled and stacked waist high around one side of the kennel. Shortly before my arrival, the platoon had employed local Vietnamese laborers to fill and stack the sandbags around the kennel. One day, several hours after the Vietnamese departed the area, one of the sandbags exploded. No one was hurt, but after that incident, Lieutenant Fenner decided never to allow Vietnamese laborers inside the K-9 compound. We dog handlers now had the job of filling and stacking the remaining sandbags.

The dogs were kept inside the kennel after dark; the handlers slept in their own quarters. During the day, each dog was taken out of his run and leashed to his own rubber tree, his water bucket nearby. The dogs were fed in the morning and in the afternoon.

I soon learned that if a dog handler wanted any comforts in his life, he had to trade something for them. I enjoyed hearing stories the handlers liked to tell about how they'd improved on the original design of the K-9 compound.

One day, a few handlers had seen a supply sergeant from another unit preparing equipment for transport by Chinooks and C-130s on the Dau Tieng airstrip. Prefab hooch kits and corrugated sheets of tin for roofing were neatly stacked on the ground. The dog handlers had decided to offer the supply sergeant a fifty-kilowatt generator in trade for of these materials. After making sure that the generator worked, the supply sergeant smiled and the trade was negotiated.

The handlers had confiscated that generator from the air force while in Saigon, in an action known as an "emergency requisition." Most of us grunts learned never to leave equipment and supplies unattended. That air force generator had remained hidden under a tarp behind the kennel until the opportunity arose to trade it to that supply sergeant.

Everyone had participated in cutting the planks of timber and hammering nails to assemble new hooches between the rows of rubber trees. The "K-9 Klub" was the result, and it turned out to be the most popular building on the compound. We even had a volleyball court between two rows of trees, and a basketball hoop with a plywood backboard nailed to a tree in the parking lot. The playground lifted morale and helped kill time while we waited on our next mission rotation.

Two huge metal water barrels were suspended on wood framing for showering under the trees near the hooches. A wood pallet became a floor. A water truck came by every few days to fill the containers. Some of the rear-area-type jobs, like the water-delivery service, were given to short-timers, those lucky infantrymen with thirty days or less before going home. Having a job that didn't involve enemy contact was one of those unwritten short-timer benefits practiced throughout the combat infantry units. I guess the army made up these wartime benefits as they went along.

A typical day as a dog handler in base camp was different from a typical day in the jungle. In base camp, we got up at six or seven A.M. We shaved, put on jungle fatigues, and ate some chow. After breakfast, we went to the kennel to feed the dogs, refresh their water, and clean the runs. A few handlers were assigned other cleanup chores, such as burning the shit in the outhouse. A rather patriotic crew of handlers painted our outhouse red, white, and blue, but it wasn't long before Lieutenant Fenner got a call from higher headquarters to have it repainted olive drab.

Other chores included cleaning the K-9 Klub, getting supplies, filling sandbags, and repairing hooches. Dog handlers worked at a leisurely pace; no one busted butt to get any chore done.

The bond between the handler and his dog grew so strong that the handler treated the animal like a human companion. It wasn't unusual to hear a handler talking to his dog like he'd talk to a person, or see a handler sitting beneath a tree, reading a book or letter to his dog.

After the dogs had been put into the kennel for the night, many of the handlers gathered at the K-9 Klub, where we got to know one another a little better. We played poker, read books, drank beer, soda pop, and Kool-Aid, and talked about girls, family, and friends back home.

The handlers had brought a tiny mixed-breed dog from the States to serve as their pet and mascot. Her name was "44." Her short-hair coat was a shiny black, and she had a long snout, floppy ears, and a long skinny tail. 44 ran all over the compound and hung around like one of the guys. One day, she ran into the road and was killed by a truck. We gave 44 a proper burial in a secluded place in the shade beneath a rubber tree.

John Burnam posing with "44." She was the unit mascot and came over with the original dog platoon from Fort Benning, Georgia in January 1967. She later died in Vietnam that same year. (Author collection)

Not long after 44's death, one of the dog handlers showed up with a tiny Vietnamese puppy he'd found on a mission. About the size of a large squirrel, it had short white hair with a few black spots, and floppy little ears. We named him "Hardcore" because he was high-spirited and chewed on everything. If we found tiny teeth marks in our boots, we knew that Hardcore had been there. He spent a lot of time roaming in and out of our hooches and chewing on whatever he found. Sadly, Hardcore was killed when he played too close to one of the more aggressive scout dogs.

Even though Hardcore met an early demise, he fared better with us than he would have in the jungle, where he'd probably have become a meal for some hungry Vietnamese soldier. Dog was a delicacy in the Vietnamese culture; they raised dogs for food just as we raise cattle. There were no large Vietnamese dogs, only scrawny and undernourished small ones. I enjoyed seeing the bewildered looks on the faces of Vietnamese villagers when they saw a full-grown, muscular German shepherd. They had no idea what a military working dog could do.

Chapter Eleven

TIMBER AND THE AMBUSH

My first German shepherd scout dog was named Timber. He was two years old and had a beautiful tan-and-black mane and perfectly shaped ears that always stood at attention. Timber was a little on the thin side and smaller in height than the other dogs. His temperament was high-spirited and aggressive, and he didn't like to be disciplined. Ollie told me that Timber would settle down after he got used to my handling. It seemed that Timber was kin to my old friend Hans. *Why do I always get the mean ones?* I wondered.

Base-camp training was essential in preparing me to lead combat patrols. The handlers of the 44th had built an infantry-blue obstacle course behind the kennel to train the dogs. Among the obstacles were a five-foot wall with a window opening big enough for a dog to jump through, and a seesaw of the type you might see in a playground. The dogs learned to walk up one side, balance the board in the center, and then walk down the other side as the board hit the ground. Hurdles were built to teach the dogs to jump on command, and several fifty-gallon drums were welded together to teach the dogs to crawl through tunnels.

We stretched out a twelve-foot section of wire-mesh fence, staked it about two feet above the ground, and used it to teach the dogs to crawl through tight spaces. For balance training, we used a long log, trimmed of branches, for them to walk across. Also, we used a narrow wooden plank as a ramp for the dogs to climb up to a horizontal ladder about five feet above the ground. The wooden ladder, constructed with twenty narrow slats spaced about six inches apart, looked much like one you'd find in a playground. Dogs aren't as sure-footed as cats, and I found it amusing to watch their awkward efforts to negotiate that horizontal ladder.

Basic obedience was the root of all training. If the dog obeyed commands, then the handler could steer him through each obstacle on the course. Initially, Timber was reluctant to obey my commands. I practiced my voice and hand signals constantly to take control of Timber and make him work for me. I soon discovered that successful scout-dog training was all about repetition, discipline, and concentrated focus on the dog. I hadn't attended the formal twelve-week training course at Fort Benning, so I worked furiously to make the best of my on-the-job training.

As Timber and I worked through the obstacle course day after day, his confidence, balance, strength, muscle tone, and obedience grew by leaps and bounds. Scout dogs had to learn to maneuver on command — to go over, around, under, and through whatever terrain, vegetation, or water hazard they might encounter during a combat mission. Timber was soon performing admirably.

Timber's only reward for his performance was the verbal and physical affection I gave him. We never gave treats to our dogs; they were on a basic diet of water and canned and packaged food issued by the military and monitored by Doc Glydon. In combat situations, it was easy to imagine running out of treats and being in deep shit with a disobedient dog and Charlie lurking in the jungle shadows. Things out there happened too fast to have to bribe or coax a dog into performing. We played on the German shepherd's natural intelligence and love for human companionship to produce split-second obedience.

The breed is known for its adaptability to almost any climate and environmental condition. Their black-and-brown coats blended well with the terrain and vegetation. Their intimidating size allowed them to take a man down quite easily, and they could be trained to be aggressive for sentry duty or to be passive for scouting. They could adapt to changing from one handler to another in a short time. The army had decided wisely that the German shepherd was the best breed for use in Vietnam.

During my training, I learned that you get out of a dog what you put into it. Dogs adapt to the handlers' personality: if the handler is lazy, his dog is likely to act accordingly; if the handler is an energetic go-getter, he'll have an A-1 partner.

The scout dog has to learn his master's scent, the pitch of his voice, what type of physical gestures he uses, the pace he walks, his general mood and disposition, and which are the most important commands he gives. The more the handler and his dog work together, the more responsive they'll be to one another. Consistent training creates understanding, teamwork, and unconditional loyalty.

One of the harder parts of being a handler was interpreting what a dog already knows. I learned more about scouting from my fellow handlers, Ollie and Mike "Mac" McClellan, than from anyone else. The key, they taught me, was to keep my eyes on the dog at all times. A dog's natural instincts will tell you what he smells, sees, and hears, and when danger is near.

Timber, not I, would be the real point man. It would be my job to translate his dog language into English, so I could convey to everyone else what he was telling me. When Timber and I worked together, he was the one in charge, and I was relegated to being his interpreter. That was a funny revelation, because, before joining the dogs, I thought I'd be in charge and make all the decisions; now it was I who was to follow and take signals from a dog.

Ollie and his dog, Erik, worked with precision as a team. They were something special to watch. Ollie used silent arm and hand signals to control Erik at distances well beyond the length of the standard-issue leash. Ollie worked Erik off leash while in base camp and on combat missions, and Erik responded quickly to each of his commands. Their movements struck me as an art form. I hoped I could teach Timber to be as disciplined and well trained as Erik.

Mac McClellan was considered the top off-leash handler in the platoon. Watching Mac and his dog, Achates, work was an excellent learning experience as well as great entertainment. Seeing the communication and movements between handler and dog was like watching dance partners who'd been together for a long time. Like the other handlers, Mac and Ollie were formally schooled in handling military working dogs and mastering scouting techniques.

Training was the key to successful preparation for combat missions. The more you trained with your dog the more you learned about what the dog sees, hears, and senses, and about his physical reactions to those senses. Between missions, training was at the discretion of the handler. The only hard-and-fast rule was that a handler had better be ready to go on a mission when scheduled.

I felt less prepared than my fellow scout-dog handlers. Sentry-dog training had given me basic knowledge, but it hadn't prepared me for anything like what I was about to face. The functional use of sentry dogs was vastly different from that of scout dogs. I preferred the intricacies of deploying scout dogs. A sentry dog was trained primarily to guard and attack. The scout dog was deployed in more complex and diversified maneuvers. The scout-dog handler had to learn how to read the dog's body language as it moved naturally, which presented the primary challenge of interpretation. That made my scout-dog assignment much more difficult, but more interesting and challenging. Even though the danger was greater in combat, I wasn't uneasy about learning and performing my new job. I looked forward to my first real scouting mission with Timber.

I reported to the commanding officer of Company B, 2nd Battalion, 22nd Mechanized Infantry (the Regulars). The unit dated back to 1866. Their motto was "Deeds Not Words," and they were commonly referred to as "the Triple Deuce." Their encampment was within walking distance of the K-9 compound. Since we worked with a different unit each time we went out on a mission, and the turnover rate in most combat units was a constant, it was my job to brief the company commander or platoon leader on the capabilities and limitations of the scout-dog team and where to best deploy the dog in a tactical formation. When I arrived, the CO, who was new to the use and deployment of dogs, directed me to brief the platoon leader and platoon sergeant Timber and I would be supporting.

The platoon leader had never had scout-dog-team support, so I briefed him on what Timber and I could do. He, in turn, briefed me on his unit's next mission, using a map and grid to point out the objective. The brigade's Long Range Reconnaissance Patrol (LRRP) had recently located a large concentration of VC operating several miles west of Dau Tieng. A long column of APCs (armored personnel carriers) had assembled on the main road leading out of Dau Tieng. The first leg of the mission was to travel on several dirt roads until we reached a point near the target area. I knew that riding inside or sitting on top of an APC would neutralize Timber's effectiveness, but he and I would just have go along for the ride until we were able to dismount and do the work we had trained to do.

On reaching the target area, we were to get off the road and break trail through the jungle about half a mile until we reached a large clearing where the APCs would form a defensive perimeter. When that was set up, Timber and I would join foot patrols to search for VC. The area on the map was considered uninhabited and hostile.

I explained that negotiating our way through dense jungle terrain rather than open areas would be difficult, as it shortened the distance of a dog's alert to a target and allowed for little reaction time. One of the scout-dog team's objectives would be to locate and check out the narrow trails that zigzagged through the terrain. These were dangerous, but I knew that we had a better chance of getting an alert with a dog than by sending a soldier to check them.

Timber was frisky and eager to go on our first mission. The APCs lined up on the road, one behind the other, engines running and ramps up, ready to move out through the main gate. On top of the APCs, several armed grunts wore helmets and flak vests that increased body temperature in the hot sun. Fifty-caliber machine guns were manned in their turrets, and radios squawked as we prepared to move out. Timber and I followed at a quick step closely behind the platoon leader.

M-113 U.S Army Military Personnel Carrier. Pictured is 44th Scout Dog, Erik (Ollie Whetstone's dog) and members of the 2nd Battalion, 22nd Infantry (Mechanized). Better known as "Triple Deuce." This was the type of vehicle Timber and I had been riding in during the ambush–1967. (Photo courtesy of Ollie Whetstone)

The smell of diesel fuel filled the air. The platoon leader stopped close to the front of the column, turned, looked at me, and pointed to an APC. Its ramp was already down, so Timber and I climbed aboard. The driver yanked a hand lever, and a greasy cable slowly pulled the heavy metal ramp door up until it locked in a closed position, eliminating the light from outside. Inside the APC, we had to shout to be heard above the engine noise.

I wasn't fond of APCs. A scout-dog team was useless riding inside any type of vehicle, and large APCs presented an easy target for a VC rocket-propelled grenade (RPG), which was designed to kill and destroy helicopters, bunkers, buildings, ammunition dumps, and whatever else they hit. Nonetheless, I had no choice about my assignment. It was my first scouting mission with a mechanized infantry unit and I would have to make the best of it.

The Russian-made RPGs were lightweight, fired very quickly, and reloaded easily. Like their American counterparts, the Lightweight

Antitank Weapon (LAW), RPGs were deployed by resting them on top of a man's shoulder. One disadvantage of the LAW was that it could fire only one shot, while the RPG could be reused. The elusive VC didn't make as easy targets as we Americans did; they didn't ride around in jeeps, trucks, tanks, or helicopters. Their strengths were their knowledge of the terrain, ability to strike without warning, and the quickness with which they could escape.

Inside the APC troop compartment, two other infantrymen accompanied Timber and me. The manually operated hatch over our heads was locked open. If you didn't mind standing, you could look out over the top of the APC as it motored down the road. Sometimes the rifleman would sit on top of the APC to enjoy cooler air and view the countryside. If the enemy attacked, the men on top could easily and quickly pile inside and return fire from a standing position. For that ride, I sat quietly with the leash on Timber, who was lying down on the cool metal floor.

I thought about many things during that trip, like my unfamiliarity with the crew. I had no idea how Timber and I would work out in a mechanized infantry unit. I didn't feel a part of the camaraderie that the others displayed. Whether I'd be accepted by the crew was still a question, but I'd come to do a job, not make a bunch of new friends.

Timber growled and bared his teeth each time one of the crew tried to touch him. They quickly backed off as I shouted, "No, Timber! No!" Timber stopped showing his teeth as long as the soldiers kept their distance. Since my mission equipment didn't include a muzzle, I held Timber close on a short leash and explained to the others that he was a little aggressive around new people. I assured them that he'd get used to them over time. I was telling a white lie, though: Timber was an aggressive dog, period; he'd even bitten me a few times. I don't think Timber liked his job or Vietnam. He was like a grumpy draftee with an attitude of "Let's get this crap over with!"

One of the grunts commented, "I have a dog at home. He's a Lab. No way would I send his ass over here to fight this fucking war."

Another said, "Fuck that! I don't know shit about what you and your dog are supposed to do for me. All I know is that he wants to bite my ass."

This crew had never worked with a scout-dog team before I arrived on the scene. I did my best to explain how scout-dog teams worked in the field. The grunts appeared interested, but I didn't think I had gained their confidence. They seemed to take a wait-and-see attitude. But, what the hell, at least I was getting to know them a little better, even if it was their testy side.

I hope they're not like this for the whole mission, I thought. *If they are, working with this crew is going to be a real bummer.*

While the long, noisy column of APCs clattered down the road for several hours, I couldn't hear any war activity. As we came to a stop, the radio started to squawk with chatter; from what I could hear, I gathered that we were to break up the convoy, get off the road, and head into the jungle. I stood up through the open hatch to take a look around. Heavy dust irritated my eyes, so I sat back down.

The APCs moved off the road and into the jungle, heading for a clearing. As a passenger sitting inside, and without looking at the field map, I had no way of knowing which clearing was our destination or how far we'd traveled. The tracks under the APC slowly cranked and ground their way through thick brush. Leaves and small branches, along with bugs and fire ants, began to fall through the open hatch and land on us, so we battened down the hatch. Then we had to quickly kill the fire ants that had fallen inside because those little predators hurt like hell when they sting. Another of Mother Nature's tropical pests, they always attacked without provocation.

The APC moved forward, bulldozing everything in its way and leaving a wide path of mashed brush and a newly created trail in its wake. The engine roared and the exhaust pipe spewed plumes of black smoke. The brush crackled beneath the APC's heavy metal treads. It was slow and bumpy as the tracks struggled to get over rocks, stumps, stubborn trees, and bushes.

There was no doubt in my mind that if Charlie was in the area, he was tracking us and knew where we were heading. The lead track was responsible for setting our direction and breaking the trail for the others to follow. Inside my APC, our ride was a little smoother on the path that the leader had created. After about half an hour of trailblazing through the bush, the APCs entered a huge clearing. Looking out at the surrounding area, I saw that the APCs were assembling into a giant defensive perimeter. It reminded me of a wagon train circling the wagons in that Old West TV show "Rawhide."

With all its antennas sticking out, the command APC was easy to spot. I watched it set up near a clump of trees toward the center of the perimeter, and figured that we must have reached our first objective. When we'd positioned ourselves defensively and organized into foot patrols, Timber and I would finally get our chance to show what we could do.

When my APC stopped and the driver lowered the ramp, I got up. Timber followed me outside. I saw APCs strategically spaced on either side of ours. The gunners on top of the APCs pointed their guns to the front. I introduced myself to the track commander, a sergeant, and asked him about the next phase. He said we'd set up camp for the night, send out some outposts, and deploy foot patrols in the morning. I told him I was ready to take the lead when the patrol assembled. The sergeant nodded and told me I'd get my chance the next morning.

It was mid-afternoon and hot as hell sitting in the open. Crews milled around, talking, assembling their gear, checking their weapons and ammunition, and setting up defensive positions. I tied Timber to the track and poured drinking water into my steel pot for him. I'd brought four canteens—three for Timber and one for myself.

My weapon, the latest model of the M-16—a CAR-15—had a retractable metal stock. When extended, it served as a rifle, yet fired the same 5.56 caliber steel-jacketed bullets as the M-16. Internally, it had the same mechanism as the M-16, but the CAR-15 was much shorter, lighter, and easier to carry. I could hang it from my shoulder by a sling and fire it from my hip with one hand. The rifle had little or no kickback when I fired it that way, a feature that allowed me to manage Timber on the leash and shoot simultaneously.

Most of the grunts carried the standard M-16. Some carried M79 grenade launcher, M-60 machine guns, or 12-gauge shotguns. I was the only one sporting the new CAR-15. I felt like hot shit because my weapon got second looks from the grunts hanging around the track. I had backpacked twenty clips of ammunition, which amounted to 200 rounds; two grenades, a hunting knife, food, water, a poncho, and a poncho liner to wrap up in at night.

My backpack held enough food for three days, but if I had thought ahead, I could have lightened my load to dog food and two canteens of water, because I was working with a mechanized infantry unit. Inside the APCs, the grunts stored all the food and water they needed, using the vehicles as pack mules. I learned that the men who rode in APCs only carried one canteen of water and a few meals of C-Rations when they went on patrol, because they never ventured far from their supply on the track.

When it rained, mechanized infantrymen usually slept inside the cover of their APCs. I was learning new things all the time on this trip. *Leave it to grunts,* I thought. *If there was a way not to have to carry their shit, they would capitalize on it.* I could understand why they were so proud of those luxuries that I hadn't had when I worked with the regular always-on-foot infantry—"ground-pounders," as we sometimes called them.

I was getting hungry, but I fed Timber first. I checked his food package for bugs before giving it to him. Bugs were everywhere in Vietnam, and they'd get into anything except a metal cans of C-Rations. There were probably some that could eat through cans. Timber ate the semi-moist packaged food as fast as I put it down, and then slurped up the water I poured for him.

I took a can of beefsteak and potatoes from my stash and soon realized that I hadn't packed a can opener. Most of the time, I had a P38 attached to the dog tags chained around my neck. Now the damn thing was missing. I felt embarrassed to ask for one from grunts I didn't know very well. I was a new face to those guys, and to have forgotten to pack my P38 might make them think of me as a greenhorn. I was a veteran, but they didn't know that or anything about my first tour as an infantryman.

I thought, *Aw, what, the hell, I gotta eat, don't I?* So I asked a guy from New York if I could borrow his P38. He was about five feet seven, weighed a husky 175 pounds, and had jet-black hair and a crusty black mustache. He spoke with a heavy New York accent and was quite friendly but had that inner-city, tough-guy attitude.

The soldier said loudly, "My P38? Sure, you can borrow it, but I'll have to kill you if you don't give it back." He immediately burst into laughter and told me to keep it as a souvenir of the 2nd Squad. I was relieved when he asked me to join him for chow. As we ate our C-Rations, we talked about where we were from. Timber lay quietly on the ground beside the APC, sheltered from the hot late-afternoon sun.

Suddenly, activity on the radio picked up. Troops quickly moved around the two tracks on either side of me. My track commander yelled, "Saddle up! Hurry! Let's go! Come on! Let's Go! Go! Go!"

I hustled to gather Timber and my gear, leaving my half-eaten can of C-Rations on the ground. Clutching my backpack in one hand and Timber's leash in the other, I scrambled up the ramp into the track and sat, with Timber between my legs on the bench seat near the hinged ramp. The other guys quickly loaded their gear and sat facing Timber and me.

Within seconds the driver had started the engine, raised the ramp, and moved forward. The sergeant was on the radio. I leaned over to ask him what was going on. He told me that a bunch of armed NVA troops had been spotted from the air, heading away from the perimeter. His squad was the closest to them, so he'd been ordered to close in and engage the enemy. The sergeant laid his compass on the map and pointed to a strategic area not too far from where the enemy appeared to be heading.

During the pursuit, Timber and I were in the lead APC. It was moving as fast as it could go. We bounced around and hung on.

The APC crashed into the brush. Small trees and bushes splintered as we plowed over them. When the terrain became rougher, the APC slowed down, mashing whatever was in its way, then dipped down with a jolt when the treads hit something solid. It felt as if we were stuck in a ditch. The treads kept grinding underneath us. The driver tried to climb up and over the sides of the depression. A thick pall of diesel fuel and stagnant smoke filled the air as the engine revved and the metal treads spun in place. The driver backed up and then slammed forward repeatedly, trying to break free. Inside, we rocked back and forth until, finally, the APC climbed up over the bank and into more jungle growth.

The machine gunner on top ducked under tree limbs. Looking up, I couldn't see the sky. Green vegetation was falling in on top of us. It felt as if we were inside a blender. Then there was a deafening BANG! and the APC stopped in its tracks. I could have sworn I was inside a metal drum that someone had just hit with a sledgehammer. The explosion's force ripped through the thin panel covering the engine. Black smoke streamed from the driver's compartment, filling the inside of the cabin. I noticed that the driver was wounded in the right leg as he quickly scrambled up through his hatch and out of the APC. Simultaneously, the .50 caliber machine gun on top began firing. I looked at the other two soldiers across from me. They looked startled and said nothing. All this took place in a matter of seconds.

There was no way to reach the handle to lower the ramp because it was in the driver's compartment. My survival instincts took over and I grabbed the small emergency door handle and yanked it open. With my boot, I pushed the heavy metal door as hard as I could. It swung out on its hinges and latched itself open.

With Timber's leash in one hand, I grabbed my CAR-15 and a bandoleer of magazines. I dove through the open door and lay flat on my belly in the dirt behind the smoking track. I pulled on Timber's leash as I tried to crawl away, but was stopped cold. The end of his leash was trapped between the ramp and the door; it must have gotten caught when the ramp door closed as we rushed inside.

The other two grunts had already dived through the opening and were crawling away. I frantically pulled and yanked to free the leash, but it wouldn't budge, so I cut it with the hunting knife I'd bought in Okinawa. Only about ten inches of leash remained to connect me with Timber. He panicked and jumped up and down trying to free himself from my grip. The shooting and explosions increased to my front and on the left.

I crouched on my knees, leaned against the back of the APC, and tried hard to control Timber's panic. I quickly looked around and realized that the APC was sitting perpendicularly on a dirt road. Its back provided some protection from the incoming bullets. The front of the APC was on fire. Nothing but the flat, narrow dirt road spread out to my right. I didn't detect any shots coming from that direction. I couldn't see the left side of the road. Another stationary APC stood directly behind me in the path we'd made in the jungle. The rest of the column was stopped behind it.

The shooting increased. The VC fired on the APC column from its front and left sides. I saw my track commander lying on top of the burning APC, firing the .50 caliber machine gun directly to his front. The vegetation on both sides of the dirt road was thick and dark. I couldn't see the enemy through it, but could feel his bullets hammering the APC close to my position.

I aimed into the thick jungle to the front of the APC and fired several rounds on semiautomatic. Charlie returned fire immediately. I still couldn't see the enemy, but I could feel his presence, and realized that I'd become a sitting duck behind the track in the middle of the road. Deciding to seek better cover, I got on my stomach and crawled away, dragging Timber from the flaming track. We made it into the jungle about fifty feet behind the APC. Timber continued to growl and jerk away from my grasp. I was determined not to let him run. If he ran away, he'd surely be killed, and I'd never have forgiven myself. *We're in this together and we'll stay together,* I thought.

I scanned the jungle for signs of enemy movement. Charlie was still invisible. The column of APCs was to my left. I could hear

American weapons firing, and the turret-mounted heavy machine guns blasting away. Small-arms fire from Americans and VC filled the air with constant cracking noises. I heard another loud explosion nearby. Through the thick vegetation, I saw black smoke and red flames coming from a second APC. I hung on to Timber and hugged the jungle floor.

Two APCs, pinned down by enemy fire from the left and front of the column, had definitely been knocked out of action during the first few minutes of the attack. Charlie had hit my APC first, which probably meant that the ambush had sprung along the left side of our column.

Bullets zinged through the air around my position, chopping jungle foliage everywhere. Nothing was coming from my right side, which led me to believe that we were in an L-shaped ambush. The short leg of the L was the front of my APC; the long leg was the left side of the column of our four APCs. The VC we had chased had maneuvered us into their trap.

Timber was going crazy. Crawling around to find a better fighting position, I discovered a wounded American soldier. Timber growled at him, but I kept my dog at bay. Timber was scared and didn't want to be in that situation any more than I did. In shock, the soldier sat on his knees, eyes glazed over, staring blindly into nothingness. He had no weapon and no helmet on his head. I recognized him as one of the crew who'd been in my APC. A chunk of shrapnel stuck out from his forehead. I pulled the wounded man to the ground and tried to comfort him. I had no first-aid bandages—only my CAR-15, a bandoleer of ammunition, and Timber. With my free hand, I tore a strip of cloth from my fatigue jacket and used it to soak up the blood dripping down the soldier's face, then helped him to crawl to a nearby tree.

Still struggling desperately to get away, Timber kept nipping at me. I was getting pissed off, so I slapped him hard across the snout with my free hand. That only upset him more. I realized that I'd lost my composure. I shouldn't have struck my dog. There was too much confusion, and too many things to concentrate on at once.

The whole situation was out of control. For the first time, I began to wonder if I'd survive.

The constant rifle fire, exploding grenades, and chatter of machine guns were deafening. I fired into the jungle in front of the track that was still blazing in the road. Although the shooting was to my left, I didn't want to shoot over the heads of the Americans positioned around the APCs. I was fortunate to have a good firing position from behind the thick base of a tropical tree whose large roots grew a few feet above the ground and connected to its base. For protection, I wedged between the tree roots with Timber and the wounded soldier. Even if the man had had his weapon, he was too deeply in shock to defend himself.

There was another APC on fire to my left behind the one I'd vacated. It bothered me not to have both hands free, but I kept returning fire into the thick jungle to my front, aware that I needed to conserve ammunition.

I figured Charlie would eventually surround and trap us all. I had no idea how large a force we were up against. The nonstop firing was brutal. I thought there must be more than a platoon of VC for them to be putting out so much firepower. Maybe there were fifty enemy soldiers attacking us—I couldn't be certain.

We had started out with four APCs. Now I could only hear two of them firing their machine guns, a distinctly American sound, as Charlie didn't have .50 caliber weapons. Now I was certain that we were trapped in an L-shaped ambush, which allowed the VC interlocking fire and maximized their killing zone without causing them friendly fire casualties. Charlie had pulled off this attack very well.

Charlie's going to come around on my side any time now. I'm not prepared to hold off an all-out assault. He's definitely got the advantage and will overrun me.

On the right side of the burning APC, I was receiving intense fire from across the road to my front. I could tell by where the bullets were landing that Charlie knew my exact location. I couldn't see the enemy through the jungle but I knew they were there. I had no idea whether I was hitting any of them when I returned fire. Charlie appeared to have been dug in, and seemed to know where all the Americans were positioned.

I kept reloading and firing on semiautomatic. Trying to maintain my confidence, I thought that Charlie probably suspected that American reinforcements would be here soon. On the downside, I also knew that the enemy's bullets and rocket-propelled grenades could take less than a second to kill us all. I kept thinking, *Reinforcements won't be here in time. We're all going to die.*

The attack wasn't typical of how Charlie operated. Usually, he'd hit fast and run like hell before we could regroup and reinforce. This time, Charlie wasn't running. I figured he was preparing to move in for the kill.

Timber kept on fighting to get free. I refused to let him go and tried talking softly, hoping he'd calm down. The wounded soldier was still alive, lying quietly on the ground between the tree roots. If Charlie charged across the road, I decided I'd switch to full automatic and take out as many of them as I could before they wasted me.

I didn't see any other Americans near me, so I assumed that I was the only one defending our right flank. My mind raced frantically: *If Charlie realizes I'm the only man defending this side, he'll overrun my position. Why hasn't he attacked already? Maybe he's getting ready to. Maybe he knows I'm low on ammo. I'll make every shot count! Reinforcements have to get here soon. I can't hold out much longer. My grenades are in the burning APC—going to get them would be suicide. Timber's gone mad.*

All these thoughts were driving me mad. For the first time while serving in Vietnam, I felt completely isolated and vulnerable.

BOOM! A tremendous explosion filled the air. The ground shook, and so did I. The APC I'd escaped from had blown sky-high. Timber let out a pained cry and went down on his side. At the same instant, I felt the heat of stinging shrapnel burning into my face and left hand. I could feel small cuts on my face. Blood trickled down my cheeks. My hands and arms had tiny cuts too. My muscles were tense. Timber was bleeding badly from his right rear flank. I had no bandages, so there wasn't much I could do to cover his wound. Timber lay on his side in pain and panted quietly. I'd been lucky once more; I was still alive. The tree had taken the brunt of the shrapnel. I looked to my left front where the explosion had occurred. The APC had been reduced to a smoking slab of metal resting on its tracks in the middle of the dirt road.

Then it became strangely quiet for a few moments. My eyes anxiously darted around looking for any kind of movement. I saw nothing, but I heard groans nearby. The shooting started again on the left side of the column of APCs. The soldier firing his .50 caliber machine gun on top of the burning APC had disappeared with the explosion. I knew that there was no way that he'd survived. Several 50 caliber brass casings, hot to the touch and split wide open from the exploding powder, were scattered near my feet, their black metal links still connecting them.

The other APCs on my left were too close for comfort. One was still smoking, and I figured it was only a matter of time before it blew up. Soldiers moved around on the ground, using the protection of the APCs to defend themselves. I decided to help another wounded soldier nearby, so I left Timber and crawled over to him. Too hurt to move, Timber didn't follow me. I recognized the soldier as the fellow from New York who'd given me his P38 to open my C-Rations. He was the most mind-boggling sight I'd ever witnessed in combat: that poor soldier, suffering from severe wounds, crawled aimlessly on his hands and knees. The sleeves of his shirt were torn away, exposing nothing but the remains of his arms—white bones and joints, most of the flesh gone. Chunks of flesh had ripped away from his thighs and back. I couldn't understand how that man could still be alive and crawling around in such a condition.

The wounded soldier grabbed me by the shoulder and stopped crawling. He looked as if he recognized me. Then, slowly, he rolled over on his back, his eyes staring up at me. He moved his mouth, trying to talk, but I couldn't understand a word he said. I couldn't stop staring at him, either.

Then something happened that I'll never forget for as long as I live. As the wounded soldier stared at me, his body began to glow a soft white, as if a light fog were slowly covering him. That lasted only a few seconds. When it disappeared, the soldier wasn't breathing anymore. I knew he was dead. I closed his eyes and slowly moved away. I'd seen my share of men die in Vietnam, but I'd never seen anything like that before. Had I watched that man's spirit leave his body? I didn't really know.

Then I thought about the tragedy of the situation. A man I'd barely known was now dead, and his face was burned into my memory. I knew I'd never recall the experience without feeling the profound sadness and senselessness of that moment.

I felt helpless and hopeless. The shooting seemed to never stop. I returned to the tree to check on Timber and the other wounded man. Timber wasn't moving anymore, but he still breathed. I told him he was going to be okay, and assured him that I'd get him out of there. I don't know whether Timber understood a word I said, but he didn't move.

The other soldier was alive and still in shock. Small-arms fire poured in on us. Spotting movement in the jungle across the road, I fired on semiautomatic. The movement stopped. I might have silenced one VC, but I wasn't going out to confirm the kill.

I kept firing single shots at invisible enemies wherever I heard something. I looked around and spotted more wounded Americans huddled in the vegetation behind nearby trees. Some were curled up on the ground, crying in pain and unable to continue fighting.

I left the safety of my position again to try to help. I found the platoon leader I'd met at the start of the mission. Badly burned, he sat with his back propped against a tree. His smoking fatigue jacket had welded to his flesh. His right arm was mangled.

With the numbness of a man in shock, the lieutenant asked, "Do I look okay?"

"You look fine, sir. Everything's going to be all right," I said, trying to give him some shred of hope to hang on to.

The lieutenant said, "Before we abandoned the burning APC, I radioed for air strikes on our position."

There was nothing I could do for the lieutenant, so I returned to the tree to check on my dog and the other wounded man.

American artillery and air strikes zeroed in on our positions and dropped their loads. Nothing is more frightening than the incredible thunder of exploding artillery shells and bombs within a stone's throw of a soldier's position. Those jets couldn't possibly see where we were under the jungle canopy. I hugged the earth near a tree, kept my head down, and held Timber to the ground. Even though Timber had lost some blood, he came to life when the artillery and bombs exploded, but he quickly wore himself out struggling to get away from me again, and then finally gave up and lay still.

The fighting seemed to last forever and I was in a state of sensory overload trying to absorb all that was happening. It was hard to believe that anyone would make it out of there alive. I knew it was only a matter of time before I'd be hit. I tried to keep my wits about me and stay focused on the VC who were still out there.

A numbness began coming over me. I'd never experienced such a feeling. For some reason I now felt mentally and physically strange. I was exhausted and thirsty, and the numbness spread quickly through my entire body. Something weird was happening to me and I couldn't shake it off.

Suddenly, I heard a commotion in the brush to my right. It was the first time there had been noise on that side of the jungle. The numbness intensified. *This is it!* I thought. *The gooks are coming for me now. It's all over! Charlie's at my doorstep, and he won't be taking prisoners. I'll fucking kill myself before I let those fuckers get me.*

The noise grew closer. My adrenaline spiked. Nervously, I aimed my CAR-15. My body shook uncontrollably as I listened and waited, eyes wide open, for something to happen. Then I heard voices call out from the brush, "Don't shoot! We're Americans!" I lowered my weapon and sat there shaking and staring aimlessly. American soldiers poured into the area; they were going to prevent us all from being wiped out—I had been saved.

I was still in a daze when one of the soldiers came over. He stooped and brushed the ants and dirt from my naked arms and offered me water from his canteen. I couldn't speak or stand, still unable to shake that strange numbness. The soldier told me to stay where I was and that he'd be back. Another soldier tended to the wounded man lying next to me. Fresh troops moved all around the area.

I could hear the leaders shouting, "Let's get these wounded men some help over here! Check out those APCs for survivors! Help that man over there! Set up a firing position! Oh, my God, we have some dead Americans here! Cover them with ponchos!"

The shooting and explosions had stopped. The only sound was the American voices. Silently clutching the short leash still attached to Timber, I sat and watched helplessly as American troops helped the wounded and covered our dead. It was a complete mess.

Why is this happening to me? Why can't I get up?

A huge armored wrecker drove past the tree where I sat. Right in front of me, without warning, it ran over a land mine, which exploded. Everyone hit the ground in an instant. I didn't even flinch. Dirt and debris flew everywhere. I just sat there and watched, not responding or talking, as if I were locked deep inside myself, looking out.

Our rescuers loaded the dead and wounded into APCs idling on the road. Two soldiers approached me. I recognized Mac McClellan, my fellow dog handler from the 44th Scout Dog Platoon.

Mac said, "John, I'm going to take care of Timber. You need to let these guys get you into the APC and to a hospital."

I shook my head and yelled, "No! No! No! I can take care of him!"

Mac pried my hand open to take Timber's leash. He picked up my wounded dog and carried him away. Two soldiers helped me to my feet and into an APC. As we rode off, I sat, wordless and not moving a muscle, feeling totally withdrawn and useless. When the APC stopped, the soldiers helped me get up. They put me on a stretcher. I lay very still, staring up at the darkening sky. I heard and saw choppers everywhere.

A face appeared and looked down at me, eyes fixed on mine. I glanced at his collar and noticed the white cross indicating that he was a chaplain. My eyes welled with tears that blurred my vision. The chaplain hugged and blessed me. He told me that the Lord was with me now, that I was safe and needn't worry. The chaplain walked beside the stretcher as two soldiers carried me to the waiting medical evacuation chopper. The Medevac lifted off and I was on my way to a field hospital. My body felt paralyzed, but my mind was clear and active.

When the chopper landed, I was carried into a tent that smelled like medicine. Looking up at the bright lights overhead, I realized I was inside a field hospital. Wounded men on stretchers and tables were all over the place. A nurse with a mask over her mouth asked me where I hurt. I couldn't speak; I lay there on my back and stared at her. The nurse shined a bright light into my eyes. I didn't even blink. She cut away my fatigue jacket and trousers and checked over my entire body, cleaned the cuts on my face and arms, and then stuck me with a needle. I soon passed out.

I awoke the next morning on a cot in a recovery tent. Feeling a little sore, but otherwise fine, I sat up and looked around the room. I no longer felt the strange numbness. *What the hell happened to me out there?*

The room was filled with soldiers all bandaged up and lying on cots. A doctor came over and told me to lie down again. I explained that I felt fine and wanted to check on Timber. The doctor said they had no patient by that name, and that I had no serious wounds; I had suffered a bout of traumatic combat shock and battle fatigue and would soon be released. I told him that I'd been on many missions and seen plenty of combat, but no such thing had ever happened to me before. "Why this time?" I asked.

The doctor believed that this type of medical condition occurred when a soldier's resistance to violent combat wears down and his system has had enough. He explained that the consequences of combat could linger for a while, but that I would recover soon. Cautioning me to take it easy for a few weeks before heading out on another mission, the doctor said he'd release me from medical care the next day.

When I arrived back at the 44th, Mac welcomed me and said that Doc Glydon had patched up Timber. Most of my gear had burned up in the APC, but Mac had put my weapon on my cot. I went to my hooch to rest. It was hard to believe that I'd been gone only a few days.

I pondered the events that had led to the ambush and all those casualties. I thought about Timber jumping all around and how difficult he'd been to control. I was still pissed off that he'd tried to run away, but I felt even more upset at having struck him. I certainly didn't want to ride in another APC for as long as I lived.

I looked at the P38 attached to my dog tags and instantly flashed back to that poor soul from New York who had given it to me. That young man died in the middle of nowhere and there had been nothing I could do but watch. I replayed that battle over and over in my mind, the faces of all the nameless men I'd fought beside flashing through my head. *God rest their souls,* I prayed.

I briefed the K-9 platoon leader, Lieutenant Fenner, on the mission. After listening intently, he said he was happy that I was okay. That was about it. The lieutenant wasn't one to dwell on the details; as a leader, he wanted me to recover and try to forget.

Doc Glydon told me that Timber had been a frightened animal when he was brought to him. Shrapnel had badly chewed up Timber's right rear flank. Doc said that the dog had lost some blood but would recover.

I went to the kennel and found Timber lying on his concrete run. He didn't respond much when I called his name, so I went inside and sat beside him, talking to him and stroking his soft, furry body. I apologized to Timber for striking him and asked his forgiveness.

Timber showed no liveliness the whole time I was there. It was too early to expect much. Timber was obviously having a hard time dealing with all that had happened to him. Hell, I knew how he felt! I wondered if either of us would ever get over what we'd been through in that jungle. Would Timber ever be the same dog as before? I knew I'd go on other missions, but would I be okay? Only time would tell.

A week passed. I continued feeding and caring for Timber, and his wounds appeared to be healing. I took him out of his run several times and tried some basic obedience exercises, but he didn't respond to commands as before. He had no snap and lacked his usual aggressiveness. My instincts told me that Timber wouldn't be ready for any missions in the near future. I wasn't sure what I wanted to do.

As much as I loved Timber, and felt sorry for him, I decided that the best thing for both of us was for me to ask Lieutenant Fenner for a different scout dog. The lieutenant agreed: if I didn't feel comfortable handling Timber anymore, I could replace him with any other available dog.

I thought about that APC mission many times during the days I spent recovering in base camp. I never had the chance to work Timber the way we'd trained to work. Regardless of my title as a scout-dog handler, I was, in reality, an infantryman. We'd entered that ambush with four APCs, each carrying four to six men. Charlie's ambush had surprised us, trapped us, and picked us off one by one. His RPGs, grenades, rifles, and machine guns had kicked American ass that day, but the final deathblow, which I'd been so sure would come, never had.

I didn't know how many enemy troops paid with their lives. I thought I'd killed a few, but I never saw their bodies. Charlie had drawn us into that spot to kick our butts, and we fell right into his deadly trap. Only a handful survived the attack. Without the timely rescue, I'd have gone home in a coffin.

Mac McClellan, the 44th's poet, expressed so well what it had been like to ride in an APC and become an easy target.

Kaiser Coffin

Aluminum-hulled hearse, carrier of cattle.

Made by Detroit to take men to battle.

Gas tank high on the left-hand side.

Charlie found out, and a lot of men died.

Gasoline tanks in the floor and wall,

One rocket hit, and you're in a fiery ball.

Beer-can aluminum, two inches thick,

A browning fifty will go through slick.

Can it stop anything except a trifle?

You're safe as can be from a Daisy air rifle.

— Michael "Mac" McClellan, 44th Scout Dogs, 1967

Now, I had to put that traumatic experience behind me and focus all my strength on healing and on preparing for my next mission. I'd have to cope with all the uncertainties of learning how to handle a new scout dog—my life and the lives of others would depend on my succeeding.

Chapter Twelve

MEET CLIPPER

It took several days for me to decide which of the available dogs I wanted as my next partner. I selected a fine-looking dog named Clipper. I was excited from the first time I saw that dog, and he took to me as if we'd worked together before.

The military permanently marked Clipper as its own by tattooing the serial number 12X3 inside his left ear; we both wore dog tags—I just had to wear metal ones around my neck.

Clipper had an official military medical record, as did each scout dog in the 44th Scout Dog Platoon. It contained information such as who had donated or sold him to the military, the date and place of his entry into military service, his age, weight, height, training record, and a photo of him in profile. Doc Glydon maintained a record of all the medical treatment provided to each scout dog assigned.

Clipper was docile and very smart. A handsome dog of about eighty pounds of toned muscle, he had a healthy black-and-brown coat, big brown eyes, and great-looking ears. Clipper walked with a sense of pride, intelligence, confidence, and control. In my opinion, he was a perfect specimen of a German shepherd, even though he wasn't a purebred animal by show-dog standards. He'd let any American soldier pet him, no matter where we were.

Whenever Clipper was around the local Vietnamese people, friendly or otherwise, he became agitated and aggressive. One reason was that the Vietnamese looked, talked, smelled, walked, and ate differently from Americans. Secondly, all the scout dogs were trained to hunt those characteristics, and were rewarded with love and affection when they found them. Besides, to keep the dogs from getting used to them, Vietnamese weren't allowed inside the K-9 compound.

John Burnam and his loving partner, Clipper,
44th Scout Dog Platoon compound–1967. (Author collection)

Between missions, Ollie and I decided to do some dog training together. We found a perfect place inside the base camp's outer defensive perimeter, within the rows and rows of tall rubber trees behind the kennel area. The trees offered the added advantage of shade from the hot and humid climate.

I wanted to teach Clipper how to recognize tripwires and alert me to their presence. Also, I needed to learn how to clearly recognize when and how Clipper alerted to specific targets, so I could quickly relay that information to the other soldiers on the mission. I had to learn what Clipper would do when he sensed different kinds of danger. How would he alert me when he suspected that there were enemy hiding in foxholes, behind or up in trees, or standing in full view? At what distance from the stimulus would Clipper alert when he detected human or metallic movement, noise, or smell? Did he alert the same way on a man as he would on an animal or a booby trap? To learn the answers, I had to work with Clipper on each training situation, and recognize the specific type of alert his body language conveyed in each one.

During our training sessions, we set up a different mock situation each time. Often, we'd use captured enemy clothing, equipment, and weapons to prepare our dogs to alert us on particular sounds and scents. In one training scenario, we'd send a fellow dog handler far enough into the woods so that I wouldn't know exactly where he was. While our decoy hid behind a tree or some other form of cover, I'd keep Clipper distracted by walking and playing with him in another area, allowing several minutes to pass before we'd begin the hunt. Then, I'd command Clipper by slapping my hand against the side of my left leg—Clipper's signal to heel and sit.

When it was time to go, I'd work Clipper on a six-foot leather leash. I'd tug the leash, signaling him to move to the end of it, and then give the command "Search!" Keeping the pace slow, as if we were walking point on a live patrol. I'd walk behind Clipper, my eyes on the back of his head and ears at all times, monitoring any physical reactions outside his ordinary behavior.

As we headed toward the hidden target, I observed Clipper's neck and head rising sharply and his ears popping straight up and forward. Clipper stopped, stood erect with his mouth closed, and stared straight ahead for just a moment. Then the alert was relaxed. If I didn't have my eyes on him at all times, I'd have missed that first quick signal that he had heard or sighted something. Clipper turned and gave me a quick glance. I interpreted his reactions as a strong alert. I quickly got to one knee, as I was taught, and looked in the direction Clipper's head had pointed. He sat quietly and waited for his next command. I put my weapon on the ready and scanned to our front. I'd still seen and heard nothing. We moved only twenty or thirty yards toward where I'd assumed the target decoy was hiding.

I got up slowly and tugged Clipper to move out again. He obeyed, moved a few more feet, and gave the same strong alert again. I knew he'd spotted something to the front, but I could tell only the target's direction, not how far away it was.

There were hundreds of trees all around. The question was, which one hid the decoy? I decided to keep moving forward. Clipper continued in the same direction; when he got within thirty yards of one particular tree, he stood erect, ears up, and refused to go any farther. Then the decoy came out from behind the tree. I grabbed Clipper around the neck and hugged and praised him for doing such a great job.

As it turned out, Clipper's first alert had been about a hundred yards from the decoy. Using these training techniques helped me learn how Clipper alerted on a human hiding behind a tree. I began repeating the exercise over and over, even in the rain. I learned that wind, heat, humidity, density of vegetation and terrain, surrounding noises, and the movement of others influenced how strongly and how far from a target a scout dog could alert. During our sessions, Ollie was a terrific tutor, always patient and understanding, as he thoroughly explained and demonstrated the training techniques.

Sometimes, we'd dig foxholes and have men hide in them, or we'd hide military equipment in the woods and in foxholes to see how the dog could alert on a scent carried by the wind, or saturated in the air without a wind factor, or after a heavy rain. Over time, I learned to read Clipper's reactions by concentrating on the movements of his body, head, and ears. I was gaining confidence in what Clipper could do and totally amazed at his consistent accuracy.

We couldn't conduct training missions outside the Dau Tieng base camp. Everything beyond the barbed wire was considered hostile. We had to be on an actual mission for me to learn whether Clipper's alerts would be the same in the various terrain conditions outside our base camp as in training sessions. I wondered how Clipper would work when fatigued by the heat, and how he'd handle marching long distances through the jungle, or moving across a lot of open terrain. After all, Clipper wasn't a machine; he was a dog, and before his induction into the army, he was a family pet.

Walking point was one of the most dangerous jobs in South Vietnam. Since that is what a dog handler did, he had to stay focused constantly. The enemy usually had the advantage of spotting the American point man first. With a scout-dog team, though, the tables were turned: we gained the advantage, because a dog's instincts, vision, and sense of smell and hearing were hundreds of times more acute than a human's. Clipper was like a walking radar beam.

Even though we expected to go on missions and knew that we'd always be situated in the lead of a combat patrol, it was normal for a scout-dog handler to be a little apprehensive.

On missions with Clipper, I carried my own ammunition and equipment, as well as his water and food supply. Clipper relied on me to recognize when he was thirsty, hungry, tired, hurt, or sick. We bonded as a team because we always took care of one another. Over time our bond would only get stronger.

When Clipper alerted, my job was to drop immediately to one knee, determine what the alert meant, and, as quickly and quietly as possible, relay the information to the men behind me. The platoon leader would then assess the situation and determine whether the patrol should act on the alert, check it out, ignore it, or proceed with caution. Even though I briefed the platoon leader ahead of time, if he had never worked with a scout-dog team, it was difficult to predict how he'd react when Clipper alerted.

Most patrol leaders trusted the dogs' instincts and my assessment of the situation; some, however, didn't like the idea of a scout-dog team making such assessments, and would often ignore the team's warning. Sometimes they'd get away with it; other times they paid a price. When I worked Clipper out front on point, I insisted that every strong alert he gave be checked out. I didn't like the crap-shoot of ignoring his signals.

If soldiers checked out Clipper's alert and we didn't make enemy contact, Clipper and I resumed the lead and continued pushing in the mission's direction. If Clipper's alert resulted in enemy contact, and if the situation allowed, we moved quickly back inside the patrol's main body. Our job was considered complete after the enemy was engaged.

Standard operating procedure for every mission was that when the fighting was over, and if casualties were light, the scout-dog team resumed the point position and continued the mission. If casualties were considered heavy, the entire platoon was usually replaced by a fresh unit. As an infantryman and scout-dog handler I'd been trained to follow that process, but things didn't always go as planned. Sometimes, the handler and his dog were so far out in front that they got trapped between the enemy and American lines when all hell broke loose.

Since I'd been in combat before, I took my base-camp training with Clipper seriously. I knew I'd have to rely on him. I'd experienced negotiating jungle conditions, open terrain, rivers, creeks, villages, hills, valleys, rice paddies, nighttime operations, and various weather conditions. Now I had to adjust to working with a dog under those same conditions and rely on him more than I had on any human I'd ever worked with. The patrol behind Clipper and me would watch out for our flanks and rear, and depended on Clipper for an early silent warning of danger to their front.

I wanted to earn everyone's respect and confidence by doing my job and, hopefully, saving lives in the process.

Chapter Thirteen

DEATH IN THE KENNEL

Specialist Four Fred DeBarros and his scout dog, Tinzer, were original members of the 44th Scout Dog Platoon that trained at Fort Benning and arrived in Vietnam in January 1967. They were next on the rotation schedule to scout for an infantry unit on a search-and-destroy mission in the jungles surrounding Dau Tieng. After a few days in the bush without enemy contact, Fred was ordered to join a small detachment of the platoon on a night-ambush operation that would set up alongside a narrow dirt road the Vietcong had been using.

It was dusk when Fred's detachment of ten infantrymen reached a suitable ambush site inside some thick vegetation a few yards off the dirt road. Complete silence was the norm; everyone quietly settled into hidden positions for what Fred thought would be a long, boring night, like most ambushes he'd supported.

After an hour it was fully dark, and the surrounding jungle came alive with its characteristic nocturnal noises. That was when Tinzer started fidgeting; he kept turning to face the rear of the ambush, rather than in the direction of the road like everyone else. Fred thought it was probably just an animal moving through the darkness behind them, which was a common alert, so he ignored Tinzer's movements and kept pulling him around to observe the road. This went on for a while before Fred realized that Tinzer was really trying to tell him that it something other than an animal might be moving behind them.

As a precaution, Fred quietly passed the word down the line to advise the detachment leader that Tinzer was alerting to the rear and that it could be human scent and movement. The leader was quick to react, passing the word back along the line to quietly change positions and train their weapons rearward.

Shortly after they were all in position to defend the rear, a small force of Vietcong attacked with small-arms fire at close range. The firing was intense from both sides as muzzle flashes and tracer bullets lit up the night. As Fred kept shooting though the darkness in the direction of the muzzle flashes, Tinzer lay by his side without moving or barking.

After a long exchange of concentrated fire from both sides, the enemy broke contact. Everyone stayed vigilant the rest of the night, nervously waiting for the enemy to launch a counterattack, but it never happened. At morning's light the weary detachment found three dead enemy soldiers nearby and some blood trails leading off into the jungle. The Americans were extremely lucky to have suffered no casualties.

Fred said that Charlie had to have spotted the detachment—including the dog and him—setting up the ambush, and decided to wait until the Americans got settled before sneaking up behind them. We all knew that the enemy could easily have surprised them and possibly wiped them out that night, if not for Tinzer's unwavering attention to the rear, and Fred's astute judgment in reporting it. Tinzer got lots of hugs and praise from Fred for saving lives.

Mission after mission, German shepherd scout dogs alerted American patrols of ambushes, snipers, and booby traps. Their bravery and courageous hard work in hostile conditions of terrain and tropical heat, often under fire, saved American lives. The enemy tried to counteract the the scout-dog teams' success by rewarding any soldier who killed scout dogs and their handlers.

On November 9, 1967, several scout-dog teams from the 44th

Scout Dog Platoon in Dau Tieng were out on combat missions supporting local infantry units. It was a typical quiet evening in base camp, with all of the dogs sheltered in the kennel for the night. As it got dark, I walked to the kennel to say goodnight to Clipper. Then, after hanging out in the K-9 Klub until after ten o'clock, I hit the sack. Most of the other dog handlers had already turned in.

After midnight, I awoke to the deafening sound of a nearby explosion. I could hear and feel the shrapnel splintering the walls of my hooch. I jumped up, grabbed my CAR-15, slipped my bare feet into jungle boots, and went flying into the screen door. I tripped and fell to the ground outside. It was pitch-black except for the blinding flashes of light coming from a barrage of exploding missiles. Clad only in underwear and unlaced boots, I darted to the shelter of one of the two bunkers outside our quarters. Once used as shipping containers, the bunkers were huge rectangular steel boxes partially buried in the ground and protected by sandbags. Portholes had been cut through the walls on all four sides to provide ventilation and create a 360-degree field of fire. We had no radio communication between the bunkers. After entering one, my hands and body shook uncontrollably; it was terrifying to awaken at night, in the safety of my base camp, and find my life in immediate danger.

While everyone ran to the safety of the bunkers, I heard at least ten explosions. Dog handlers crammed inside the shelters and huddled tightly in the limited floor space. Looking around, I realized I wasn't the only one in underwear and unlaced boots. Hell, some guys were barefoot! We were all wide-eyed and shocked: this was the first time the K-9 compound had come under surprise attack and taken direct hits from enemy mortars.

Another volley of shells whistled down, exploding in trees and on the ground. I shuddered with fear at the metallic sounds of shrapnel striking and piercing objects all around us.

On the K-9 compound, which was several hundred yards inside the primary defensive perimeter of Dau Tieng, the bunkers provided the only safe area to fight from. The enemy was somewhere inside the nearby rubber trees and not far from the base-camp perimeter.

Although there was no way to account for everyone, it appeared as if, by some miracle, no one had been wounded while running to the safety of the bunkers.

Each bunker was fully stocked with weapons, grenades, and plenty of ammunition. Between barrages of mortar fire, the dog handlers nervously waited to see the silhouettes of enemy soldiers assaulting the compound. If we spotted the VC, it would mean that they'd breached the perimeter.

We loaded weapons, pointed them out the portholes, and waited for targets to appear. During the relentless VC barrage, one round exploded on the top of the bunker I was in, and we all flinched simultaneously. The bunkers had never been tested like that; we didn't know how safe they'd be, but our bunker held up, making us feel more secure.

The kennel was across an open area from the bunkers; we couldn't see it very well through the dark shadows of the rubber trees that surrounded the compound. Months before the attack, we had filled and stacked sandbags waist-high on the side of the kennel facing the bunkers. On the night of the attack, the back of the kennel was still unprotected: no sandbags shielded the dogs from shrapnel or the bullets that flew over the ground on that side of it.

During the bombardment, the dogs barked in panic. They were used to their handlers being with them during dangerous situations. I knew Clipper felt confused, wondering where I was and when I'd come and move him out of harm's way. Because of the frequent explosions inside the compound, it was too dangerous for us to leave the bunkers. As long as the dogs kept barking, we handlers assumed they were okay, though several of the men wanted to get their dogs and bring them inside the bunkers. Lieutenant Fenner ordered us to quiet down and stay where we were.

We could hear small arms and machine guns firing in the near distance. We assumed that Charlie had decided to assault our camp's perimeter of defense, which was well fortified and manned twenty-four hours a day, seven days a week, 365 days a year. If Charlie somehow got through the perimeter, the K-9 compound was the second line of defense. I wondered how long we'd be able to hold off an enemy assault.

The scout dogs were the only ones unprotected from a ground attack. Caged inside their runs, they couldn't get out. If Charlie got to them, each dog could be easily killed without having an opportunity to fight back. Every dog handler's worst fear became reality when several 82mm mortar rounds hit the tin roof over the kennel and exploded, sending deadly shrapnel in every direction.

"They hit the kennel! They hit the kennel!" one handler screamed.

"Oh, my God!" another yelled.

The scene inside the bunkers was chaotic. We strained to see through the portholes. The roof of the kennel had been visibly damaged. We knew that one or more of our dogs had either been wounded or killed. The question was which dogs? Several of us started to leave. Lieutenant Fenner screamed, "Everyone stay in the bunkers! That's an order!" It would have been suicide to go outside at that time.

Indescribable dismay filled the eyes of my fellow dog handlers. We couldn't do anything but wait as more volleys of missiles exploded outside. I worried that Clipper had been wounded or, worse yet, killed. Several more explosions damaged trees near the entrance to our small compound. I figured there was a VC spotter hiding nearby, zeroing in on the compound and directing the attack with deadly accuracy.

To our surprise, a jeep, its lights on and no doors or canvas top, suddenly roared through the compound entrance. Someone shouted, "That's our jeep! Who the hell is it?"

A man jumped out of the vehicle and ran toward the bunkers. Sergeant Barnett was halfway out of his bunker, motioning the man to hurry, when a mortar shell landed and exploded near them. We watched in horror as the impact blew the driver to the ground facedown. A large piece of flying shrapnel shattered Sergeant Barnett's elbow. The jeep lurched forward from the blast, its engine dying when it was a few yards from the bunkers.

Sergeant Barnett and another man dragged the driver inside the bunker. Someone turned on a flashlight to identify him. It was "Kentucky," one of the new men in the platoon. The front of his body and his hands were unscathed. but his backside, from head to buttocks, was bleeding and peppered with gray-and-silver shrapnel slivers. He looked more frightened than racked with pain. A closer look at his wounds indicated that Kentucky wasn't in life-threatening condition, but he definitely needed medical attention. A dog handler got some field dressings from the first-aid kit and wrapped up Kentucky's larger wounds and Sergeant Barnett's injured elbow.

Had he sat down or lain on his back, Kentucky's pain would have been unbearable. Two dog handlers helped him to stand, as that position would be less painful. Kentucky didn't complain — he tried to tough it out. Most of the handlers had experienced the brutality of combat, so it was easy for us to imagine how bad Kentucky must have felt. We knew that when the blood from all those splinter wounds dried, Kentucky had better not try to move or he'd suffer pure agony.

Lieutenant Fenner asked Kentucky why he'd driven a jeep into the middle of a mortar attack. Kentucky explained that he'd been visiting a friend across the compound when he saw the flashes of light and heard the explosions. The area Kentucky'd been in wasn't under attack; wanting to help us, he'd driven the jeep as fast as he could. "Hey," he said, "I almost made it before that mortar hit me from behind."

A voice in the bunker blurted, "Kentucky, you're fucking nuts! You should have stayed put!"

Shortly after we brought Kentucky into the bunker, the mortar shelling stopped. The only noises we could still hear were the pitiful sounds of our scout dogs crying out in the kennel. In underwear and boots, carrying our weapons at the ready, we darted one by one from the bunkers. We moved quickly over shards of glass from the jeep's blown-out windshield and debris from the trees and kennel.

After a shelling like that, there was always the danger that one of us might step on an unexploded mortar round lying on the ground.

We also knew that the VC might have breached the perimeter and could be waiting behind rubber trees or lying in the weeds seeking targets. Even so, we braved the dark unknown to reach our dogs. The closer we got to the kennels, the louder the dogs howled. They knew we were coming and were frantic to get out of the runs. I couldn't imagine how they must have felt being trapped and helpless while awaiting rescue.

A few of us stepped inside the open entrances at either end of the kennel, while others checked the surrounding area for signs of the enemy. We could hear dogs groaning in pain.

A voice cried out in the darkness, "My dog's hit!"

Only a few feet inside the kennel, I stopped in my tracks, worried about what I might see. Clipper's run was close to the middle of the kennel. I took a deep breath and hoped I'd find him alive and unhurt. I moved closer to his run. Someone flipped on the overhead lights, revealing a sickening sight: large pools of blood marked the entrances of several dog runs. Splinters of wood and structural debris littered the concrete floor, and the tin roof had gaping holes.

The repaired roof of the 44th Scout Dog Kennel after a deadly enemy mortar attack on the night of November 9, 1967. (Author collection)

By now, most of the dog handlers had made it inside the kennel. Several sobbed as they held their wounded and bleeding companions. Some of the dogs lay in pools of blood inside their runs. Others limped because of their wounds.

I hurried to Clipper's run. He was pawing at the door and trying to get out. I opened the door and went inside. Clipper jumped all over me with his bloody paws. I touched and examined every inch of his body. Although Clipper's paws were bloody from clawing at the door, he had no wounds at all. He was so excited to see me that he couldn't keep still. I sat on the floor, hugged him tightly, and cried like a child. Feeling partly responsible for his having been helplessly caged during the attack, I told him how sorry I was that I hadn't been able to protect him.

The sight of the other dogs' suffering devastated me. The smell of their blood saturated the air. Doc Glydon was away on R & R (rest and relaxation), so he wasn't available to tend to the wounded and dying.

On that awful night, Ollie, who was scheduled to rotate back to the States in just a few months, found his scout dog, Erik, serial number 36X3, in his kennel run, bleeding to death. Erik had taken several shrapnel wounds, and both his lungs were punctured. Ollie held his limp friend in his arms and cried, crushed to know that his best friend was slowly dying in agony. No one could save Erik's life.

Mac came over to Ollie, sadly offered him his weapon, and told Mac that he couldn't bring himself to use it, even to relieve Erik's suffering. He asked Mac if he'd take care of the awful task. Visibly shaking, tears streaming down his face, Ollie stood on unsteady legs. Without looking back, he walked away from Erik and Mac. After Ollie left the kennel, a single shot rang out.

In releasing Erik to heaven, Ollie had made the hardest decision of his life. The thought of losing his best friend must have been unbearable. Ollie had trained with Erik back in the States, and had worked with him on countless missions in Vietnam. We considered Ollie and Erik one of the best-trained scout-dog teams in the platoon.

*Specialist Four Ollie Whetstone and his beloved Scout Dog,
Erik – 1967. (Photo courtesy of Ollie Whetstone)*

I'd learned a great deal about scout dogs from Ollie, and I held him
and Erik in the highest esteem as soldiers and friends. They'd been
through lots of scrapes with the enemy over the past ten months,
and there was no telling how many lives had been saved by Erik's
alerts and courage under fire. On that tragic night, Ollie had to watch
helplessly as the kennels were bombed, only to find Erik bleeding to
death. It was incredibly painful for him and for the rest of us.

Dan Scott's dog, Shadow, serial number 9X00, was in the run
next to Clipper's. Barely breathing, Shadow lay in a pool of blood.
Dan had been on the other side of the base camp during the mortar attack and couldn't get back to the K-9 compound in time to do
anything for his dog, so, Sergeant Dan Barnett tended to Shadow
after making sure his own dog, Sergeant, was okay.

Doc Glydon's absence was deeply felt that terrible night. Doc was
used to making medical decisions about the dogs; now it became
our duty to make tough choices about the injured and dying. Sergeant Barnett stood over Shadow, struggling over whether to put
him out of his misery or allow the dog to suffer in hopes that he'd

somehow recover. Barnett assessed Shadow's wounds and decided that he was too badly hurt to be saved. Shadow was slowly dying from massive loss of blood. In the absence of Dan Scott and the veterinarian, Barnett decided Shadow's fate. He fired a single bullet into the dog's head. Barnett was visibly shaken—this was one of the hardest calls any dog handler ever had to make.

44th Scout Dogs Shadow and Clipper were friends and lived next door to one another in the Kennel–1967. Shadow's handler, Dan Scott, was devastated because he was not there during the enemy mortar attack that took the life of his beloved dog. (Author collection)

When Dan Scott returned later that night to find Shadow dead from a gunshot to the head and covered in a poncho, he went berserk. Several dog handlers had to restrain him from physically attacking Sergeant Barnett. Scott believed that Shadow hadn't been mortally wounded and didn't need to be killed, that with proper medical attention and a blood transfusion, he'd have still been alive.

He pointed out that another handler's dog had been saved despite having suffered severe face and jaw wounds. But Sergeant Barnett had done what he thought was best for the dog. He stood his ground and defended his decision. Nevertheless, Dan called Barnett, "the Dog Killer." Having worked together for eight months, Dan and Shadow had become inseparable. I wondered if Dan would ever recover from Shadow's untimely and unfortunate death.

A medical vehicle took Kentucky and Sergeant Barnett to the Dau Tieng field hospital. We all pitched in to help clean wounds and patch up the dogs who'd survived. I washed the kennel's blood-stained concrete floor. Other handlers picked up debris and hunted for unexploded mortar rounds.

Before long, the morning sun was shining. Even with all we'd gone through, none of us looked tired, probably because we were so keyed up all night. We paid our respects by giving Erik and Shadow proper burials. While someone led us in prayer, Dan and Ollie interred their friends. We marked their graves in the scout-dog cemetery, which was in a quiet spot away from the kennel and sleeping quarters, under the shade of rubber trees.

Later that morning, someone yelled, "Formation!" and we assembled in front of the orderly room next to the K-9 Klub. Lieutenant Fenner announced that Major General Mearns, commanding general of the 25th Infantry Division, was flying in from his headquarters in Cu Chi. The CG planned to visit the 44th and evaluate the damage to our K-9 compound. Lieutenant Fenner ordered us to clean up, shave, and get into proper uniform.

Later that day, someone spotted a clean jeep heading to the compound. We were alerted and gathered in the parking area in front of the K-9 Klub. Several jeeps drove under the 44th Scout Dog sign marking the entrance of our small compound. When the vehicles stopped, Lieutenant Fenner walked to the lead jeep, which had two white stars on small red flags attached to the front bumper, and saluted. Major General Mearns returned his salute, stepped out of the vehicle, and shook the lieutenant's hand. It was the first time that a distinguished military officer had visited the K-9 compound since its construction eleven months earlier.

Fifteen dog handlers gathered to greet the general; we hung out in a very loose group that anyone would have hesitated to call it a military formation. We weren't showing disrespect, but we weren't used to showing snappy protocol, either. At least each of us was properly dressed and had a baseball cap on his head.

Major General Mearns addressed us, expressing his sorrow about the scout dogs who'd been lost and the handlers and dogs who'd been wounded. He explained how important scout dogs were to the infantry mission in Vietnam, and praised the successful contribution of the 44th to the mission of the 3rd Brigade, 25th Infantry Division. It was obvious that the CG was well informed about several recent K-9 missions that had saved American lives. His brief speech over, the look in his eyes was sincere as he shook hands with each dog handler.

The general took Ollie Whetstone and Dan Scott aside. Spaeking to them privately, he asked Ollie how long he had before he rotated back to the States. Ollie told him his rotation date was in January, just two months away. Major General Mearns promised Ollie that he'd be home for Christmas. Then he asked Dan the same question. Dan replied that he was scheduled to rotate in four months. The general told Dan that, regrettably, he had too much time left to justify ordering an earlier rotation date. After talking to Ollie and Dan, the general toured the damaged kennels and the rest of our compound. He ordered his attending staff officers to make sure that repairing the kennel would be given top priority for the engineers.

Having quickly learned the advantage we got from using scout-dog teams against them, the VC were now doing all they could to eliminate them. I was very grateful that Clipper had lived, so that he could help me and others make it through the battles yet to come. Deeply saddened over our losses, I prepared for my next mission—to hunt down the enemy with extreme prejudice.

Chapter Fourteen

TRAPPED

A few weeks after the demoralizing attack on our compound, the kennel had been repaired and we were going about our business as usual. Those of us who were healthy continued to support the infantry units of Dau Tieng.

On November 25th, Dan Scott, Mike Eply, Ed Hughes, Ollie Whetstone, Mac McClellan, Dan Barnett, and a few others were socializing in the K-9 Klub when a fight suddenly erupted between Eply and Hughes. During the scuffle, Eply went flying through the screen door and hit the hard ground outside. Hughes ran out to punch him again. Lieutenant Fenner came out of nowhere and stepped between them to end the altercation.

Eply complained to the lieutenant that his ankle hurt so badly he couldn't go on his assigned mission in the morning. Lieutenant Fenner, clearly angry, ordered Ed to take Mike's place.

Ed turned to Mike, hostility in his voice, and said, "Eply, if I get killed out there tomorrow, I'm gonna come back here and kick your fuckin' ass."

Mike said nothing as he limped away, but I'm sure he thought about the possibility of Ed's returning from the dead to exact his revenge.

Despite the brawl between Ed and Mike, they were both good men. We nicknamed Ed "the California Boy." He and I were good friends. Before joining the canines, Ed explained, he was assigned to the Old Guard to provide security for the Tomb of the Unknown

Soldier at Arlington National Cemetery in Virginia. He boasted that, for a soldier to be an honor guard, he had to project the image of a Hollywood model with exactly the right height and weight and physique. Short, stumpy guys weren't considered for that assignment. The public visited the tomb every day, he said, and the guards had to stand tall and always look clean-cut. There were no excuses for failing to strike the right pose.

Ed was tall and had the ideal physique for that job, and I could picture him in a perfectly tailored army dress-blue uniform, his shoes and boots spit-shined every day, though most of us dog handlers had never seen dress blues.

Ed demonstrated how to march properly with stiff, sharp, snappy movements as he paraded around like a toy soldier. He'd learned a marching rhythm that the rest of us had never seen before, and we got a kick out of watching him demonstrate Old Guard rifle drills with his M-16. Yup, among the scraggly scout-dog handlers of our platoon, we had ourselves a true blond-haired, blue-eyed California boy.

I got up early the next morning and greeted Ed in the kennel while he was with his dog Sergeant. I let Clipper out of his run. As usual, Clipper raced past me and headed to his tree, where he'd sit until I arrived to hook him to the twenty-foot leash and fetch him a fresh bucket of water.

Each dog had a tree with his name on it. I nailed a small piece of wood from an ammunition box to Clipper's tree and painted CLIPPER on it in large black letters. Below his name I wrote in small letters, War is Good Business – Invest Your Dog. At the time, I thought that was a pretty cool slogan.

While cleaning Clipper's run, I couldn't help noticing the faded bloodstains in Shadow's and Erik's empty runs — a constant reminder of what had happened to them. I wondered if they'd be replaced. We hadn't had any new dogs in the eleven months the platoon had been in Vietnam.

When I returned to Clipper's tree with my field gear, he became excited, wagging his tail and pacing back and forth. It always amazed me how a dog knew when it was time for a mission.

I met Ed near the compound entrance, where he and Sergeant were ready to leave. As the sun peeked over the trees, we walked onto the main dirt road leading to our respective units of assignment. Along the way, we talked, agreeing to get together and exchange stories after the mission. I didn't ask Ed about the fight with Mike because it didn't seem an appropriate issue to discuss at the time.

Ed and I split up when we reached the infantry battalion area, so I could search for the "Company A" unit sign while Ed looked for his outfit. They weren't difficult to find. Because pride was such an important part of army life, every unit marked its territory with its name, unit crest, unit patch, and logo. We knew we'd found our mission assignments when we saw soldiers milling around and preparing their field gear.

When I arrived at Headquarters, Company A, I recognized the company commander by the two black bars attached to the front of his helmet. He finished his conversation with several lieutenants, acknowledged my presence, and introduced me to the platoon leader Clipper and I were assigned to support. After we shook hands, the lieutenant knelt to pet Clipper. He seemed pleased to have a scout-dog team with his unit, and Clipper loved the attention.

The platoon leader briefed me on the mission. Choppers would fly the platoon into a landing zone close to the Cambodian border and west of Dau Tieng. My platoon was to hit the ground first and serve as the company's point platoon, the scout-dog team in the lead.

Other platoons were to follow after the first platoon had secured the LZ. Then each platoon would split up and maneuver into tactical sweeping formations. Our orders were to sweep the South Vietnam side of the Cambodian border for several miles. Battalion reconnaissance teams had reported large numbers of North Vietnam Army regulars and Vietcong throughout the area. No other American units were operating in that remote area, which was considered a primary NVA infiltration route from Cambodia into South Vietnam. The infamous Ho Chi Minh Trail was just inside Cambodia and stretched all the way into North Vietnam.

On the field map, the terrain appeared to be fairly flat with thick vegetation and jungle. A few large natural clearings ran alongside the border. American troops were never to cross into Cambodia to search for or pursue the enemy. I told the lieutenant that someone needed to direct my forward movement while I was working the point position, to make sure I didn't venture into Cambodia. He smiled and assured me that I'd stay advised as long as I didn't get too far ahead of the platoon.

The border between South Vietnam and Cambodia may have been clearly designated on the map, but it wasn't marked on the ground. Where we were going, there would be no villages, signs, fences, walls, outposts, roads, or other ground markers to identify the boundary separating the two countries. On the ground, Vietnam and Cambodia looked the same. Looking at the map, I knew it would be easy to cross into Cambodia accidentally. Besides, who'd have reported us if we accidentally crossed the border?

The area of operation (AO) we were going into was designated as a hostile free-fire zone, which meant that I could lock and load, fire first, and ask questions later. I preferred that scenario to the limited-fire zones where I could only lock and load after the enemy fired at me first, and operating in no-fire-zones, which were usually in densely populated areas, just plain sucked; it was like walking around with a target on my chest. The enemy had the upper hand to begin with, because he blended right in with the population. Evidently, in no-fire-zones, it was okay for us to have casualties, but we couldn't inflict them for fear of killing innocent noncombatants. I doubted whether the people who made up these rules had ever served as infantrymen.

American and Vietnamese government leaders were making and controlling the rules of war. Vietnam was classified as a *conflict,* not a war, but soldiers were killing each other just the same.

The ground rules for fighting the Vietnam "Conflict" should have been left up to the men who were fighting it. If Charlie didn't abide by any rules of war—and he surely didn't—why handicap Americans with restrictions? Vietnam was no gentleman's war. Soldiers on both sides were serious and used every trick possible to hunt and kill each other. I believed that American soldiers put themselves at a disadvantage by fighting within the confines of those ridiculous fire-zone rules.

I told the lieutenant, "Get real! It's a bunch of bullshit that we can't pursue Charlie into Cambodia. Those multiple fire-zone re-strictions are a crazy idea!"

He replied, "Just do your job, soldier!"

I learned that the company was at full strength, with four pla-toons of about 150 fighters. My platoon would be breaking trail when we reached the landing objective; the other three would follow not far behind.

Ed and I had both been assigned to the same mission, and not knowing anyone in my platoon, I wondered where he and his dog, Sergeant, were positioned in relation to my company.

The platoon split up for transport into chopper-sized groups. The morning sun was heating the air; I thought it might get over 115 degrees at the top of the day. My backpack was crammed full of the usual stuff: I had three days' food and water and ex-pected to be re-supplied in the field. My gear weighed about fif-ty pounds. I listened to some guys complaining that they were carrying over sixty pounds on their backs. No one was going to feel sorry for them and offer to carry part of their loads. I had at least a hundred rounds of ammunition for my CAR-15, but I'd forgotten to pack any grenades. I moved out to the Dau Tieng airstrip with my chopper group and the rest of the platoon. The choppers were warmed up and ready to fly; their door gunners' M-60s were freshly oiled and loaded. I climbed aboard with sev-eral infantrymen I didn't know.

When we were airborne, Clipper stood up and leaned forward, sticking his head out the open door, his usual tactic when riding in a chopper. His eyes squinted, and his mouth hung wide open, his tongue dangling to one side. This was his favorite position, and who could blame him? He was a dog, and dogs liked that natural air conditioning as much as the troops did.

Clipper knew I had a solid grip on his leash as he leaned out the opened door, stretching the leash taut. We'd done this before, and he felt confident that I wouldn't let go of him.

On these copter rides, the weight of Clipper leaning out the door for the entire ride really tired my arm. After a while, I'd yank on his leash to pull him back inside. When I did, Clipper would back off and lie down beside me for about a minute. Because he enjoyed the view and the cool air felt so good, Clipper would get back up and again assume the leaning-out-the-door position. Again, I would yank him inside, a back-and-forth routine that went on during every chopper ride. What was a dog handler to do?

On this mission, I thought of a possible solution: I decided to take up a little slack in Clipper's leash and clutch it tightly in my fist. I figured that when Clipper got up and assumed the leaning-out-the-door position, I'd just let the slack go. Well, I did, and Clipper freaked out. He fell forward enough to think he might be falling out of the chopper. His ears and the hair on the back of his neck stood straight up like the quills on a porcupine. When he turned to me, his eyes were as big as golf balls. Clipper dropped to all fours so fast that he scared himself. On his belly, he hugged the metal floor of the chopper, and scooted backwards to get next to me. He gave me that doggy dirty look, which I interpreted as, "Hey, John, have you lost your freakin' mind? You just about got me killed!"

I just hugged Clipper and said, "Hey buddy, are you okay? I just saved you from falling out. You must have slipped on something. Let me check your paws."

Clipper was really too frightened to be interested in my explanation. My ploy worked, and Clipper never again leaned out while standing up. His new technique was to stay on all fours, crawl to the edge of the door, and flap his tongue in the wind. New techniques of dog training in Vietnam sometimes happened on the fly.

Scout dog, Clipper, ready for takeoff on his favorite ride–1967.
(Author collection)

The chopper formation in the air was quite a sight: twenty or thirty ships clustered in small groups comprised a large spread-out tactical flying formation, with gunship escorts flying below. On the ground, the enemy probably saw us and wondered where the hell we were going to land. Flying into our target area with such a formidable display of force gave me a huge feeling of confidence, almost of invincibility.

Through the open doors, I saw well-armed soldiers sitting inside the other ships flying alongside us. The door gunners' loaded M-60s were pointed downward, but we were flying too high to be in any danger from ground fire. I was delighted that the VC didn't have surface-to-air missiles like those they used in North Vietnam to shoot down our fighter pilots and bombers.

Watching the huge, heavily armed armada in tactical flight all around me, I was pumped with adrenaline. *With a force like this, how could the NVA and VC possibly whip us?*

The ships began their descent into a large LZ of flat ground with short vegetation. When we landed, I immediately jumped out and ran in a crouched position, Clipper beside me. To provide security for the ships, we headed to the tree line away from the landing area. With the choppers blowing any airborne scent away, the noise and movement made it impossible for Clipper to alert on anything in our immediate area. In that type of situation, a scout dog team was neutralized and as vulnerable as everyone else.

We drew no enemy fire as we moved into the trees. Seeking cover, the soldiers spread out quickly and crept into the woods. Though we had made no contact with Charlie, the squad leaders directed their men to stay spread apart, keep their eyes open, and keep weapons on the ready. We moved into a swift defensive position almost immediately after the entire platoon had gotten on the ground and under the cover of the surrounding forest.

The platoon leader quickly took control, assembling the lead squad, which included Clipper and me. Choppers made a lot of noise as they cotinued landing and dropping off troops in the clearing behind us. The platoon leader gave me a hand signal, pointing out the direction he wanted me to go. I told the two-man team assigned as my security to stay far enough behind us for Clipper to have full scent capability in the direction of travel. I instructed them not to get in front of the dog or me unless I signaled them, and that I'd turn periodically to check for their signals to direct my forward progress. I didn't want to get too far ahead or off track.

Clipper and I moved out through the stubbly vegetation and lightly wooded terrain. The rest of the platoon followed cautiously, eventually stretching out behind our lead. I stepped forward slowly, keeping my eyes on Clipper's head, ears, and body. Occasionally, I'd glance rearward to check my security team and get directions. Using hand signals, the troops behind me made sure I stayed on the compass heading. The farther we moved from the landing zone the quieter the surrounding jungle became.

During that initial penetration into enemy territory, Clipper didn't alert at all. I wondered whether his ears were still ringing from all the helicopter noise, or were distracted by the noise of the troops moving all around him. Since Clipper kept moving forward with what appeared to be little concern for his surroundings, I had to assume he wasn't sensing danger.

Before long, Clipper gave a mild alert by flicking his ears and canting his head ever so slightly. I stopped and knelt on one knee; everyone behind us stopped, too. Listening closely, I heard nothing; looking at the area where Clipper had alerted, I saw nothing. Unsure whether Clipper's alert had been strong enough for me to signal for help, I got up and tugged his leash to tell him to move out again.

Clipper walked another hundred yards without alerting, and then his ears shot straight up and forward. I stopped and signaled one of the security guards behind me to come up. I told him that Clipper had alerted the same way twice and that I thought that his warning was worth checking out. I couldn't say specifically what Clipper had sensed or how far away it might be. The soldier quietly moved back to deliberate with the platoon leader, who then came forward and signaled two men to cautiously sweep the front about fifty yards out and then report back.

When they returned, the men reported seeing fresh footprints about forty yards directly ahead that didn't resemble GI jungle boots. Despite my confidence in a dog's ability to pick up a scent left behind by the enemy long after he was gone, I couldn't believe it: Clipper had alerted on an airborne scent! I immediately praised and hugged him for his alert.

The platoon leader's hand signal got me moving forward again. As Clipper approached the footprints, he sniffed the ground and moved in the direction of the scent. I followed him for several yards and then aborted. The footprints headed away from our direction of travel and we were getting too far away from the rest of the troops.

Standing in tall grass about fifty yards ahead of the rest of the platoon, I signaled the man behind me to come forward. While we knelt down and talked about the situation, the platoon leader arrived on the scene. I whispered to him that Clipper was getting a fairly good scent and seemed to want to track the trail of footprints. The leader directed a squad of men to follow the fresh tracks for a short distance and report back. When the squad leader returned, he reported that there were fresh footprints all over the place, but he'd seen nothing else. We stayed at a halt for a few minutes while the platoon leader got on the radio and made his report. Shortly afterward, we were ordered not to follow the trail of suspected enemy footprints, but to continue the mission in the direction planned.

We moved out of the grassy area and into the woods. Several hours into our mission, it was fairly quiet except for the everyday sounds of birds and insects. His head rising above the vegetation, Clipper moved forward into the jungle easily, even though the low vegetation and vines got thicker. I could see him clearly. So far, navigating that part of the jungle wasn't proving difficult.

In pursuit of the enemy, Clipper, mouth closed, paused for a moment and lifted his head high, as if sensing something directly in front of us. I stopped, dropping to one knee to scan and listen for anything unusual; I even sniffed the air. Again, I neither saw, heard, nor smelled anything out of the ordinary. Even so, I motioned the closest man behind me to come up, and told him that Clipper's alert was fairly strong and straight ahead.

The platoon leader assembled a rifle team to search the forward area. They reported a huge clearing about seventy-five yards through the jungle, but no signs of the enemy. Looking at his map, the platoon leader nodded, and then hand signaled me to push on. I complimented Clipper for the alert, hugging him and telling him, "Good boy! Good boy!" Clipper had done a great job up to that point.

We moved ahead, but standard operating procedure (SOP) dictated that we stop before entering the clearing. When coming out of the jungle, no one was supposed to enter a clearing unless the platoon leader directed. He was responsible for assessing the situation and deciding how he wanted the platoon to maneuver across a clearing.

Everyone stayed just inside the trees, waiting for orders. I noticed that Clipper began sniffing a small pile of bamboo shavings a few feet away. I figured the enemy had probably made a bunch of punji stakes there. As I pondered the pile, Clipper alerted sharply to the rear. I quickly turned to find him standing erect and staring at a tall man in clean jungle fatigues, whose only weapon was a holstered .45 caliber sidearm. He held a field map inside a plastic sleeve. I immediately recognized the two black stars sewn onto his camoflage-covered helmet. I couldn't believe my eyes—it was Major General Mearns, commanding officer of the 25th Infantry Division, the same officer who'd visited the K-9 compound after the VC mortar attack.

What the hell is he doing out here? I wondered. *Is he trying to earn his combat pay, or what? And how the hell did he get here in the first place?*

I rose to a standing position and, without saluting, nervously greeted him: "Good morning, sir." In a combat zone, it was forbidden to come to attention and salute, because Charlie might be watching; if he saw a telltale salute, the officer could get a bullet in the head.

The CG was out of view under the cover of vegetation. He smiled and asked me, "What's the name of your dog, soldier?"

"Clipper, sir!"

The general knelt on one knee and said, "He sure is frisky."

"Shake hands, Clipper!" I commanded softly. Clipper lifted his paw into the general's palm; the CG smiled and shook it. Then, while he examined his map and peered at the open clearing through the trees, he asked me several questions about how scouting worked.

The general's radio operator and several of his staff officers, all wearing clean jungle fatigues, surrounded him. They didn't say a word to me, but kept looking and smiling at Clipper.

I chatted with General Mearns for a few minutes before he turned and headed back to the main element of the platoon. I looked down at my dog and said, "Clipper, you just met the CG of the 25th Infantry, the most powerful man in the division." Clipper didn't appear too impressed.

We were told during the mission briefing that there would be an entire battalion—several hundred troops—working the area. I figured the CG had landed with us on the choppers and had been beating the bush all morning. It was quite rare for a general to show up in the jungle and hump with his troops. Unlike World War II, Vietnam had no front lines, so danger was expected everywhere we traveled outside base camps. I was impressed to see the commanding general walk in a combat zone with his men. It reminded me of seeing Lieutenant Colonel Hal Moore in the Ia Drang Valley during my first tour. I'd never forget that he gave me water and carried my pack on my very first mission.

After Major General Mearns departed, we were given a short break in place. I poured some water into my steel pot for Clipper, and hugged him for doing such a terrific job. I was extremely happy with how we were working together as a team. Clipper was a source of loyalty, comfort, and satisfaction for me. Even though I'd worked with him many times before, each mission was different and we learned new things every time we went out together. At this point in our relationship, our bond was very strong.

After about fifteen minutes, I heard some choppers overhead, flying just above the treetops. They landed in the clearing we were about to cross, picked up some soldiers, and took off. I figured that MG Mearns and his staff were the passengers. Clipper sat facing the clearing and watched everything take place. He moved his head back and forth as if searching the clearing, probing for clues as to what might be on the other side.

My friend Ed Hughes and his war-dog partner, Sergeant, were somewhere in this same area of operation. I recalled telling Ed that we'd trade stories when we got back to the K-9 Klub. *Oh, boy, have I got a tale to tell about how Major General Mearns came up to me and shook Clipper's paw!*

The platoon leader finally gave me the command to move out

across the clearing. Clipper and I slowly moved out, exposed to whatever might be waiting for us. I was tense looking at the other side of the clearing, which was several hundred yards away. As we walked farther into the clearing, I glanced to my rear: my two bodyguards were spread out ten yards to my left and right rear. The rest of the platoon spaced themselves apart and cautiously moved forward. I could feel a light wind, but had confidence that Clipper wouldn't miss a scent of danger.

As we moved deeper into enemy territory, my eyes stayed glued to Clipper's head and ears. Suddenly, his neck and head went rigid and his ears popped up, then he cocked his head to one side, giving his strongest alert of the day. I immediately got down on one knee. Crouching low, I looked and listened but couldn't see or hear anything unusual. I turned around and noticed that everyone behind us had also stopped and taken a knee.

My right knee was beginning to hurt from kneeling on the hard ground. A long time had passed since I'd jumped from that chopper in the central highlands and had a punji stake shoved through it—a hell of a painful memory indeed. Now I had to keep moving and deal with the lingering pain of that old injury.

I felt uncomfortable being so exposed, in vegetation no higher than my boot tops. Clipper's ears and head remained erect, so I decided not to push our luck by proceeding. I turned and motioned to the man behind him. The platoon leader moved up forty yards to join me. He asked for my thoughts, and I told him I had a bad feeling about going ahead.

The platoon leader wasted no time. He motioned for the nearest squad leader, who directed two fire teams of three men each to move forward and sweep the area. After reconnoitering, both fire teams returned and reported having seen a long, wide, and recently used trail about fifty yards away, but they'd made no contact with the enemy. The platoon leader signaled for me to lead on.

When Clipper and I reached the trail, which ran perpendicular to the mission's direction of travel, we saw fresh footprints and the tracks of wheeled carts and oxen leading into Vietnam from the direction of the Cambodian border. These certainly weren't the prints we'd expect of peasant farmers moving around. Besides, there were no farms or villages in the area.

The platoon leader figured the Cambodian border must be less than half a mile away. This trail had to be a branch leading off the main Ho Chi Minh Trail. Since the tracks were so fresh, he thought that a heavily armed, battalion-sized NVA or VC force must have moved into South Vietnam from Cambodia within the past day or so. He used a grease pencil to mark the location of the enemy movement on his map.

I took the lead and crossed the trail, heading toward the facing wood line, less than seventy-five yards out. We were now traveling parallel to the Cambodian border. Before long, Clipper stopped and stood erect, his ears pointed high and forward; the muscles in his shoulders grew tense and began to twitch.

When I looked back, my security guards motioned for me to keep going. The platoon leader must have decided to ignore Clipper's alert. I was a bit puzzled, but got up and tugged on Clipper's leash. He started stepping side to side as if he didn't want to go forward. Then, several shots rang out over our heads. Instantly, we dropped to prone positions on the ground. Clipper was on his belly, his head up and pointing in the direction of the tree line ahead. I hugged him close and told him what a good dog he was. He licked my face.

There was a momentary silence as I strained to spot the shooter. I saw nothing but a wall of green ahead. Behind me, everyone lay prone in the short grass, trying to figure out where the shots had come from. Someone decided to fire an M-16 over my head into the wall of trees; right away everyone else started shooting.

I knew that if a sniper was hiding in a tree, the entire platoon was visible to him. From the direction of the shots, I thought that Clipper might have been Charlie's first target. We were definitely not out of a sniper's range of fire, because the rounds had gone over our heads. Charlie was either a bad shot or Clipper and I had been mighty lucky.

John Burnam and Clipper preparing for a patrol near the Cambodian Border—1967. (Author collection)

The firing stopped when it became apparent that our side was doing all the shooting; then there was a lengthy silence. The platoon leader ordered two squads to fire and maneuver until they reached and secured a position at the edge of the trees ahead. As the squads tried to fire and maneuver, several more shots rang out from the jungle. Voices behind Clipper and me were giving orders to get up and move out on line. I got to my feet and tugged Clipper to move forward along with everyone else.

Several more shots came from the jungle ahead. Again, the entire platoon dropped on their bellies and poured a deadly barrage into the trees. Clipper didn't move while I placed several rounds where I thought the shooter was. I patted him on the back and told him he was a good boy. Several men flanked us, taking up firing positions.

Directly behind me, a voice shouted, "Get up and move out on line, soldier!"

I wasn't about to move, because I didn't feel safe exposing myself to a sniper who I felt was zeroing in on me and Clipper, so I ignored the voice and remained flat on my belly in defensive firing position. When I looked up, a tall man with two black bars on his helmet was standing over me. It was the captain, the company commander I'd met that morning. I was startled to see him glaring down at me, a disgusted look on his face. He yelled, "I said get up and assault the tree line!"

I looked at him as if he was crazy and replied, "Sir, why don't you call for artillery or air strikes before we go into those trees?"

"Soldier, I said get up and assault!"

I finally obeyed and moved forward with everyone else. Charlie didn't fire a single round while I closed in on the tree line with the rest of the troops.

By the time Clipper and I reached the edge of the wall of trees, there was a lot of fussing and shouting going on. Everyone seemed to be in a state of confusion, uncertain of what to do. Clipper and I stopped among a bunch of troops who were standing around, waiting for the next command. There was too much activity and noise for Clipper to be effective. At that point we were useless as scouts.

The platoon leader approached, and told me that one of his men had spotted a bunker not far from us. He asked if I'd use my dog to check it out.

On other missions, Clipper had avoided going into bunkers, foxholes, and tunnels. I learned that you never force a dog to do anything he didn't want to do, especially in enemy territory. I told the lieutenant, "Clipper doesn't like going into holes in the ground, but I'll go with you to see if he gets an alert."

The lieutenant told me that he'd lead the way. He moved out at a quick pace; Clipper and I followed him closely. A few yards after we had passed the last man in our platoon, Clipper raised his head and alerted up into the trees. I didn't give it a second thought, because there was too much activity all around for the alert to be accurate.

It wasn't long before the three of us were by ourselves. The lieutenant snaked a path through the thick jungle vegetation. The nearest American was at least twenty yards behind us. At point-blank range muzzle flashes lit up in my face. The lieutenant's body slammed into my chest like a sack of rocks, knocking me onto my back and making my helmet fly off my head. Because I was still hanging on to his leash as I fell, Clipper rolled over on top of me.

Directly to my front, Charlie opened up with automatic rifle and machine gun fire. Fortunately, I'd fallen near a small tree. I rolled behind it, Clipper at my side. Rifle and machine gun fire opened up from behind. Clipper and I were caught in the crossfire between my platoon and the enemy. With an arm around Clipper, I hugged the ground. The firing from both sides got so intense that it chopped up the vegetation like the blades of a lawn mower. Charlie was dug in and shooting at us from camouflaged underground bunkers.

Clipper and I were trapped, unable to move. I knew that the lieutenant had absorbed the initial fusillade. He had to be close by, but I couldn't see him through the dense vegetation. He wasn't crying out in pain or shouting for a medic, so I assumed that he must be dead.

My platoon and the enemy troops fired furiously back and forth over our heads. *I guess Charlie doesn't see Clipper and me,* I thought, *or maybe he thinks he's already killed us!* I decided not to make any sudden moves and give Charlie a second chance. I slowly moved my rifle to a firing position. As I got the barrel up by my face, I noticed a plug of mud jammed inside the muzzle. *It must have happened when I fell onto the wet ground.* Trying to clear the muzzle with my finger only packed the mud in deeper. I thought of tossing grenades, but then remembered that I hadn't packed any.

Under those circumstances, it would have been suicide to break down my weapon and run a cleaning rod through the bore and chamber to clear the plug. It was more important for me to stay alive than to figure out a way to shoot. If I absolutely had to, I could risk firing my weapon, but the round in the chamber might explode in my face.

Clipper and I lay only fifteen feet from Charlie's entrenched positions. Between the exchanges of small-arms fire, I could hear Vietnamese voices whispering from his foxholes. I knew Clipper heard them, too, but he didn't make a move or a sound. My dog and I were in deep shit with no way out. My adrenaline spiked, and my heart pounded so loud I could hear it.

This was a much different situation than that of the APC ambush: this time I was closer to the enemy, had no helmet, had no functional rifle or grenades, and could be killed by either side. I didn't dare make the slightest movement or noise to draw attention to my location. I was grateful to be with Clipper, who, unlike the frightened Timber, wasn't jumping around and trying to get away.

I prayed, "God, please get us out of this deathtrap."

Minutes seemed like hours. I thought my time on earth was running out. I wanted to melt into the dirt to get away from it all. I was scared, and so was Clipper — I could feel him shivering underneath my arm.

I found it peculiar that I could simultaneously hear Charlie whispering in Vietnamese and my comrades shouting in English. Not long into the firefight, I heard the deafening sound of artillery rounds exploding behind Charlie's positions. Shrapnel splintered the trees and shredded the vegetation all around us. The Americans were walking the artillery closer and closer to our positions. Between volleys, the exchange of small arms and machine gun fire continued.

I lay silently holding Clipper and trying not to move a muscle. To my surprise, something touched my foot. I spun my head around and saw an American soldier, one of my designated security guards. We made eye contact but exchanged no words. He gave me a thumbs-up and motioned me to move back to the rear.

As quietly as I could, I slowly turned around on my belly. Clipper followed. When I tried to crawl away from the tree, my backpack caught in some vines and moved them. Charlie must have spotted the movement. Rifle fire erupted again. Somehow, I broke free and crawled away with Clipper at my side. I anticipated feeling the agony of a bullet entering my body or hearing Clipper groan from being shot. Charlie was either shooting too high, or we were as flat as the rotting leaves on the jungle floor.

To my rear, the distinct sound of an M-16 echoed—the soldier who'd relieved me was providing cover for our escape. I flinched at the sound of a grenade exploding behind me. I hesitated briefly but didn't turn to look.

As I crawled, an American soldier appeared before me and motioned me to stay down. He fired over my head. As Clipper and I passed, I saw a dead Vietnamese in khaki clothes dangling from a tree by one bare foot. His arms hung down below his head, fingers almost touching the pool of blood dripping from his body and soaking into the earth. I quickly moved Clipper around the hanging body and took cover behind a nearby tree.

Behind the American lines, there were dead and wounded on the ground everywhere. I broke down my CAR-15, ran a cleaning rod through the bore to release the clump of mud, and took up a defensive firing position. I quickly checked over Clipper's entire body, feeling for holes and looking for blood. Clipper didn't wince in pain as I touched him. He was okay. It wasn't long before the artillery barrages halted and the shooting trickled to a stop.

That was the way such firefights usually began and ended. Charlie had either been eradicated or had decided to break contact, it was hard to tell. Reinforcements from another platoon reached the perimeter and took up firing positions. A medic worked on a wounded soldier nearby who screamed that he was going to die. The medic tried to calm the wounded man, stop the bleeding, and patch him up, but to no avail; the soldier died, and the medic quickly moved on to assist another.

I saw the lieutenant's lifeless body being carried in a poncho. The platoon sergeant, now in charge, told me that, after the captain had been shot, the company commander had killed a VC who was in a tree. I remembered that, before the firing started, Clipper had alerted up in the trees and I had disregarded it. I now realized that Clipper might have sensed the danger there. Guilt pierced my heart for the captain who'd paid the price for my mistake. The platoon sergeant also told me that the soldier who'd come to save us while we were trapped in that crossfire had been killed. My platoon had killed several enemy soldiers in a bunker near that tree.

The sergeant explained that most of the casualties had happened during the first few seconds of fighting, as everyone stood waiting for the lieutenant to check out the bunker. He said it had been chaotic getting everyone out of the open clearing and under cover of the jungle. He believed that his men should have automatically formed a defensive perimeter and assumed firing positions on the ground. Instead, many of them were standing or milling around waiting for something to happen. Baiting us with the sniper, Charlie had sucked us right into a trap.

I told the platoon sergeant that Clipper had done his best under the circumstances. The sergeant placed no blame on me. "You did your scouting duty and are lucky to be alive," he said. "When the shooting started, I thought the lieutenant and you and the dog had all been killed."

The sergeant knelt, stroked Clipper's head, and told him that he was a good dog. Then he got up, shook his head, and walked away.

The sounds of helicopters, small arms, and machine gun fire echoed in the distance, signaling that someone else was getting into the shit. The entire area must have been loaded with pockets of hard-core NVA troops protecting the exit paths of the Ho Chi Minh Trail.

The reconnaissance team who'd scouted that area before the mission had done a good intelligence job. Now it was up to the infantry to fight smarter and defeat the bastards. Even though the other fight was going on nearby, my platoon wasn't ordered to assist, so I rested under a tree with Clipper and gave him some water. I listened to the squawking of the field radio and the distant noise of a firefight, and watched my fellow soldiers receive medical attention.

A soldier came up to me and asked, "Is your name Burnam?"

"Yes!" I answered.

The soldier handed me a helmet with my name written on the headband inside. He said it had been lying near a bunker next to the bodies of the lieutenant and another soldier. He couldn't understand how the dog and I had survived without a scratch.

Before I put on my helmet, I checked it over. There wasn't a mark on it. Clipper didn't have a scratch, either, and appeared to be dealing with the whole situation better than I was.

Clipper had been a brave and competent soldier that day, alerting us to danger and then showing courage under extreme circumstances. Many of the troops came by to pet him for good luck. One called Clipper "the invincible scout dog." I chuckled at that. I hugged Clipper and said, "Pal, for all the hell you've been through, you just earned yourself a Bronze Star and a Combat Infantry Badge. Thanks for all those great alerts."

Scout Dog, Clipper, taking a well earned nap after a hard day's work – 1967. (Author collection)

I knew the army didn't award medals or badges to war dogs for exceptional performance of duty or for bravery and heroism. The army officially recognized scout dogs only as military combat equipment. In four months, I'd be rotating back to the States. Clipper, on the other hand, didn't have a rotation date; his orders were to serve his country in Vietnam for the rest of the war. I didn't want to believe the naked truth about what Clipper's fate would be.

What the hell do the army brass and the politicians know about Clipper and how he's risked his life to save others? I thought. Clipper was a soldier, not a piece of equipment. He displayed uncompromising loyalty and obedience. He knew what he'd been trained to do, and he was a hell of a lot more responsive and trustworthy in carrying out his duties than many of the humans I'd met during the war.

How did the army know what my dog was mentally and physically capable of? How many lives would Clipper have to save to be recognized as something more than equipment? I thought it was cruel and unjust to punish a dog by making him walk point for the entire war. The army had recruited and trained Clipper to save lives. Shouldn't they treat him with respect and give him a rotation date, too? These were questions I could never ask out loud. As a lowly grunt, I had to follow orders and never question the decisions made by people at higher levels of authority. Sitting under that tree, I pondered the mystery of why Clipper and I were still alive, and thought about my dog's true fate.

Later, I heard that the platoon's casualties during that skirmish — six men killed and eleven wounded — were considered light. It was decided that we hadn't suffered enough losses to be relieved of our mission. The platoon sergeant briefed me on our new orders: I was to join the rest of the company to set up a defensive perimeter for the evening in the very field we'd crossed. The next day, the company would continue its mission, hunting NVA troops along the Cambodian border.

After a short mission briefing by the platoon sergeant that afternoon, it was time to saddle up, move into the clearing, and set up for the night. Assuming our usual position out in the front of the platoon, Clipper and I headed into the clearing to join the rest of the company. Clipper alerted like crazy. We didn't have to check out his alerts, because American soldiers were in the area all around us.

A sister company had reconnoitered the battlefield to clean up any remaining pockets of enemy troops. They'd discovered a small enemy base camp, but it was abandoned. It looked as if Charlie had ambushed us in his back yard. Now, except for leaving behind a few of his dead near our positions, the enemy had disappeared. Knowing that we couldn't pursue them there, the enemy had probably run for the Cambodian border. I knew that if this had been my old unit, the 1st Battalion, 7th Cavalry, the CO would have dropped artillery and napalm before sending one soldier after a sniper. We all knew that using a sniper to lure Americans into a trap was a common tactic.

There was no way Clipper could have alerted on that bunker, because the lieutenant had been walking directly in front of us. But if Clipper and I had taken the lead, it would have been lights out for both of us. We must have had a guardian angel watching over us that day—I just hoped our angel would stick around.

Moving across the clearing that afternoon, Clipper and I entered a company-sized perimeter of more than a hundred American soldiers. They were everywhere, digging chest-deep foxholes, clearing firing lanes, planting claymore mines, and setting up trip flares. The company was prepared for a counterattack, every man on full alert. There would be little or no sleeping on the perimeter that night; none of us wanted to get caught by surprise.

Clipper and I took up a firing position behind a bush well inside the perimeter, where I felt a little more secure. We got lucky and weren't assigned perimeter guard duty that night. In the past, when I pulled guard duty, Clipper was so naturally good at it that I could sleep all night if I wanted to. Whether in the field or in base camp, I wasn't a heavy sleeper; I tended to awaken at the slightest unusual noise. After all we'd just been through, I knew I wouldn't even catnap easily.

As darkness settled in, a helicopter appeared overhead and landed under the green smoke signal inside the large perimeter. I figured it was a supply ship and, not needing any supplies, I paid little attention to it. A few minutes after the chopper took off, I recognized a fellow dog handler, Sergeant Durbach of the 44th Scout Dog Platoon. I wondered what Durbach was doing out here without his dog. As Durbach approached me, I noticed that he looked fresh and clean-shaven, and his jungle fatigues weren't dirty. I, on the other hand, was filthy from a long day's humping and crawling along the damp jungle floor.

The sergeant carried a CAR-15 and had a light pack strapped to his back. We greeted one another with smiles and a handshake. As we sat on the ground, Durbach stroked Clipper's head and back, but he appeared nervous, his face conveying that something was bothering him. He forced a smile and asked me how I was doing.

"John," he said, "Ed Hughes and his dog, Sergeant, were killed today."

I couldn't believe what I was hearing. My eyes welled with tears.

Durbach filled me in on what had happened. After Ed's chopper had landed, he and Sergeant ran for cover along with the rest of the troops. When Ed reached the jungle wall, he moved inside to seek cover and was shot at point-blank range. The VC then shot and hacked Sergeant to death with a machete. Durbach speculated that the dog had died fighting, but that Ed was taken by surprise and probably died instantly, never knowing what hit him.

Durbach said that the NVA had overwhelmed the rest of Ed's platoon and forced them into a hasty retreat back across the landing zone, where they set up a defensive position and held off an enemy assault. The NVA retreated into the jungle where Ed and his dog lay dead.

I asked Sergeant Durbach how he knew so much if he hadn't been there. He said Lieutenant Fenner had received a call from 3rd Brigade headquarters in Dau Tieng. They told him that a dog handler and his dog were killed in action while on patrol near the Cambodian border. All the casualties, they said, except for the handler and his dog, had been recovered. It was apparently too risky to try to recover Ed and Sergeant at that time, so they'd left them behind.

"What a bunch of bullshit!" I said. Those fuckers can't leave Ed and Sergeant out there alone all night. So, they sent you to get me to help recover Ed and Sergeant? Well, I'm ready. Let's go get some more men and fucking do it!"

Sergeant Durbach put his hand on my shoulder and said, "John, sit down and let me finish."

Then he told me that Lieutenant Fenner had sent him out about three hours earlier to size up the situation and report back. Since the attack, Ed's platoon had been reinforced with two more platoons and had set up in defensive position not far from Ed and Sergeant. Durbach had received a status report from the company commander of Ed's unit.

The CO had already decided to assemble two squads and send them across the clearing to locate and recover the bodies. Durbach arrived in time to accompany the patrol. When they'd found Ed and his dog, the NVA were long gone. Ed had been stripped of his weapon and gear, including his boots and his scout'dog patch. Sergeant's body was lying near him; his left ear was missing, as were his leather leash and harness. Both bodies were recovered without incident and sent home to Dau Tieng. Durbach's next task had been to locate me.

Using a field radio, Durbach had been able to find my exact position within minutes. I was less than a mile from where Ed and Sergeant had died. Durbach caught a ride on a re-supply chopper operating in the area. I told Durbach that I'd heard a firefight in the distance after our battle, but it hadn't occurred to me that it might have been Ed's unit under attack.

Sergeant Durbach asked me for details about our fight. I gave him a blow-by-blow account of our near-fatal encounter with Charlie.

On Thanksgiving Day of 1967, I was thinking, *What the hell do we have to celebrate or be thankful for?* Even after listening to every detail about Ed's death, I couldn't believe he was gone, killed without even a chance to fight back.

Durbach and I sat silently for several minutes. I reflected on how much I'd enjoyed Ed's friendship and humor. Though I'd only known him for six months, I thought Ed was a wonderful person. Now I'd never see him again. The incident between Ed and Eply at the K-9 Klub, which led to the two of them switching places for that mission, now played over and over in my head. "Eply, if I get killed out there tomorrow," Ed had said, "I'm gonna come back here and kick your fuckin' ass!"

Sergeant Durbach coordinated my return to Dau Tieng so I could provide a field report to my unit. In the morning, we left on the first available chopper. Durbach briefed Lieutenant Fenner on Ed Hughes, and I provided the details about what had happened during my mission. After the briefing, all I wanted was to take a shower, put on clean, dry fatigues, and read my mail.

No one in the platoon could believe Ed and Sergeant were dead. Of course, every dog handler wanted to hear about it. I must have repeated the story twenty times that day. I didn't talk to Eply, but I could imagine how he must have felt about that incident.

The day after the debriefing, the entire 44th assembled at a field chapel to pay their last respects to Ed and Sergeant. The chapel was a large green tent with several rows of folding chairs and a makeshift altar. We held a memorial service without bodies — by now, Ed was in a morgue somewhere in Saigon.

To my distaste, the chaplain gave a sermon filled with military jargon. He said something like, "Ed hasn't left us. He's gone on to serve a higher commander, the celestial six."

That term, "six" was used in common military radio jargon as part of a commanding officer's call sign. I wasn't the only one to cringe at the chaplain's eulogy: Dan Scott and many of the other handlers were livid about his choice of lingo for that service. We wanted to hear something beautiful and poetic from the Bible, not language that sounded like a military mission in the afterlife. I vowed that that would be the last time I'd ever attend a formal religious service for a fallen comrade in Vietnam. I'd deal with it in my own way, instead.

A few days after Ed's death, Lieutenant Fenner asked me to join Sergeant Durbach to escort Ed's dog, Sergeant, to a military morgue in Saigon. Veterinarians wanted to complete an autopsy on the dog, and Saigon apparently had more extensive veterinary medical facilities than our field hospital. The second part of my mission would be to positively identify Ed's body in the morgue.

Edward Cowart Hughes III, nineteen years old, now rested in peace. He'd be going home to his grieving family in Garden Grove, California.

I would be returning to Dau Tieng to risk my own life and Clipper's on missions yet to come against the same enemy that had taken the lives of Ed and his faithful partner Sergeant.

Edward Cowart Hughes— Killed in Action along with his faithful Scout Dog, Sergeant, near the Cambodian Border on November 26, 1967. I was working Clipper in the same area and ducking for cover during an ambush when he was killed.
(Author collection)

Chapter Fifteen

BOOBY TRAPS

Dense forest surrounded the Ben Cui and Michelin rubber tree plantations that stretched about ten square miles east and north of Dau Tieng. Half a mile north of the airstrip stood a small range of steep foothills covered by a thick canopy of jungle foliage.

On a military grid map, the plantations were identified by thousands of tiny green circles divided into square grids with the many dirt roads that were used to harvest the countless rows of rubber trees. One grid equaled 1000 square meters. Resident Vietnamese workers lived in the many small hamlets scattered throughout both rubber tree plantations. A combination of numbers and letters such as AP 2, AP 12, and AP 13, was used to mark the location of each hamlet on our grid maps.

Every so often, a blue-and-white civilian helicopter flew into base camp. It would stick out like a sore thumb, since all the military aircraft and equipment was painted olive drab or camouflage. The civilian choppers belonged to business partners of the Michelin and Ben Cui rubber plantations. Scuttlebutt had it that these companies were concerned that we, the U.S. Army, were destroying too many of their precious rubber trees. Apparently, they wanted payment for each tree we damaged or destroyed. They were unhappy that we were tying our dogs to the trees, because the chains rubbed the bark raw and the dogs were digging too many holes. They complained about all the wooden hooches that the dog handlers had built between the rows of rubber trees.

I never learned whether the army paid for damaged and destroyed rubber trees. In the K-9 platoon, "Fuck 'em all," was the general response to the businessmen's complaints. I had no idea what kind of diplomatic relations the army had, or what deals were made with the plantation owners. As a grunt, I didn't give a shit; I just didn't want civilians snooping around the K-9 camp.

I reflected on what my former first sergeant had warned me of in Okinawa: "There are spies out there. They want classified information about what we do. Don't talk or try to figure them out; they're professionals. Report everything to your security officer immediately. Do you understand, soldier?"

We dog handlers figured that we owned the rubber trees while we occupied them and fought a war to keep the South Vietnamese from being invaded by the communists from the north. Besides, the rubber trees offered us no safe haven; we had to defend every inch of what we maintained. The VC and NVA used the trees and dirt roads between them to set booby traps for American troops. We knew that the enemy lived inside the hamlets at night and, if we weren't patrolling, during the day.

I found the scout-dog business a never-ending learning experience. Since booby traps surrounded us, I needed to know whether Clipper could detect tripwires. When conditions were favorable, he was better than I was at seeing, hearing, smelling, and sensing danger from great distances. I knew Clipper was bright, a proven combat veteran war dog, and a great partner. I didn't think he'd ever intentionally walk through a tripwire stretched between two trees. I assumed Clipper would avoid that type of danger, but I had to learn what alert he'd give when he came near one.

One morning, before I cleaned Clipper's run, I walked to the rubber trees behind the hooches. I had a roll of regular OD (olive drab) tripwire —thin, fairly strong, and pliable—taken from a trip flair. I tied a strand knee-high between two trees and twanged it with my finger to assure that the wire was as tight as a guitar string.

After I cleaned the kennel and played with Clipper, I put him on leash and choke chain, and we headed in the direction of the trip-wire. Clipper walked ahead without pulling, just as he did when working on a mission. We went to an area of short grass that was clear of obstacles. The tripwire was set up about seventy-five yards away. I didn't want to walk a straight line to the target, so I tugged the leash left or right to direct Clipper through the rubber trees. As we moved deeper into the trees, Clipper didn't alert. We came closer to the tripwire, but I still saw no sign of an alert from him. When he was about fifty yards away from the target, Clipper gave a weak alert with a slight movement of his ears, but he didn't stop walking.

When the wire touched his head, he ducked under it, so I jerked the leash and said, "No Clipper! No!"

Clipper turned and looked at me as if to say, "What did I do wrong?"

I moved Clipper's head close to the wire and clutched it in my hand. I got down on one knee, looked Clipper in the eye, and showed him the thin green wire. Then I gently tapped the wire on the black tip of his nose. Each time I tapped Clipper's nose, I raised the in-flection in my voice and said, "No Clipper! No!"

I talked to him as if he were a trainee. I said, "Clipper, that is a fucking tripwire. Do not cross it. Do you understand? Do you have any idea what might happen to us if you crossed it? Boom! That's right, BOOM!"

Clipper responded to the word "no," but I doubt he understood anything else.

I walked Clipper around a bit to calm him, and then let him ap-proach the wire again. Clipper gave a weak alert and, as before, walked under the wire. We continued to practice, but Clipper did the same thing each time. He surely must have tired of hearing me say, "No, Clipper! No"

Finally, I decided to add a blasting cap to the end of the tripwire, so that if Clipper tripped the wire, the popping sound it made would get his attention.

The firt time Clipper went through the wire, it triggered the blasting cap, startling him. I quickly went to one knee and said, "Clipper, that's what I'm talking about. You just killed us! He looked at me with a blank expression.

After we practiced with a loaded tripwire several times, Clipper finally decided to stop and sit a few feet in front of the tripwire. I was so excited and proud of him that I hugged him and said, "You're the best scout dog in the platoon—the greatest fucking dog in the world! Good boy, Clipper! Good boy!"

We had actually accomplished a new trick! I made Clipper repeat the exercise day after day until I was sure his behavior hadn't been a fluke and that we were on the same wavelength. Sure enough, Clipper had really learned not to go through the tripwire. He would either sit in front of it or avoid it entirely by going around it.

To make the training tougher, I put several wires in different locations, to see how Clipper would negotiate more than one. I learned that if Clipper came directly upon a tripwire, he'd sit in front of it more often than he'd go around it. I also learned that if he sensed the wire from a distance, he'd go around it. I was quite pleased to have made so much progress with Clipper in just few weeks of training.

I still had no idea how effective the tripwire training would be when Clipper worked in thick brush or moved across wooded terrain, down trails, or among the rubber trees. I always dreaded trails and tried to avoid them, especially in very remote jungle. Pathways around populated areas weren't as hard to negotiate. It was only common sense that staying in the bush was safer than walking on smooth dirt trails, which were perfect for the enemy to stage ambushes and hide punji pits and explosive booby traps.

The Cong were savvier than Americans, because the bush was their natural turf. Most of us teenage American grunts had never traveled outside the States, let alone seen a jungle. The closest I'd ever come was thumbing through a *National Geographic* magazine. The NVA were masters of guerrilla warfare tactics long before I was born. We Americans were infants, learning how to walk and talk our way through that war.

By conducting these training sessions, I thought I'd created one more trick to keep my dog and me alive while we walked point. Still, I didn't intend to volunteer our services as an expert booby-trap-detection team.

The day arrived when my name came up on the rotation schedule for another mission. I'd be working with the 2nd Battalion, 12th Infantry (White Warriors), whose motto was "Led by Love of Country." That unit was organized back in 1861 during the Indian Wars.

"The two/twelve," as it was commonly called, consisted primarily of foot soldiers who were sometimes transported in trucks or choppers to air assault into an LZ. I preferred working with foot soldiers, especially after my ambush experience with a sister battalion of armored personnel carriers. Working with the mechanized infantry had become one of my greatest fears.

I reported to the 2/12, which was just down the road from the K-9 compound. I thought, *There's one good thing about living in a small base camp: everything's within walking distance.* Brigade G2 (military intelligence) had information concerning a VC buildup around Dau Tieng. The enemy was reported to be operating out of hidden base camps in the nearby jungles surrounding the rubber plantations. At night, VC were infiltrating the hamlets and reconnoitering our base camp's perimeter to assess our strengths and weaknesses. They knew a lot about our capabilities, such as how many helicopters we had, when they flew in and out, the exact locations of our ammunition dumps, where our main communications bunkers were, and how many troops were inside.

At least twice a week they attacked our airstrip with mortars, wreaking havoc on our aircraft operations. The mortars were mainly coming from the foothills north of Dau Tieng, and east from somewhere in the rubber trees and surrounding jungle. Retaliatory artillery and air strikes on the suspected locations didn't fix the problem. Helicopter gunships weren't effective enough without someone on the ground to help them pinpoint their strikes.

Now, infantry foot soldiers and scout-dog teams were deployed to search out and destroy those VC and their hidden base camps. Someone once told me that the infantry was called the "Queen of Battle." When no one else could get the desired results, the Queen of Battle was sent in to finish the job. I thought that sounded too much like a bunch of women fighting the war. The army should have called the infantry the manlier "King of Battle," but that title was already taken by the artillerymen.

Clipper and I were going on a two-day mission with the 2/12 infantry. My assigned platoon would be flown by helicopter several miles east of Dau Tieng, and be dropped off in a clearing from which we'd search the surrounding jungle. On day one, our job was to patrol the jungles east of the Michelin plantation in search of the VC and their base camps. On day two, we were to sweep west through the rubber plantation all the way back to our base camp.

Another company of the 2/12 had the job of conducting search-and-destroy operations in the northern mountain sector of the rugged foothills. Most of the VC mortar attacks had been coming from that area.

Charlie's shelling equipment consisted of an 81mm mortar tube, base plate, sighting mechanism, and a bunch of mortar rounds. Charlie could quickly and easily assemble the weapon, fire, disassemble, and move off before any retaliatory strike arrived. These highly mobile mortar squads were deadly accurate, and they were difficult to detect unless flushed out by ground troops.

The mission reminded me of the time I was hill jumping in the central highlands, hunting for the same type of mobile enemy attack squad.

The American infantry had similar capabilities in its arsenal, but American artillery required vehicular or aircraft transportation. The smallest artillery pieces, 105mm Howitzers, fired explosive shells that were much bigger and deadlier than mortar rounds. Charlie wasn't equipped with such large artillery; he carried all his weapons on his back.

The 2/12 was given the order to hunt down and eliminate Charlie's mortar teams. To get to the mission site, we flew east by chopper, escorted by gunships. Clipper and I were in the lead formation's second troopship. The door gunners' post-mounted M-60 machine guns were loaded and ready for firing. It was a short ride over the rubber trees to the nearby jungle. The choppers descended into a small clearing and landed under the all-clear green smoke signal.

Clipper and I jumped out and darted to the jungle wall to our front. Its outer skirt was too thick to get through without a machete. The platoon leader ordered one of his men to take point and cut a path for the rest of us. Clipper and I followed the man with the machete as he hacked his way forward. We were useless at that point in the mission, as the machete's loud chopping diminished Clipper's ability to sense danger ahead.

With such thick vegetation, the platoon leader had to pull in the flank guards. He tightened up the column so he could maintain tighter control and accountability. The point man continued to slowly cut his way forward through the vegetation — the thickest jungle Clipper and I had been through. It reminded me of the vegetation in the central highlands where I'd been a year earlier with the 7th Cavalry. I had no dog back then, but we sure could have used a great one like Clipper.

The platoon continued to make its way deeper and deeper into the dark jungle. Looking up, I couldn't see the sky or sun through the jungle canopy. My right knee had begun to ache a bit more during each mission. I had hoped it would hold up for a few more months until I got out of Vietnam for good.

If we got hit by Charlie, our position would pose a major problem: it would be hard for air and artillery support to locate us on a map. Our AO (area of operations) was colored dark green for thousands of square yards around us. If we needed artillery support, it would have to be walked in from the mapped reference points. If we relayed the wrong coordinates, we risked having artillery dropped on our heads. Regardless of the what-if scenarios, we had no choice but to keep moving under the thick vegetation. Since another entire company of infantrymen was operating in the same area, we had the assurance of support—if only we could rendezvous in time.

Not long into the journey, thunder roared overhead. It soon began to rain, and drops of water made their way through the thick canopy and down onto the platoon. Millions of raindrops splashing on the leaves and branches helped muffle the sounds of our movement. The man with the machete kept switching it from hand to hand, so we could walk at a steady pace through the rain-soaked jungle. The pace man walked behind Clipper and me. His job was to count the number of steps we'd traveled. Periodically, the lieutenant halted our progress to get the pace man's count, and to use map and compass to check our distance and direction of travel.

Our jungle fatigues and boots were sopping wet from the heavy rain and tromping through the soaked and rotting debris. That trail we had forged with machete and boots would disappear in a few days; that was how fast vegetation grew back after it had been cut or mashed into the soil by human feet.

Then there was the unavoidable thorny vegetation we called "wait-a-minute-vines," which scratched deep into our exposed wet arms and hands and ripped holes in our fatigues. When a grunt rolled up his sleeves, cuts, scratches, and thin scars could be seen running up and down both arms. The wounds immediately distinguished an experienced infantryman from a crowd of new men or REMFs (rear-echelon motherfuckers). One could almost guess how much time a grunt had spent in the bush by the number and age of the scars on his body. Veterans took their licks from Mother Nature without whining about it; new guys were still learning to just take the hit and forget about it.

The rain and sweat washed away our trickles of blood. The jungle was alive with insects, spiders, snakes, and other weird-looking critters crawling on the ground or sitting on the leaves and branches around us. The rain made it easy to spot the huge spider webs. When someone spotted a snake, each man quickly passed on the word "Snake!" I don't think any of us youngsters knew a poisonous snake from a nonpoisonous one—we just feared them all.

As we moved forward, Clipper startled me by jumping up and down as if he'd stepped on hot coals. I looked down at him dancing around, groaning, and furiously biting at his paws. The point man had apparently stepped on a decaying log, crushing it open, and hundreds of large wingless insects swarmed out. Clipper had stepped right on them and they attacked. I leaped over the log, pulling Clipper away and trying to brush off as many bugs as I could, stomping on the ground to keep the disturbed insects from climbing up my boots and pant legs.

A man behind us said, "Your dog is going to get eaten up out here."

"No shit, Sherlock!" I replied.

I moved to the side and let the others pass. A soldier stopped to help me get the bugs off Clipper. Eventually, Clipper calmed down, so we moved on to catch up to the man with the machete. I'm sure that if Clipper could talk, he'd have asked me for some boots to wear and a soothing chopper ride back home.

The rain finally stopped. There was still no sign of Charlie. All I heard were birds and flying insects and the sounds of grunts slapping their exposed skin to kill mosquitoes and other bugs. The sound of the machete cutting through vegetation became less frequent as the jungle thinned out. The platoon leader decided to halt and give us a short lunch break. Flank guards were posted, and machine guns were manned to the front and rear of the column.

I sat on the wet jungle floor, my back against a big tree. Clipper didn't seem to mind my examining him for bugs and bites. He had lots of bite marks on the tender areas of his paws. I brushed his steel comb through his furry back and neck, checking for ticks. Clipper enjoyed the grooming. I found some bloated, peanut-sized purple wood ticks attached to his skin. I lit a cigarette and used its red-hot tip to burn them off. Clipper was happy to be rid of his little pests. Clipper would get a dip in a vat of medicine when we got home.

I expressed my love for Clipper by hugging him and telling him that he was doing a good job and was very brave. I gave him fresh water and a package of dog food. He showed his appreciation by licking all over my filthy, sweaty face. After nourishing himself, he lay down on his side, leaning against me, and licked his sore paws. I ate a jungle-temperature can of ham and lima beans and washed it down with some cool water. The smell of American cigarette smoke filled the air. I wondered if letting Clipper breathe that smoke might dull his sense of smell.

Glancing around, I saw the steam rising from damp jungle fatigues. Squad leaders quietly moved about, making sure that we were all okay and that we buried our trash. All too soon, the order was given to saddle up. I spotted the radiotelephone operator next to a tree, the lieutenant talking into the handset. After he finished, I asked him if Clipper and I could take point since the jungle was no longer dense. He nodded his assent.

A West Point graduate, the lieutenant possessed impressive leadership skills. He walked and talked with the confidence of an organized and well-trained officer. When he spoke, his squad leaders listened and obeyed his instructions. I preferred being with a unit that had that kind of discipline. Working with many units was the nature of our job as a "scout-dog team for hire." I found that the organizational structure was pretty much the same from unit to unit, but the leadership and discipline ranged from poor to outstanding.

As a scout dog handler it was harder for me to get to know anyone in the field very well, and working with that platoon was no different; names just didn't seem to stick in my head for long. But one thing that made me welcome was that the grunts loved to see and pet a dog. Clipper gave them some comfort, offering up his paw when they'd say, "Shake!"

Kenny Mook had been my best human buddy. He'd have loved Clipper. Now Clipper was my new best friend, and we'd been together longer than Kenny and I had. Sure, I had a lot of dog-handler friends back in base camp, but we never traveled together on the same missions. I had no idea how they had worked in the field or reacted under fire. I assumed that they managed things in the bush the same way I did.

Few handlers worked with any unit long enough to develop

friendships; besides, we walked point most of the time. My relationships with the infantrymen I worked with amounted to casual conversations at best. We were never together long enough to form strong bonds.

After the lieutenant approved my request, I took the point and told the flank guards not to get ahead of Clipper, explaining that they would diminish his scouting effectiveness. Clipper started forward, slowly picking his way through the jungle. I watched his head and ears for any sign of an alert.

Soon, Clipper alerted, his ears up high. As the rest of the platoon got down and security was implemented, the platoon leader sent a fire team to investigate. They returned with a negative report. As Clipper and I continued forward, he alerted a second time. Again, the platoon leader took no chances and dispatched a fire team. Again they returned with nothing to report. The leader came up to me and asked why I thought Clipper was alerting. I admitted that I didn't know exactly why. I said I wasn't sure what was out there, but maybe Charlie had left a fresh scent or was hiding up ahead, or a base camp could be nearby.

Suddenly, something came dashing and crashing low in the brush a few feet in front of Clipper. He alerted in amazement and I flinched with surprise. Before I knew it, whatever had crossed our path had disappeared.

The lieutenant came up and asked what we'd seen. I told him I thought it had been a small animal that we'd spooked, and all I'd seen was the vegetation moving as it blew by us in high gear.

The platoon leader decided to send out a patrol to sweep the area fifty yards to the front. The fire team returned and reported finding the edge of a base camp with well-worn trails directly ahead. Assuming that Charlie's not having engaged the fire team meant that he was either gone or hiding in wait, the platoon leader assembled his squad leaders to check out the report. Then he came up to my position, said I was doing a good job, gave Clipper a pat on the head, and thanked him for the alert. He told me to enter the base camp with the first squad and an M-60 machine gun team. I followed the squad as it spread out and began cautiously stepping through the jungle at the edge of the base camp. The second squad was right behind us; the rest of the platoon remained in reserve.

I had a flashback to the time I'd followed the platoon leader to check out a bunker, and he'd been killed in front of me. That wasn't such a good memory to dwell on at the moment, so I tried to erase it from my mind. Not long into our forward progress, everyone in front of me swiftly took a knee. I knelt right behind them, ready to fire my CAR-15. Preparing for that mission, I made sure to pack several grenades—I was never again going to get caught without them.

A soldier signaled me to move up. Clipper led the way. We were now a few short steps inside the edge of a Vietcong base camp. Weapons at the ready, the first squad spread out and carefully penetrated its interior.

Enemy base camps varied in size, depending on their purpose and how much of a force they housed. Some camps were used as training sites for local guerrillas, while others were fortresses. For the most part, VC camps were underground, leaving only a few exposed signs of their existence. The vegetation was carefully cleared away, leaving a few paths. The jungle floor of the camp we now explored had recently disturbed vegetation, but there were no occupants.

Clipper alerted wildly, but there were too many Americans moving all around for me to get too excited. The VC base camp appeared to be about one acre, and could probably accommodate a company-sized unit of fifty to a hundred soldiers. It had "spider holes"—tiny bunkers—all around and well-trod paths throughout. Even thought it appeared empty, it had been much used. Charlie could spring up at any time. Clipper and I continued the search; two other soldiers followed us for security.

Inside one of the bunkers, someone found a pile of Chinese communist grenades. I knew from experience never to touch a pile of enemy grenades that were lying around, because they might be booby trapped. Someone used C-Ration toilet paper to mark that bunker, warning others to leave the grenades alone. Those primitive black-powder bombs had cast-iron heads, shaped like tiny pineapples, attached to hollow bamboo handles with strings hanging out of them. Pull the string, toss the grenade by the handle, and—BOOM! These grenades worked well, but American grenades had a more complex design and were much deadlier.

Clipper alerted to something on the ground and started sniffing at a clump of cut branches. I recognized it as a cover for something hidden below. I pulled Clipper away in case it was booby trapped. I motioned everyone nearby to find something for cover. From behind a tree, I used a bamboo stick to move the brush away, thankfully not triggering an explosion. As I peered from behind the tree I realized that what Clipper had found was a buried fifty-gallon drum full of what looked like crushed green weeds. As I approached it, I smelled marijuana. I couldn't believe it—Clipper had found Charlie's pot stash!

Scout Dog, Clipper, being playful after a job well done—1967.
(Author collection)

Word quickly spread throughout the platoon about the great marijuana find. No one said anything when some grunts grabbed and stuffed handfuls of weed into their pockets. Everybody who came by wanted to know who had found the stash. Well, Clipper was the hero once again. It didn't take much to excite a bunch of grunts.

The platoon leader got on the radio, reported the findings, and ordered the marijuana destroyed. One squad leader stuck a flare down inside the drum of weed and ignited it. The scent of pot smoke carried throughout the base camp. I got out of there before I got high, and I wasn't sure how Clipper's senses would be affected if he got loaded.

After we completed our search, we moved a safe distance from the base camp. The bunkers containing war supplies were blown up with C-4 (plastic explosive). The force of the explosions scattered dirt and debris all around us, but no one got hurt.

The lieutenant called for a spotter round of artillery so he could pinpoint our location. A bit later, an artillery round whistled through the air and exploded a few hundred yards away. Satisfied, the platoon leader marked his map; the coordinates could be used later to destroy the VC base camp with an artillery barrage or a bombing run.

The vegetation was thin as Clipper and I moved out on point. Flank guards were posted about ten yards on either side of the column. We departed without incident and soon reached a small clearing. It was getting too late to travel any farther, so the lieutenant decided we should set up camp for the evening inside the clearing. Clipper and I took a position inside the perimeter, near the platoon leader's command post (CP).

Half the platoon had to be awake throughout the night. The lieutenant was hoping the VC would pass our way on their return to their base camp. Clipper remained alert, but nothing out of the ordinary happened that night.

The next morning, Clipper and I assumed the point position and slowly moved through a heavily wooded area with knee-high undergrowth. Clipper stopped at the edge of a tiny clearing with ankle-high grass. About half the size of a basketball court, the clearing had a small tree near its center. I followed Clipper as he crossed the clearing. When he reached the tree, he sprang up and over me as if he had been launched from a catapult. He let out a loud yelp. I hit the ground, thinking that Clipper must have been hit.

As I lay there, Clipper stood on his hind legs, his right front paw stretched high above him. He twisted and turned, trying to get loose from something that was suspending him. No shots had been fired. I was totally confused, but soon realized that Clipper had been caught in an animal snare. I released his right paw and checked him; he was shaken but uninjured.

Turning around, I saw two soldiers lying on the ground, shaking their heads in laughter. Embarrassed that Clipper hadn't sensed and avoided the animal trap, I hurried to the other side of the clearing to continue the mission. As we walked, I kept wondering what had happened back there. *How could Clipper step into an animal snare? We had so much tripwire training. Maybe I should have trained him to detect snares, too. Has my dog lost his instinctive edge? Did the pot smoke impair his senses? Maybe Clipper's tired of the bush and getting lackadaisical. Has he had enough rest, food, and water? How could he need anything when we've only been on the move such a short time?*

Finally concluding that Clipper had made a mistake, I thought *So what? It happens to everyone. What about me and that after-shave lotion in the Ia Drang Valley, or the time I almost killed the squad leaders by accidentally discharging my M-16 on full auto? Besides, Clipper's just a dog, not a robot.*

Most important, no one had been hurt. I realized that I couldn't blame Clipper. I needed to clear my mind of all these thoughts and doubts and stay focused. A lot of people were depending on us. I was grateful when Clipper and I made it to the edge of the rubber plantation without further incident.

The platoon leader stopped us at the edge of the plantation and reset the tactical formation for movement through the wide rows of trees. I felt relieved when no one said anything to me about what had happened with Clipper and the animal trap. The squad leaders spread their men out and moved flank guards to the far right and left wings of the main element.

Continuing to walk point, Clipper and I passed row after row of rubber trees. It was quiet and we spotted no Vietnamese working that sector of trees. The age and density of the vegetation between and around the trees made it easy to tell which sectors the Vietnamese had and hadn't worked. We knew that hamlets had to be approached with caution, but we were under orders not to fire inside a hamlet for fear of wounding or killing noncombatants.

About a hundred yards into the advance, we heard several explosions in the near distance, followed by small-arms fire. The platoon leader halted us. I looked back and saw him talking on the radio; then he started running and passed me. He pumped his fist up and down over his head and yelled, "Double-time! Double-time!"

The entire platoon started running to keep up. That pace didn't last long, because the weight of our heavy packs forced us to slow down. The platoon leader, still in the lead with his radiotelephone operator (RTO), finally slowed to a quick-step. Clipper and I were right behind him trying to keep up. The rest of the platoon spread out behind us to maintain the formation's quick pace and discipline through that open area.

The sound of shooting stopped; I waited for it to start again, but it didn't. Minutes passed and still I heard no rifle fire, so I assumed the attack to be over. I heard distant choppers, but couldn't see them through the rubber trees. It sounded as if we were still several hundred yards away from the action. Squad leaders shouted to their troops to stay alert. We began to move more easily, maintaining a brisk pace through the tall grass and weeds between the trees.

When Clipper came upon a steep ravine with a creek of running water below, we abruptly halted our progress. A narrow footpath led to a log that bridged the creek. The platoon leader directed two riflemen to cross first, a distance of about thirty feet, while the rest of us provided cover. After the advance team reached and secured the other side, we carefully crossed over the thick log one by one.

Clipper cautiously stepped onto the log. He crouched low, looking as if he were hugging it. Step by step, he steadily picked his way across the log in a crouch. I was careful to give him enough slack in the leash as I followed behind him. It took us a little longer than the others to get across, but we made it. I was glad that I had Clipper in a harness; with a collar or choke chain on, the leash would have snapped his neck if he'd fallen from the log. I had no doubt that our crossing-the-log training course had helped prepare Clipper for that real-life obstacle. When we got to the other side, I gave Clipper a big hug and praised him for a job well done.

We had all reached the other side without anyone losing balance and falling into the creek. The platoon leader motioned the lead squad to move out quickly. Clipper and I assumed the point position, with the platoon leader, his RTO, and two riflemen directly behind us. The rest of the platoon spread out in a tactical formation to the left, right, and behind. The leader kept telling me to move faster, so Clipper and I quickened our pace.

Clipper gave a strong alert to the right front. He stopped and stood rigidly, head and ears pointing to the right. I took a knee, quickly looked in that direction, and spotted troop movement about a hundred yards away through the rubber trees. Immediately, I praised Clipper, "Good boy Clipper! Good Boy!"

His RTO beside him, the platoon leader got flat on the ground next to me. He got on the radio and learned that we were to the rear of a sister platoon ahead of us. He directed me to move toward where Clipper had spotted the troop movement. I got up, tapped the bottom of the twenty-round magazine to ensure it was properly seated in my CAR-15, and made sure that the safety lever was on safe. I yanked Clipper's leash to motion him to move out.

It was quiet as we penetrated deeper into the rubber trees toward the American lines. Even though Clipper kept alerting directly ahead, I didn't stop until we spotted an American soldier waving us forward. When I reached him, the platoon leader stopped me from going any farther. I knelt on one knee, and Clipper got down on all fours.

We'd arrived twenty minutes after first hearing the sound of shooting; crossing the creek had taken most of that time. We stayed put while the platoon leader headed for our sister platoon's command post (CP). I sat next to a soldier from the other platoon and asked what had happened. He told me that his platoon had spread out and moved through the rubber trees. Then, when they got into the killing zone, concealed VC had triggered command-detonated mines, which struck down the front of the platoon, killing a few men instantly and wounding several others. He said the rest of the platoon had fired in the direction of the explosions, but Charlie never returned fire. The platoon's advance halted while they awaited medevacs and reinforcements.

I saw gunships and slicks in the air. Several landed on a road not far from us to pick up the dead and wounded. When the platoon leader returned, he changed our mission, ordering us to merge with the platoon ahead and sweep through the hamlet area. There was a possibility that the VC who had detonated those mines might still be hiding in the hamlet, among the women and children who lived there. We were not to shoot while inside the hamlet unless we had a clear target of aggression. As he talked, I noticed that the nearby area of rubber trees had been well worked by the Vietnamese; there was little or no grass and weeds between the rows.

Weapons at the ready, we moved out cautiously, Clipper and I leading the rear squad of our sister platoon. Shortly, I stepped on something that felt weird and rubbery under my boot. I looked down and saw a human hand, but didn't stop to think about it. I had to keep moving until I reached the outer perimeter of the lead platoon.

Moving forward along with us, American soldiers were spread throughout the rubber trees. We weren't far from the hamlet when Clipper's ears had perked up. I hadn't stopped because I'd assumed that Clipper was alerting on the hamlet's inhabitants.

A soldier to my right said, "Hey, Dogman, check out the bomb lying against the trunk of that rubber tree."

I glanced at the tree trunk and saw a huge warhead at its base. The soldier told me that his platoon had discovered it after they were hit by the mines. He explained that the VC probably hadn't had time to rig it as a booby trap or they'd have already detonated it. Instead, an American soldier had booby trapped it for the VC. If anyone tried to move it or tamper with it, that bomb would explode. Clipper couldn't stop alerting on that booby trap until he'd completely lost sight of it.

When we arrived at the hamlet, Vietnamese women and children quickly came out of their thatch-roofed huts to greet us. Clipper became agitated, growling as they approached. I held him back as the other soldiers entered the hamlet. I held my finger on the safety lever of my weapon, just in case I had to flick it to semi-auto and fire. More soldiers entered the village and started searching for the VC who had detonated the mines.

As they searched, I heard someone shout inside one of the huts, "You VC? You kill Americans? Where VC? Bullshit! You lie!"

A thorough search revealed only the hiding places of women, children, and old men. We couldn't figure out where the VC hid, but they couldn't have just vanished. I began to think that one of the women, an old man, or even a child could have detonated the mines. I trusted no one.

The hamlet was filled with activity, its residents confused and scared as soldiers completely surrounded the twenty or thirty huts and conducted interrogations. The Americans were having major communication problems until a few Vietnamese interpreters were flown in to translate.

Because the Vietnamese were afraid of Clipper, I stayed a safe distance from the activity, not participating in the search for fear that Clipper might bite someone. If I let him loose, he'd attack the first Vietnamese he found. I decided to take advantage of Clipper's aggressive behavior and use him to guard against any anyone trying to leave the village.

Several of the Vietnamese women and old men were taken into custody and loaded into choppers for further interrogation in Dau

Tieng. When the situation had calmed down, several Vietnamese women carrying baskets of bananas moved quickly past Clipper and me and offered the fruit to the American troops.

I was part of the first group of soldiers ordered to leave the village and move across the dirt road and into the rubber trees for our final push to Dau Tieng. Once in the trees, the troops spread out in a sweeping formation to cover a maximum of ground in our hunt for the enemy. After Clipper and I had moved past a few rows of rubber trees, we were ordered to stop and hold our position.

We waited several minutes while the rest of the platoon departed the hamlet to join us. Finally, the signal was given to move out again. Clipper and I slowly moved between the rows of trees, troops spread out to our left, right, and rear.

As we passed between two trees, I heard a shattering explosion to our immediate right. I hit the ground and dragged Clipper down beside me. We didn't hear any shots. Then I heard the sounds of an injured soldier a few feet away. I quickly crawled over to him. He lay on his back, rocking in pain, his legs and boots covered with blood.

I yelled, "Medic! Medic!"

When the medic arrived, he cut the young black soldier's boots off and treated the wounds on his legs and feet. Scanning the ground, I discovered a broken tripwire attached to a short stick that was stuck in the ground. The other end of the wire was tied to a rubber tree. I thought, *That could have been Clipper or me, if we'd been one more tree over,* I thought. *Would Clipper have alerted on that booby trap?* I'd never know the answer.

Clipper had demonstrated that he could detect trip-wired booby traps in a mock situation. Now, he'd have to detect them out here, or more of these men would be injured or killed.

After a helicopter had evacuated the wounded soldier, I told the platoon leader that I'd take the lead. I asked him to move the rest of the platoon into a column and follow behind my dog's lead. I gave the leader no chance to respond as I quickly turned and took the lead. Glancing behind, I noticed that he had ordered the troops to form a single column behind us.

Clipper is in charge now, even if he doesn't know it, I thought. *If anyone can get us through this area and safely home to Dau Tieng, Clipper can.*

With the outer perimeter of the Dau Tieng base camp less than half a mile ahead, I kept my attention glued to Clipper's head and ears as he guided me forward. Clipper gave a faint alert to the left, hesitated briefly, then moved right. Seeing nothing in that direction, I didn' stop. I had to trust Clipper's movements through the knee-high weeds and thick grass below his head. It was easy to walk through, and Clipper had no problem negotiating a path.

John Burnam and his trusty Scout Dog, Clipper, in the search mode—1967. (Author collection)

Clipper gave another weak alert to his right and then moved left. He performed that maneuver again and again with little hesitation or stopping. A short time later a voice from behind ordered me to halt. Looking back, I saw a long column of American troops snaked through the rubber trees. We stopped briefly and then moved out again. That stop-and-go situation occurred several times during the journey. I wasn't entirely sure why we were stopping; no one behind me said anything and I didn't ask. They could have been checking something out or reviewing the map for direction of travel or someone might have spotted trip-wires or booby traps.

Clipper's alerts weren't strong enough for me to worry about danger and stop the column. He seemed to be moving deliberately, but I saw nothing out of the ordinary. I decided to just keep my eyes on Clipper instead of trying to figure out why he was walking the way he was. I was grateful that there'd been no more explosions. So far, Clipper had led us on a safe path.

When we finally reached the outskirts of the Dau Tieng base camp, I stopped short of the concertina wire and spotted soldiers standing next to their bunkers and staring at us from the other side. I dropped to a knee and waited for the rest of the platoon to catch up. My right knee was aching again, but I knew that I'd soon be safe inside the K-9 compound.

While I rubbed my sore knee, several soldiers caught up with us. One stopped and told me to wait for the platoon leader; another smiled as he passed by. In a column, the soldiers moved along the barbed-wire fence toward the gate.

The lieutenant I worked with throughout the mission had finally shown up. When I stood up to greet him, he smiled and thanked me for getting his men through all the other booby traps. Then he knelt and gave Clipper a hug and told him what a great dog he was.

I was puzzled, so I asked, "What 'other booby traps,' sir?"

Looking at me as though I should have known the answer to that, he said, "When your dog changed directions for the first time, one of my men spotted a grenade tied to the base of a rubber tree, with a tripwire leading to another tree. After you and the dog changed directions several times, my men got wise to what was going on and started searching for booby traps. The times we stopped were to mark the booby traps the dog helped us avoid."

He explained that the marked traps would be detonated after the entire company was safely through the area. Finally, I realized that Clipper's deliberate changes in direction were to avoid those booby traps and tripwires. I'd seen none of them because I hadn't stop to search. Then I remembered that Clipper had performed that maneuver during our training sessions, going around a tripwire when he didn't feel like sitting in front of it.

The platoon leader told me that it was brave to have taken the lead when I didn't have to. He said, "If it hadn't been for Clipper some of my men could have been wounded or killed. I'm recommending you and Clipper for the Bronze Star." The lieutenant shook my hand and, as he walked away, turned and said, "I'm going to ask for you two the next time I need a scout."

That was the finest compliment Clipper and I ever received for doing our job.

I smiled, waved, and gave the lieutenant a thumbs-up. I looked down at Clipper and tapped my chest. He jumped up and rested his forepaws on my shoulders. I looked into his big brown eyes, gave him a bear hug, and told him what a great warrior he was and how proud I felt to have him as my friend and scout.

I thought about the lieutenant's words. This was the first time anyone had ever wanted to recommend me for a medal. I felt honored, but knew that all the credit belonged to Clipper. He'd been the meritorious hero; I was just the lucky guy behind the leash, grateful to have such a wonderful companion to lead us to safety. There was nothing more valuable and rewarding than to know that others had lived because of Clipper. My trust and confidence in him increased enormously that day.

Behind the rest of the troops now, Clipper and I moved through the gate. Walking with my head high, I smiled all the way home to the 44th Scout Dog Platoon. The training had paid off and lives had been saved. I was relieved that another mission was over. Watching my dog walking ahead of me I said, "Thanks again for another safe mission, Clipper!"

Chapter Sixteen

THE CAPTURE

It was early in the morning when Clipper and I got an assignment to report to Company A, 2nd Battalion, 12th Infantry. Brigade intelligence had reported that a NVA courier routinely traveled, sometimes alone, between the provinces of Tay Ninh and Dau Tieng. They wanted him captured and brought back alive for interrogation.

I quickly got my gear together and fetched Clipper from his run. He was wagging his tail and ready to go when he saw that I had my field gear strapped on my back and my helmet on.

We reported to the mission's combat patrol leader, a lieutenant, who showed me his field map marked with the most likely places to trap and bag our target without killing him. That type of mission was normally reserved for long-range reconnaissance patrols (LRRPs), but those teams must have been busy with other missions, so the 2/12 infantry got the job.

Choppers lifted us off at the crack of dawn, and we headed toward the majestic Black Virgin Mountain, an inactive volcano. "Nui Ba Den," as the Vietnamese called it, jutted up from the ground about 3000 feet, towering over the Tay Ninh Province about eighty miles west of Saigon. Its steep summit, capped with a thick green blanket of dense, rugged jungle, was usually shrouded by clouds and mist. The highest peak in the area, Nui Ba Den was easily seen from miles around.

The U.S. Army 5th Special Forces Group had captured the summit in 1964. When we flew close, we could see the 25th Infantry signal corp's VHF and FM relay station towers and some other tall antennas atop the mountain. The signal corps relayed communication between units of the 25th Infantry Division located in Cu Chi, Tay Ninh, and Dau Tieng. The summit of Nui Ba Den was heavily fortified and appeared nearly impossible to reach by foot from below. The VC used the lower slopes as observation posts and radio relay positions, and constantly harassed the American troops stationed on top with sniper fire and mortar attacks.

The majestic and massive Black Virgin Mountain (Nui Ba Dinh)
as seen from atop a lookout tower in base camp–1967.
(Author collection)

Four combat infantry platoons were assigned to the mission to capture the enemy courier. Each had a separate area to reconnoiter suitable ambush sites. I didn't know why I was the only dog handler assigned to the mission; we could have used four scout-dog teams, one attached to each combat platoon.

Green smoke signaled our landing in a small clearing less than a mile from the base of Nui Ba Den. We quickly moved away from the aircraft and under the cover of the jungle. The patrol leader motioned me to take the lead. Clipper and I moved into the jungle, which wasn't too dense to navigate, and were soon about a hundred feet ahead of everyone else.

The patrol leader frequently signaled me to stop while he checked the map and distance to a trail we were trying to reach. For several hours we cautiously moved parallel to Nui Ba Den. Clipper eventually gave a strong alert, ears and head held high. I stopped, dropped to a knee, and motioned the nearest man forward. A three-man fire team was dispatched to check out the alert. On returning, they reported a well-used trail less than 200 feet ahead. The patrol leader moved up to my position and evaluated the map coordinates; according to the map we were on target.

Clipper and I quietly approached the trail under the cover of the surrounding vegetation. The platoon didn't yet want to risk exposure by getting on the trail, and I didn't want them to get ahead of me for fear of their scent contaminating the area and throwing off Clipper's sense of smell. We moved quietly, using all the proper methods of a successful patrol: radio silence, camouflage, and concealment.

Eventually, we set up an ambush alongside a natural fork where two narrow trails intersected. It was a spot that provided excellent concealment and lines of sight in either direction. The platoon leader strategically positioned each man about five feet inside the surrounding vegetation. Clipper and I were at one end of the ambush, which gave him the best chance to alert if any VC came down the trail. The other platoons supporting the operation were within a one-mile radius of our position.

The plan was to surprise and capture the courier, not kill him. The ambush platoon waited several hours, quietly swatting mosquitoes and killing bugs, ants, and spiders. Some men catnapped, but most stayed vigilant, reminding me of a spider waiting for prey in its web. As the hours went by, the sky darkened until nothing within even a few feet remained visible. We stayed alert in stationary positions all night, but nothing happened.

*John Burnam taking a break at the ambush site near the
Black Virgin Mountain – 1967. (Author collection)*

As dawn light chased the shadows away, the men stirred. No one
was allowed to light cigarettes because the smoke might alert the
enemy to our presence. Of course, we didn't really know whether Charlie had already located us, or whether we'd succeed in am-
bushing him.

As the morning progressed, Clipper suddenly alerted toward the
trail. I immediately informed the man next to me, who passed the
warning down the line. In the dim light, I spotted the target of Clipper's alert: an NVA soldier in khaki uniform and straw hat, riding

a bicycle, a rifle slung over his back. I got a major adrenaline rush as I watched the enemy come closer, realizing that I was the first man he'd reach. Clipper remained silent, ready to pounce. The enemy soldier appeared to be alone and relaxed. He had two canvas bags draped over his bike's back fender.

This must be our man, I thought.

When the courier was right in front of me, I turned Clipper loose; he darted into the road, lunged, and knocked the NVA soldier off his bike. The man landed on his back. I gave Clipper the command "Watch him!" Clipper growled and showed his teeth but didn't attack. The enemy soldier looked so completely surprised that I thought his eyeballs were going to pop out of his head. Immediately, the rest of the patrol surrounded the man, weapons pointed at him. Clipper's growling and barking kept the frightened man squirming on his back in the dirt. Someone quickly stripped him of his rifle.

I handed my CAR-15 and Clipper's leash to the nearest soldier and told him to hold back the dog. Remembering my wrestling days, I was convinced that I could contain the prisoner without using a weapon. I reached down and rolled him onto his stomach, straddled his body, and spread his arms and legs. He was so scared that he pissed his pants while I searched him.

In one of his pockets I found a worn Zippo lighter engraved with the 1st Infantry Division shoulder patch and the slogan "Big Red One." As far as I knew, the Big Red One didn't operate near Tay Ninh province; I thought they were way up north. The canvas bags attached to the bicycle were filled with Vietnamese currency and documents. I was sure we had the NVA courier that army intelligence was so eager to get their hands on. I didn't want to think how this North Vietnamese soldier had gotten that lighter. *The bastard must have taken it off a dead American,* I thought.

It was honorable for a soldier to be wounded or killed on the battlefield, and normal procedure was to take weapons, ammunition, and military documents from enemy wounded or dead. It's disgraceful, however, to rob them; a soldier's personal effects should be returned to his family no matter which side he's on. But the war in Vietnam wasn't a gentlemen's war; it was as brutal and ugly as the death and destruction it left in its wake.

I was in complete control of the prisoner now. If he tried to escape, I'd tackle and pin him in a wrestling hold he couldn't wriggle out of, or I could command Clipper to attack him. *There's no damn way that guy's getting away,* I thought, my blood boiling. I was hoping he'd try to resist or escape; if he did, I'd have an excuse to vent my rage at his having robbed a fallen American, but the prisoner was too scared to move a muscle or even show an expression of defiance.

After I completed the body search, two soldiers took over. They tied the man's hands behind his back, taped his mouth shut, and blindfolded him. The patrol leader radioed for a chopper to get us out of the area immediately. Under cover of the jungle, we hustled to the pickup point, where several choppers arrived. They flew my platoon and our prisoner to Dau Tieng. I was grateful that Clipper and I had accomplished another mission and there'd been no American casualties. I hoped that all my future missions in Vietnam would be that successful, but in that undeclared war, safety was never guaranteed.

Chapter Seventeen

LIFE BETWEEN
MISSIONS

Returning to base camp after a mission was always a welcome comfort. Our K-9 Klub was the best place for us to unwind and try to forget our on-the-job troubles.

Sergeant Way, 44th Scout Dog Handler, and an American Red Cross volunteer enter the K9 Klub – 1967. (Author collection)

Huddled within the wooden buildings of our sleeping area, the K-9 Klub served as mailroom and lounge. It was modestly furnished with tables, chairs, a refrigerator, a bar, and portable air conditioners. Screened-in windows covered with scrapped sheets of clear plastic kept the cool air inside. The club was even wired for electricity to accommodate those modest but important morale-lifting conveniences.

Good times and bad with family and friends back home was always a hot topic of conversation. Some guys bragged about all the girls waiting for them. Others talked about going to college, getting a job, and starting a business. Nobody voiced aspirations of making army life a career.

The *Stars and Stripes* newspaper reported the war's current events throughout Vietnam. Many of the dog handlers passed time reading books, outdated magazines, and hometown newspapers. We played cards and drank canned soda pop and Ballantine and Pabst Blue Ribbon beer. We especially enjoyed Kool-Aid, because it spiced up the nasty taste of the local water supply.

Dan Barnett, Staff Sergeant, Squad Leader, 44th Scout Dogs, having coffee and a cigarette, early in the morning, somewhere in the bush – 1967. (Author collection)

News of our fellow dog handlers who were in hospitals recovering from wounds was always a major topic. Kentucky, wounded during the kennel attack, was wounded a second time, shot in the buttocks by a VC sniper during a search-and-destroy mission. Another dog handler, Randy Cox, was severely burned while he and his dog were inside an armored personnel carrier that was hit by an enemy rocket. His dog died of burns. Randy was evacuated to a hospital burn unit in the States and did not return to active military service.

In May 1967, I read a story in the 3rd Brigade's newspaper about Mike Phillips and his scout dog Beau. Mike was a twenty-year-old, curly-haired redhead from Cleveland. Beau, his German shepherd partner, had an aggressive attitude. They trained together at the Scout Dog Training Center in Fort Benning, Georgia, and arrived in Vietnam with the original members of the 44th Scout Dog Platoon in January 1967. Both had tasted the bitterness of war.

According to the story, Beau had been wounded on two occasions, the first during a three-day mission. Phillips and Beau had been scouting for an infantry unit near a large clearing when Beau alerted. Phillips had immediately recognized the danger, signaled the men behind him, and dived for cover. The Vietcong opened fire, but Beau's alert had halted the American patrol short of that ambush's kill zone.

During the ensuing firefight, a bullet from an enemy AK-47 rifle struck Beau in the front leg. Phillips protected Beau by covering him with his body while returning fire. The Americans, who suffered only light casualties in that battle, defeated the enemy. If not for Beau's alert, American casualties could have been greater. Beau's wound wasn't grave, and Doc Glydon patched him up for duty.

That put Mike and Beau back in action for Operation Junction City, in a rugged area of War Zone C. Sitting in a clearing, the two were preparing to move out when enemy mortar rounds began exploding all around them. During the attack, Beau and Phillips were wounded. A piece of shrapnel passed completely through Beau's middle, breaking his backbone. Phillips' right arm was pierced by another piece of shrapnel. Beau's wound was so serious that he was evacuated to a hospital in Saigon. In Dau Tieng a death certificate was filed because no one expected Beau to survive, let alone rejoin his war-dog platoon. Beau was a tough dog, however, and refused to give up. He made it through the surgery and was rehabilitated back to health. A month later, Beau returned to duty with the 44th. His death certificate was torn up and thrown away.

Specialist Four Ollie Whetstone taking a nap after digging his foxhole. His faithful Scout Dog, Erik, keeps watch–1967. (Author collection)

I preferred to work Timber and Clipper on leash, but Ollie and Mac and other dog handlers sometimes worked their dogs off leash without having any control problems. Roger Jones did the same. Roger won the Trainee-of-the-Cycle award at the scout-dog training school in Fort Benning, Georgia. In June 1967, Roger and his dog, Ringo, were supporting a platoon on a mission when they got into a firefight. Unleashed, Ringo bolted from the chaotic scene. Lieutenant Fenner and Bob "Doc"Glydon felt accountable for every scout dog and handler, and were furious when Roger returned without Ringo. They filed a "Report of Survey" form charging Roger with suspicion of negligence. It could have resulted in court-martial proceedings, but Roger was never punished.

```
┌─────────────────────────────────────────────────────────────────────┐
│              REPORT OF SCOUT DOG OPERATIONS                          │
│                  (USARV Reg 11-2)                  RCS:  AVHGC-7     │
│                                                                     │
│  TO: Commanding General      FROM:  Commanding Officer    DATE 4 July, 1967│
│      Hq, USARV                      44th Inf Plat (Scout Dog)        │
│      ATTN:  AVHGC-PO                APO 96268                        │
│      APO 96307                                                       │
│  1.  Period of Report:    1 June,67 to 1 July, 67                   │
│  2.  Number of Scout Dog Teams Assigned:  3.  Number Available for Operations:│
│      4 July,67   24 dog teams assigned        19                    │
└─────────────────────────────────────────────────────────────────────┘
```

Report of Scout Dog Operations (USARV Reg 11-2) — RCS: AVHGC-7

TO: Commanding General, Hq, USARV, ATTN: AVHGC-PO, APO 96307
FROM: Commanding Officer, 44th Inf Plat (Scout Dog), APO 96268 DATE 4 July, 1967

1. Period of Report: 1 June,67 to 1 July, 67
2. Number of Scout Dog Teams Assigned: 4 July,67 24 dog teams assigned
3. Number Available for Operations: 19

4. NUMBER OF PATROLS:

Combat	SD	SC	Ambush	Outpost	Recon	Longe Range	Village Search	Other	TOTAL
	242	9					30		281

5. Number of Scout Dog Team Days Worked During Reporting Period:
   19 different dog teams worked during period.
6. Number of Patrols with No Contact:
   around 200
7. Enemy: (KIA, Prisoners & Material)
   2 Bullock plows, 1yoke, 3 base camps, 10 booby traps, 2 squads of VC, 2 weapons, medical supplies, documents, foxholes and trenches, rice, uniforms, batteries, canteens, sandals

8. Handlers: WIA 0   KIA 0
9. Dogs: WIA: 0   KIA MIA-1

10. Remarks:
    One handler lost his dog out in the field. The dog's loss is being determined by a report of survey as to if it was the handler's fault.

11. Major Extended Operations:
    Operations DIAMONDHEAD and UNIONTOWN

* Attach copies of patrol reports where significant contact was made. Forward through channels to CG, USARV, ATTN: AVHGC-PO, APO 96307. Send information copy directly to CG, USARV, ATTN: AVHGC-PO, APO 96307.
TYPED GRADE & TITLE OF PLATOON CO: ROBERT D FENNER, 1 LT, 44th IPSD   SIGNATURE:

USARV Form 302-R (12 Apr 67)

An official copy of a Report of the 44th Scout Dogs Operations for operations "Diamondhead" and "Uniontown" for the month of June 1967. (Document courtesy of Mike McClellan)

A few weeks after Roger had lost Ringo, the local *Stars and Stripes* paper carried the story of a wounded German shepherd who had followed an American combat patrol into the Cu Chi base camp. According to the story, the dog, badly wounded in the jaw, dehydrated, and hungry, had survived several days on his own, hiding in the jungle.

The dog had been taken for medical attention to the 38th Scout Dog Platoon, a sister platoon based at Cu Chi, about sixty miles from Dau Tieng, Ringo's home base. Because each dog had a serial number tattooed in the left ear, Doc Glydon was able to verify that the wounded dog's serial number matched that of Ringo, Roger's missing scout dog.

Ringo had suffered a close-range gunshot wound in the face. The bullet entered one side of his jaw and exited the other. Ringo was evacuated to Saigon where he underwent a special operation performed by a well-known military dental surgeon. Roger flew to Saigon to accompany his dog through the successful surgery, and a month later, Roger and Ringo returned home to the 44th. Ringo eventually recovered from his wounds, albeit missing a piece of his tongue.

For surviving his wound, hiding in the bush, and finding an American patrol to follow home, Ringo was our hero. We admired the courage and strength it took to escape and evade being captured and killed by the enemy.

Staff Sergeant Barnett and Ringo after Ringo returned from surgery in Saigon. Note that part of Ringo's tongue is missing–1967. (Photo courtesy of Dan Barnett)

Dog handlers had unique personalities and ways of expressing their individuality. For example, my hooch-mate, Dan Scott, always had a book sticking out of his back pocket because he liked to read every chance he got. After dropping out of Officer Candidate School, Scott was reassigned to scout-dog training. Upon graduation, Scott was shipped to Vietnam and assigned to the 44th in March 1967, the same month that I returned to Vietnam for my second tour of duty.

Scott had somehow acquired a World War II relic: a twenty-five-inch-long .45 caliber machine gun commonly called a "grease gun." Although .45 caliber ammo was a standard item in the Dau Tieng supply channels, Dan had also acquired several thirty-round clips to go along with his new weapon. The gun was designed to be slung from a shoulder strap and fired from the hip with one hand.

Mac McClellan insisted on carrying his M1 rifle in the field and wouldn't trade it for anything else. Scott toted his grease gun on every mission, swearing that it never jammed when fired. It didn't have a semi automatic selector switch like the CAR-15 because it was designed to fire on full automatic. I didn't think that grease

Specialist Four Mike "Mac" McClellan and Achates inside the 44th Scout Dogs kennel area—1967. (Photo courtesy of Mike McClellan)

gun could hit the side of a barn beyond twenty feet, but everyone agreed that if the bullets didn't kill the enemy, the noise would scare him to death.

Lieutenant Fenner didn't seem to mind that some of his men preferred weapons other than the standard-issue CAR-15 or M-16.

A sense of humor was not only a way of expressing one's identity, but also of staying mentally healthy in Vietnam, so we often looked for ways to have some fun.

One day, Scott stood outside my hooch and called, "Hey, Burnam! Get out here! I have something to show you!"

Going out to see what he wanted, I found Scott holding two jars in his hands: in one was the largest centipede I'd ever seen; in the other was a monster scorpion. Before long, several other dog handlers gathered around while Scott placed the two jars on the ground. We started placing bets on which of the critters would survive in a fight. I put my money on the scorpion, because it looked meaner. When all the bets were in—about fifty-fifty on scorpion and centipede—Scott emptied the jars and forced the critters into a fight. It didn't last long: less than a minute into the first round, the centipede killed the scorpion—and I lost my bet.

Dan Scott, Mike Phillips, and I acquired a torn camouflage parachute from a logistics sergeant and decided to liven up our hooch with it. We centered the parachute's apex onto the ceiling and painted it black. We glued strands of steel wool around the dark center and spread and nailed the rest of the parachute material to the rafters and walls. We called our creative decoration *The Pussy That Swallowed Vietnam.*

While Dan, Mike, and I fantasized about women, fellow scout handler Bill Zantos found a unique way of finding a girlfriend. Two local women, each of whom we referred to as a "Mama San," operated a laundry and boot-shine service in a large military canvas tent across the road from the K-9 compound. A chalkboard listed the price they charged for each laundry item as well as the cost of boot polishing. We used Military Pay Currency, or paper money, to pay.

One of the older Vietnamese women who worked in the laundry

tent took a shine to Bill Zantos. Compared to the rest of us, Bill had a robust body, which quickly earned him the nickname "Heavy." When the dog handlers found out that Heavy was doing the boom-boom thing with a Mama San in the back of the laundry tent, they had a great time poking fun at him. Fortunately, Bill had a good sense of humor and laughed right along with us.

The 44th set up a volleyball net between two rubber trees inside the K-9 compound. Playing volleyball gave us some exercise and helped take our minds off our troubles. There always seemed to be plenty of dog handlers who wanted to play a game. We played for hours without shirts under cover of the fully-leafed rubber trees.

About once a week, firing from the small mountains north of the K-9 compound, Charlie launched mortar rounds at the Dau Tieng airstrip. We quickly learned that the maximum range of these mortar rounds brought them about 200 yards short of the volleyball court, so whenever we heard mortars exploding on the airstrip, we'd stop the volleyball game and watch.

Since the shrapnel from the mortar rounds never reached us during those random daytime attacks, we didn't need to run and seek shelter in the bunkers; we stood on the volleyball court and watched the fireworks. Most of the shells exploded in and around the runway, sending the helicopters scrambling to get airborne. During each mortar attack, Dau Tieng sounded a siren like the one used for an air raid. The attacks never lasted long—they were just Charlie's way of saying hello!

Occasionally, Charlie would get lucky and blow up a helicopter or ground vehicle, or hit a building near the runway. American retal-iatory strikes were immediate: our gunships were airborne instant-ly. With a vengeance, the Americans would fire volley after volley of artillery rounds. The infantry would patrol on foot to search the rugged and difficult mountain terrain. Scout-dog teams would also be sent out to locate Charlie's mortar squads. Once in a while we got lucky and surprised Charlie, killing him and capturing some of his mortar tubes. For the most part, however, that was a game of cat and mouse. Charlie was too smart and usually got away in time, only to return another day and launch more shells. We learned to respect those tenacious little bastards, because they were so good at guerrilla warfare.

On September 2, 1967, a hot, humid morning with not a cloud in the sky, Lieutenant Fenner decided that we should go on a road march because he thought we weren't getting enough exercise in base camp. He directed the entire platoon of fifteen or so scout-dog teams to assemble. We were to march around the entire perimeter of Dau Tieng. We decided to travel light, with only our helmets, weapons, one canteen of water each, and our dogs on leash. With the hot sun and balmy air, none of us was thrilled with the idea of a road march. Nonetheless, orders were orders, so, shortly after lunch, we formed up in single file.

44th Scout Dogs "Dog Walk" inside the perimeter and security of the Dau Tieng base camp–1967. (Author collection)

Heading out of the compound, we must have been a magnificent sight: German shepherds and scout-dog handlers stretched out for a quarter mile. As the platoon moved along the shoulder of the road, I realized it was the first time I'd seen this type of organized activity since my assignment with the sentry-dog platoon in Okinawa, where it was routine to march around in formation. In Vietnam, emphasis wasn't placed on organized training activities; usually, we rested while in base camp, and trained at our individual discretion.

Because our base camp wasn't very large, the dogs drew immediate attention as we passed infantry company areas, battalion and brigade headquarters, the field hospital, motor pools, the airstrip, maintenance hangers, and trucks and jeeps driving down the road. We figured we'd be gone just a short time. It must have been 110 degrees that afternoon, and the dusty road offered no cover to protect us from the sun and heat. We marched at a slow pace. In about two hours, the column of scout-dog teams had made a nonstop loop around the entire base camp. The dogs' tongues were just about dragging in the dirt. So were the handlers'.

We were within a few hundred yards of the entrance of our K-9 compound when the worst possible thing happened: Tony Pettingill's dog, Prince, gasped for air and collapsed near the gate. Doc Glydon was unable to revive Prince, who died of dehydration. I watched as Tony, sobbing, cradled Prince in his arms. There was nothing anyone could do for him. Prince was the only casualty of that road march, just another tragic accident that took the life of a war dog.

We buried Prince in the cemetery inside the K-9 compound next to the dogs who had died before him: Erik, Shadow, Prince, Sergeant, 44, Hardcore, and others. The grave markers were starting to add up.

44th Scout Dog, Prince, after having been placed on a stretcher by his handler, Bob Pettingill–1967. (Photo courtesy of Dan Barnett)

The army never let a grunt rest for very long. Even when we were back at base camp between jungle missions and assignments, we had to pull duty with the 3rd Brigade, 25th Infantry Division's military police detachment. That served to keep us occupied and useful.

Responsible for law and order as well as a ton of other security jobs in and around the Dau Tieng base camp, The MPs also controlled the traffic in and out of the gates. The village of Dau Tieng was off-limits to American grunts at all times; liberty passes to enter the village were never issued (there was really nothing to see or anything worth buying there, anyway). The MPs also patrolled inside the village at night.

The primary reason American troops occupied Dau Tieng was because the rubber plantations happened to be strategically located for military use as a forward fire base and as a buffer between Cambodia and Saigon. The Vietnamese used the Song Saigon River, which ran right through the village, for fishing, bathing, and transport.

Somehow, the 44th got involved in supporting MP night patrols in Dau Tieng village. Lieutenant Fenner, who maintained the duty roster, made sure that every scout-dog handler was on his list. When we weren't in the field, dog handlers were expected to go on what we dubbed "Rat Patrol."

Rat Patrol was never conducted during daylight. It started after midnight and lasted several hours. Mainly as a show of force, a scout-dog team would accompany a small detachment of MPs into the village several nights during the week. A dog handler traveled light, carrying a CAR-15, a bandoleer of ammunition, a flashlight, and a few canteens of water for his dog. Instead of a steel pot the handler wore a soft flop hat. The MPs carried M-16s and .45 caliber pistols as side arms. One MP backpacked a PRC/25 field radio to relay situation reports or call for help.

The local whorehouse, off-limits to Americans, was one of the village checkpoints. An ARVN and an American Military Assistance Command Vietnam (MACV) command post near the center of town was heavily guarded and surrounded by barbed wire and sandbags. The Rat Patrol used it as a pit stop for a cup of coffee and a place to hang out and talk with the American advisors on duty there.

Rat Patrol was conducted with clockwork precision and didn't surprise any of the locals. Every villager knew where we went and how many of us were on the team. The patrol walked the main road and the beaten paths of the village. Every now and then the patrol had to chase someone through the darkness, but the quarry always seemed to get away. The Rat Patrol wouldn't be surprising a lone Vietcong, and never snuck up on a squad of North Vietnamese Regulars setting up a mortar tube or sitting around smoking pot. Charlie was too slick for that.

Dau Tieng didn't have street lamps, traffic signals, or a town square with a huge lit-up clock. It was a poor town where people lived in small huts and mostly traveled on foot or on bicycles. In their dirt yards, chickens, oxen, pigs, and tiny dogs hung around. There were no paved roads. In fact, everything seemed to be dirt, including the floors inside the homes. Some of the businesses had a more enduring look, heavily influenced by French-style architecture, but there were few permanent-looking structures in the village of Dau Tieng.

We enjoyed going on Rat Patrol for one reason: we could visit the local bakery. Dau Tieng's Vietnamese baker used a primitive brick oven, with a cast-iron door, to bake small loaves of bread. What a treat it was to smell and taste hot baked rolls at two o'clock in the morning! The baker gave us the hot bread; he never charged us for his goods, saying that the Rat Patrol kept away the VC. Part of a scout dog handler's mission on Rat Patrol was to bring back some bread rolls for his friends.

I figured MPs were like the local cops back home, but instead of free donuts at the local late-night convenience store, they enjoyed free bread rolls at the local Vietnamese bakery. The only redeeming value in going on Rat Patrol was bringing home this welcome treat, which was just another way to relieve some of the tension of serving as a scout-dog handler. Despite the great food, Rat Patrol, along with combat missions, was wearing on my bad knee.

Soon, that old wound would force me to leave Dau Tieng and my best friend Clipper.

Chapter Eighteen

SHORT TIMER

On Christmas Day of 1967, the battalion mess hall served a big turkey lunch with all the trimmings. The past week had seen a major increase in incoming mail and packages from the States.

I woke up early that morning and felt great, even though it was hot and muggy. Everyone I ran into seemed to be in a good mood, and the dogs were barking and hungry. It was a day like any other in Vietnam for Clipper and his pals in the kennel. Same old dog food, same old rubber tree, same old water pail, same old kennel run, same old mutts as neighbors. Clipper didn't even know that he had no chance in hell of ever going back to the States to become a pet in my backyard. That was too depressing a thought, so we dog handlers didn't talk about it much.

That Christmas, I thought about two Christmases past: In 1965, I'd been in Littleton, Colorado living it up on a weeklong furlough from infantry training, with no idea that the army would ship my butt off to Vietnam three months later; in 1966, I was a sentry-dog handler with the 267th Chemical Company in Okinawa. My fear of guarding chemical weapons of mass destruction was one of many reasons I chose to return to Vietnam.

Now, on this, my first Christmas in South Vietnam, the radio played Christmas music, courtesy of the armed services radio station. Since the Asian culture was Buddhist, there were no colored lights or Christmas trees in the villages. We were separated from families and friends on the other side of the planet; no children surrounded us, sharing their excitement about Santa Claus and special Christmas toys. We couldn't shop for Christmas gifts, because there were no real stores nearby. Civilian life was just a pleasant memory, even though many of us had been civilian teenagers not long before. Although we felt light-years away from the comforts of a traditional American Christmas, we enjoyed each other's company, sharing packages of good food and colorful Christmas cards from home.

The nearby chapel offered a variety of religious services throughout the day. Still bitter about the sermon the chaplain had given for Ed Hughes, I had stopped attending church services. I was truly thankful, however, that I was well and had been spared falling sick with malaria, dysentery, or Asian flu, and that I wasn't lying in some hospital bed, suffering from another combat wound.

The K-9 Klub was where we shared care packages from home, all of which seemed to contain various types of fruitcakes. People back home figured that fruitcake wouldn't spoil on the long journey to South Vietnam. I hated fruitcake; in fact, many of the other dog handlers also detested the taste of fruitcake. We couldn't even feed it to the dogs, because we thought they'd puke. Nonetheless, we were grateful to receive them. There was always someone who'd eat the fruitcakes; also, we could trade them for something we needed. Our fellow dog handler, Coonrod, would eat just about anything. He was known to swallow large chunks of cooked hog fat just to gross people out.

A soldier wouldn't think of writing home to complain about the contents of a care package, even if it contained fruitcake. Homemade chocolate-chip cookies, oatmeal-raisin cookies, and chocolate cakes were our favorites. They arrived in cardboard boxes, wrapped and taped in plastic and tinfoil, and packed in popcorn. Those goodies never lasted long, because you couldn't eat one cookie without eating another and another. Sometimes, the packages took a beating during the long trip. Many times, the cookies arrived crumbled and the cakes mashed, but they still tasted great, and we ate every crumb.

Rumor had it that if the United States declared war on North Vietnam, we'd all be in Vietnam for the duration. The war could go on for several years, which would've been the biggest of all bummers. I didn't figure I'd last the duration of a full-blown war with North Vietnam. In my line of work, soldiers walking point and being the first exposed to the enemy got killed sooner or later. But it was taboo to allow yourself to think about death, so I convinced myself that I'd survive.

I believed the Americans could kick ass and take names all the way to Hanoi if the army unchained us from all the war restrictions and let us take and keep the ground we fought so hard to capture. As it stood, we operated out of base camps, fought the enemy, and returned to base camps, only to go out another day to the same places and do the same things again — like continuously mopping up the water from a leaking pipe but never fixing the plumbing.

A Christmas cease-fire to last a few days into the New Year of 1968 was announced throughout Vietnam. There would be no major offensive, no search-and-destroy operations. They called it "standing down." Still, the defensive perimeter circling the Dau Tieng base camp still had to be manned round the clock. Patrols were scheduled, as a minimum security, to probe right outside the perimeter during the cease-fire. This was our only insurance against one of Charlie's surprises. We didn't want to get caught with our pants down, and even though the 3rd Brigade's infantry units were standing down, they remained on one-hour alert status.

All the scout-dog teams were in base camp for the week but ready to deploy if needed. Charlie was supposed to honor the holiday cease-fire, so we didn't expect him to attack our base camp with mortars, rockets, or snipers, but there was no telling if all of Charlie's units, hiding in the jungle, had gotten the message or would obey.

In general, the Vietnamese didn't recognize Christian holidays. For me, the Christmas holiday was another day off from the war, which was a good thing. Any day I didn't have to expose Clipper and me to the enemy was a good one. I couldn't believe I was only two and a half months away from ending my tour of duty in Vietnam. My rotation month was the middle of March 1968; my twelve-month stint would soon be over. Soon, I would have accomplished my mission, even though the army had reneged on my promised assignment when I'd volunteered to return to that hellhole. I didn't care to think about it , because it still upset me. My hope was that the army would get me home in time to celebrate my twenty-first birthday on March 16, 1968.

In Vietnam, there was no such thing as a travel agent at headquarters who took requests for plane reservations and a window seat. I knew exactly how the army operated: I was just a number, a faceless man who'd be processed out when my time was up. I'd grown to expect the routine of "hurry up and wait for the unknown." I couldn't understand how career soldiers, dubbed "lifers," dealt with the army for twenty years or more—I could barely figure out how to handle the next seventy-five days.

Combat missions, combined with walking, running, jumping, and carrying a loaded backpack, had taken a heavy toll on my right knee. Over the past few months, I'd been more and more uncomfortable, feeling as if my knee was wearing out on me. After a mission, it stayed inflamed, puffy, and red for days. Every now and then it would lock up, and I'd walk stiff-legged until it unlocked. I'd feel okay after the swelling went down, but then I'd have to get ready for another mission. Though I began walking with a noticeable limp, when it came to pulling my load I was no complainer, slacker, ghost, or skater.

When I talked to Lieutenant Fenner about my knee, he agreed that I should see a doctor. After an initial evaluation at the local field hospital, the news the doctor gave me wasn't good: I'd damaged the ligaments around the fleshy area of my old punji-stake wound, and the beginnings of degenerative arthritis were developing in the joint. The doctor told me that this condition could worsen with age.

Age? I thought. *I'm only twenty years old!* I wondered what my knee would be like when I became an old man of thirty.

The doctor said that further aggravation of the knee would cause even more discomfort or permanent damage, and then I'd need another surgery to repair the ligaments. For at least a year since my surgery, I'd been pounding hard on that knee. I didn't want to go under the knife again; the recuperation period was too long and I was almost through with my tour. I knew I had to hang in for a few more months before I went home.

The doctor at the Dau Tieng field hospital scheduled an appointment for me to see an orthopedic specialist in Cu Chi, home of the 25th Infantry Division. The 3rd Brigade in Dau Tieng was a subordinate brigade of the 25th Infantry. The medical facilities at Cu Chi were more permanent and better staffed than the small field hospital in dusty old Dau Tieng.

In the middle of January 1968, a supply chopper flew me to visit the orthopedist in Cu Chi. I expected to be away from Clipper for only a few days.

Boy, was I wrong!

When I met with the doctor, I underwent another complete medical examination, including a blood workup. The doctor told me he was going to put a cast on my leg to immobilize it for a month. He asked how much time I had left in Vietnam, and I told him I was scheduled to rotate back to the States in two months. Based on the condition of my knee, he said I wouldn't be leaving Cu Chi. He placed me under medical observation and care in the Cu Chi hospital for my remaining time in Vietnam.

I thought this news was fine and dandy, but I really needed to get back to Dau Tieng to collect my personal effects and see Clipper. I'd always been bothered by this kind of quick decision making that was so typical of the army.

The hospital issued me a temporary physical profile document signed by the doctor who'd performed the examination. It ruled that I was not to do any more strenuous activity; I was restricted from running, jumping, crawling, prolonged standing, and marching for three months, which would carry past my March rotation date. I had to carry the document—my special-duty pass—in my pocket at all times.

Not having to hump the boonies anymore was great, but I really missed Clipper. My only comfort lay in knowing that my hooch buddies, Dan Scott and Mike Phillips, would take good care of Clipper while I was gone.

The doctor told me he was obligated to ensure my health and welfare. My knee would get better only if I quit abusing it. In his eyes, I was "just a kid," and he told me so. I decided to educate the doctor on my idea of a man.

I said, "I resent being called a kid or a boy. If I'm old enough to fight a war and spill blood for my country, I'm old enough to be called a man."

The graying old doctor smiled and told me that he had sons my age, but they were in college. My initial thought was that if the war continued, his sons would probably be drafted for Vietnam duty. I also had the impression that the doctor was trying to give me the gift of a valid medical reason for staying out of a combat unit. I decided not to push the "man" point with him. My health was important to me, and although I might have been a little crazy to return to Vietnam for more punishment, I sure as hell wasn't so stupid as to pass up this opportunity not to get shot at anymore.

I had never discussed with a military doctor how he felt about war; I'd formed my opinions about doctors' attitudes by observing them. I remembered the kindness of Dr. George Bogumill, the surgeon in Japan who had repaired my knee. He wasn't motivated by the war, like a field commander in constant need of fresh healthy bodies to fight the enemy. Field commanders expected a certain amount of casualties and considered infantrymen replaceable. I'd experienced that attitude many times during my military service. Doctors, on the other hand, had more caring and sensitive natures. They didn't see or experience battle, but dealt with the aftermath. They helped mend the bloody young bodies toted on stretchers from the battlefield. Sadly, a doctor and his medical staff were often unable to save those young lives. I concluded that doctors were truly a breed apart from the world of military infantry where I lived and breathed.

I didn't like being in a field hospital because it meant having to watch my fellow soldiers suffering. Hanging around the tents of Cu Chi hospital, I saw naked men sitting in ice-filled metal tubs on dirt floors. Those men were burning up with fever caused by malaria, and the sight of them made me glad I'd taken my malaria pills regularly. Some of those men would die if the doctors couldn't break their fever in time. What a way to leave that lousy war—high fever, shaking all over, sitting in cold water, and then dying. I could sense the pain those young guys were going through, but I could only watch, wait, and hope.

The most depressing aspect of being a patient in the hospital at Cu Chi was that I wouldn't get a chance to say goodbye to Clipper or my dog-handler friends. Because of the distance between base camps, communication had to be done by some kind of radio patching system. I felt a little uncomfortable going into some unit's headquarters and asking if I could make a long-distance call to check on my dog. I felt powerless to do anything out of the ordinary, since I was a stranger in these new surroundings. The hospital personnel clerk advised me that he'd contact the 44th Scout Dog Platoon and forward the paperwork authorizing my reassignment to Cu Chi field hospital.

The doctor decided not to put my leg in a cast. Instead, he wrapped it in a large flexible bandage. He advised me not to overdo physical activity, and told me to see him for checkups every few days until the swelling went down. If my knee continued to swell with fluid, it would have to be drained with a syringe.

I'd hated needles ever since a doctor back in Littleton, Colorado, had stuck one in my left ear to drain fluid that had accumulated from the punishment of high school wrestling. That ear had frequently puffed up with fluid as a result of my not wearing protective ear guards. After having drained the ear with a needle a few times, the doctor decided to lance it with a scalpel and squeeze the fluid out—a little procedure that hurt like hell. After that visit I never went back. Over time, the fluid hardened and my left ear became deformed—but it didn't hurt anymore. Wrestlers called this condition "cauliflower ear."

I was assigned to living quarters at Headquarters Company, 25th Supply and Transportation Battalion (S&T). I reported to First Sergeant Milanowski. When he noticed the CIB and Jump Wings sewn above my left breast pocket, he smiled and said, "Welcome, Sergeant Burnam!" I had finally been promoted to sergeant, E5 in December 1967. My scout-dog platoon sergeant had pinned the stripes on me in the K-9 Klub. Rear-echelon troops couldn't earn a CIB unless they were assigned as infantrymen in an infantry unit, but they respected anyone who wore it.

My promotion came a few weeks after Private First Class Ed Hughes was killed in action. The timing of the promotion and celebration was poor, but, to ease my painful memories of Ed, I had a few beers and a couple hits off a joint with my fellow dog handlers. Unlike "blood stripes"—the stripes of a sergeant killed in battle, given to the next person in line for promotion—my stripes were merit-based, so I wore the new three-stripe chevrons on my sleeve proudly. I felt pretty cool and cocky to be a sergeant—equivalent to a squad leader in rank and authority—especially when I was addressed as "Sarge."

"Top," the first sergeant at my new base camp, was trim, short, and about the same build and height as I. He sported a typical military haircut, and kept his head covered in a clean military OD baseball cap. He wore properly fitting pressed jungle fatigues and brush-shined jungle boots. Top was the perfect example of a professional career soldier. My first impression was that I liked him, and he seemed to like me, too.

Since I was a sergeant, Top assigned me to the noncommissioned officers' (NCO) quarters, which was just a green canvas tent with no special trappings. I'd had better quarters in Dau Tieng. No one below the rank of sergeant was allowed to live in the NCO quarters; NCOs were separated from the low-ranked enlisted men and not allowed to fraternize. I violated the crap out of that military protocol.

After I settled into my new digs, a runner came by to tell me to report to First Sergeant Milanowski. I hustled my butt over to Top's office in the "head shed" — the headquarters building. Top informed me that I'd been assigned to work at the Post Exchange and was to report to Sergeant Major Kelly who ran the place. With a smile, Top told me that it was the best job he could find for me, and I believed him. I thanked him and headed out in search of SGM Kelly. SGM (E9) was the highest enlisted rank in the army. High-ranking soldiers always made me nervous.

The PX was about a mile away from the 25th S&T. I walked along a dirt road that wound its way around the entire inner perimeter of Cu Chi. My knee wrapped tightly, I limped a little, but at least I no longer had to carry a sixty-pound pack and rifle.

I found SGM Kelly's office in a small detached building behind the huge PX. I spotted him through the screen door, sitting by himself at a desk, his back to the door. I knocked lightly on the wooden screen door. He didn't look up, but his deep voice told me to enter. I walked in, removed my headgear, stood at attention, and announced myself: "Sergeant Burnam reporting as directed, Sergeant Major!"

The SGM swiveled his chair around and faced me. "Do you have any experience working in a store, Buck Sergeant?" (a common nickname for a three-striper).

"No, Sergeant Major!"

"Well, you'll learn."

He told me to stand at ease and tell him about myself.

I noticed that the SGM had a Combat Infantry Badge with two stars connecting the top of the wreath, which meant that he'd been awarded the CIB three times — in WWII, Korea, and Vietnam, as I later learned. SGM Kelly had deep wrinkles around his eyes and cheeks, and looked much traveled in the army. *One war is enough for me,* I thought. I couldn't imagine serving as an infantryman in three wars. That old soldier must have been born with army blood in his veins or else was just plain crazy, but he deserved my unconditional respect. I surely wasn't about to ask him how he'd ended up as SGM for the PX.

SGM Kelly assigned me to new quarters near the PX; he told me that he didn't like waiting when he needed someone. My new accommodations were in a wooden building with a wooden floor. I had a metal bunk bed with a mosquito net rigged above it. The hooch was equipped with a refrigerator stocked with food, soft drinks, and beer. It had tables, floor lamps, chairs, and a small bookshelf stocked with paperbacks—the nicest place I'd lived since entering the army!

By that time, I'd been in Cu Chi a few weeks. When I asked the SGM for a chance to visit Clipper in Dau Tieng, he denied my request. Officially, I was no longer a scout-dog handler assigned to the 44th. The SGM told me that I hadn't worked long enough to earn time off, but he promised me a convoy trip or chopper ride to Dau Tieng before I left Vietnam in March. I'd heard army promises before, so I wasn't sure that one would be kept. I hoped it would. I sure did miss Clipper and my buddies.

My new job was driving a tractor-trailer rig to the infantry units throughout the base camp. The fully enclosed trailer was stocked with sundries such as candy, peanuts, canned finger foods, canned soda and beer, cigarettes, and Zippo lighters. Really a mobile store, the truck was a morale booster for the troops.

What a job! I thought. *To have all the food and drink I could handle.*

When I pulled up to an infantry company area and opened the doors for business, I had no problem selling the supplies and collecting the money, which I had to turn in to SGM Kelly at the end of the day. He didn't require an inventory of stock; he left that to me. My job was to keep the truck re-supplied. Occasionally, I was tempted to take whatever I wanted, but if I were ever caught stealing, I'd likely end up in "LBJ" (Long Bin Jail). I wasn't about to blow that job for some petty-theft rap, especially with just a month and a half left to serve in Vietnam. I knew I could do this PX job standing on my head.

Any infantryman would have loved to trade places with me.

When I parked the rig in an infantry company's compound, it was like the Good Humor Man had arrived. After opening the large metal door and lowering the stairs for business, a line would quickly form to come aboard. I'd position myself at the small cash register near the entrance, which was also the exit. Due to the cramped space inside, I could let in only a handful of soldiers at a time. The entering troops' eyes would light up when they saw the rows of metal baskets filled with packaged candy, canned food, and drinks.

Infantrymen were very special to me; I knew how hard they worked in South Vietnam, and I'd always smile and welcome each of them as he entered my store. I liked to make up my own rules for them. When I serviced an infantry unit smelling of fresh muck from the field, I'd yell, "Two-for-one sale today, men!" They'd smile and go crazy, buying all they could carry. Many of those young guys looked as green as I had when I first got to Vietnam almost two years earlier. I knew that some of them would never make it home to the States alive.

I'd visit a bunch of different units each day, seven days a week. When I earned a day off, I liked hanging out with the other short-timers who worked in the PX. It helped keep my mind off of missing Clipper and my other pals in the 44th.

While it was hard to believe that my time in Vietnam was coming to an end, forty-five days seemed like an eternity, and anything could happen before I went home. I certainly didn't want to become a casualty during my last month. I knew that each day would take forever to go by if I dwelled on these thoughts, so I tried not to worry about things I had no control over. I had to remain positive and do my job. I knew there'd be plenty of time to reflect on my experiences after I was safely back in the United States.

A soldier with thirty days or less to serve was called a "short-timer." Some field commanders did their best to keep short-timers out of harm's way, but a good number of short-timers still humped the boonies, and some got killed or wounded weeks or even days before their scheduled departure. The goal of an infantry short-timer was to become a REMF (rear-echelon motherfucker)—a truck driver, supply clerk, vehicle mechanic, hospital technician, personnel and finance clerk, cook, or engineer—any job that would keep him away from combat until he left Vietnam. When the infantry was out looking for a fight, the short-timers manned the base-camp perimeter.

Once a guy reached short-timer status, it was also a tradition to carry around a short-timer-stick. Some guys carved tree branches into fancy sticks, and notched them to show how many days they had left in Vietnam. As each day passed, they'd cut a notch off the stick until only a stub was left. A short-timer also marked a big "X" on his calendar at each day's end. Many of them spent much of their free time writing letters and sending stuff home.

I was surprised at some of the things short-timers tried to mail home, though their attempts to have keepsakes of their time in Vietnam were more funny than shocking. For example, there was a story of one soldier who sent home an M-60 machine gun. He broke it down into little pieces and mailed each piece in a separate package. The recipient wrote back to report what had arrived and what hadn't. The operation took several months, but the man ultimately succeeded. The military postal system had so many packages coming in and out of Vietnam that it must have been impossible for them to check each one for illegal contents.

Some short-timers got superstitious; they did only what they believed wouldn't put them in any danger. They'd avoid walking close to the perimeter for fear of getting shot by a sniper. Walking around base camp with several other men, they'd refuse to take the lead or bring up the rear. They ate with their backs to the wall so they could keep an eye on everything. Some wore their flak vests every day while in base camp; others had been known to live and sleep inside a bunker during their last thirty days. The list went on and on.

One short-timer told me, "I'm so short and bold that I can look a fire ant in the eye and still kick his ass!"

No one wanted to hang around short-timers, especially FNGs (fucking new guys) who had twelve months' service ahead of them.

It was tough enough for veterans to have to listen to short-timer bullshit. I hoped I wouldn't develop any superstitions when I had only thirty days left to serve in Vietnam—I believed that if it was my time to meet my Maker, nothing on earth was going to save me.

I also knew this to be true: somehow, I had to find a way to see Clipper and my fellow scout-dog handlers before I left Vietnam.

Chapter Nineteen

RED AND THE CONVOY

On January 31, 1968, the Chinese Lunar New Year, the North Vietnamese Army launched an all-out assault on Saigon's military district, the U.S. embassy, and almost every military fire base throughout South Vietnam, including Cu Chi, Tay Ninh, and Dau Tieng. History books would call this massive attack "the Tet Offensive." A cease-fire was in place at the time, and the enemy violated it by attacking, thinking they could win a major victory in the process. With my March departure approaching, the Tet Offensive couldn't have come at a worse time.

Fucking Charlie! I thought. *Why can't he wait until after March to do this, when I'm safe at home?*

Early on the first morning of the Tet Offensive, I heard mortar rounds and rockets exploding outside not far from my hooch, which was deep inside the perimeter. I jumped out of my bunk, grabbed my M-16 and a bandoleer of magazines, and headed for the nearest bunker. I'd never heard so many detonations all around the area. Enemy B-40 rockets whistled through the air past my bunker. I began to realize that this was shaping up to be much more intense than the mortar attack on our kennel back in November. The only thing any of us could do was stay inside and look for any VC who might breach the base camp's defensive perimeter.

Minutes went by, and all I heard was explosion after explosion outside the bunker. From what we could see through the portholes, the sandbags stacked around the bunker were absorbing shrapnel, as were our hooches. At one point, a huge blast rocked the walls, shaking dust from the sandbags around the bunker. My ears rang from the sounds of earth-shaking impacts.

Having no radio inside the bunker, we couldn't contact anyone to get a status report. Machine guns and artillery fired in the distance. It was clear that the perimeter must be under heavy attack. Several men in the bunker were scared shitless, sitting on the dirt floor, curled up against the walls, and covering their bare heads with their hands. I guessed that they'd never experienced the war so close to them. They looked and acted like REMFs and FNGs; I was sure that the only ones more frightened were the helpless patients in the base-camp hospital.

A nearby ammunition dump took a direct hit, and there was no way to put out the fire. The several ammunition caches strategically located throughout the base camp were definitely on Charlie's list of critical targets. So were the reinforced bunkers that maintained the strategic and tactical communication systems. Charlie would have a hard time taking out those targets without a ground assault. As each wooden crate of ammunition, rockets, artillery, and grenades exploded, it set off another crate, until the entire stockpile of munitions was destroyed.

The ammunition dump finally burned out, but there was still sporadic small-arms fire in the distance. It was late in the afternoon before I came out of the bunker to check the damage to my hooch. None of the nearby hooches had been destroyed by shrapnel, and the damage inside mine appeared minimal. My personal items were unharmed. Through all this, I hadn't fired one round from my M-16.

Using howitzers, an artillery battery launched flares into the air, lighting up the perimeter, allowing the men in the bunkers to see their targets better, and dissuading Charlie from attempting a sneak attack. The sky was brightly lit as the parachuted flares slowly descended.

That next morning, the base camp buzzed with activity; I reported to work as usual. The PX and surrounding buildings had sustained only minor damage.

A few days after that all-out attack, SGM Kelly summoned me. He told me that General William Westmoreland, commanding general of the military forces in Vietnam, was scheduled to give a speech that was to be broadcast over the armed forces radio to the troops stationed throughout South Vietnam.

General Westmoreland's long speech was motivational. He reported that the Tet Offensive, with an estimated 70,000 enemy troops involved in the attacks, had been a major military defeat for the Vietcong and the North Vietnamese Army. They'd been repelled overwhelmingly, the American embassy had been secured, and law and order restored on the streets of Saigon. Of all the military base camps throughout Vietnam that had been attacked simultaneously, none was in enemy hands.

American casualties were reported as minimal, but the VC and NVA had suffered thousands of dead and wounded. General Westmoreland called the Tet Offensive a great victory for South Vietnam and the American and allied forces. I waited for the general to say that all orders to leave Vietnam for the States were canceled, but he didn't, and I breathed a sigh of relief.

I could think only of Dau Tieng and wondered how Clipper and the rest of my pals had dealt with the attack. Getting news from Dau Tieng was especially difficult then, so I went to SGM Kelly and pleaded with him to find out what was going on there. He put me in contact with a SGM buddy of his who worked at the division tactical operations center. The SGM took me to the communications shed—a heavily fortified and heavily guarded bunker with a bunch of antennas sticking out of it. The shed buzzed with radio communication. The SGM got on a radio and patched me through to the 44th Scout Dog Platoon's land line.

Through some static, I could hear Sergeant Dan Barnett on the other end. He told me that everything was okay; to my relief, there'd been no dog or handler casualties. The VC had hit Dau Tieng hard but hadn't been aware that most of the infantry units were in base camp at the time. The Americans had easily driven back Charlie's attempt to penetrate the wire surrounding the perimeter. Sergeant Barnett told me that the original dog handlers and Lieutenant Fenner had already rotated back to the States, but that he had extended his tour of duty for six more months.

After asking how my knee was doing, Sergeant Barnett explained that most of the dog teams were out on patrol, supporting Tet counteroffensive operations. He told me that Clipper had not been assigned to another handler, and assured me that Clipper was my dog until I left Vietnam. Sergeant Barnett asked if I was going to get a chance to come back to Dau Tieng before rotating to the States in March. I told him I was trying all the time and not to give up on my return. Then the transmission ended.

In mid-February 1968, the 25th Infantry Division was continuing the Tet counteroffensive throughout Cu Chi's surrounding areas of operation.

I was ordered to report to Sergeant Major Kelly. I had a feeling I was in for a butt-reaming, but didn't know why. Instead, the SGM told me that with all the hell going on with the Tet Offensive, he needed experienced combat infantrymen to ride shotgun on his re-supply convoy to Saigon. He'd requested support from the infantry units, but they told him to go blow—they couldn't spare infantry troops for that kind of task. They advised him to use REMFs for the job: cooks, mechanics, supply clerks, and administrative personnel. Considering the circumstances, SGM Kelly was uncomfortable with that idea. In the past, he'd always had veteran infantry support. Several infantry combat veterans were already assigned to PX jobs, but they were all wounded short-timers, so the job landed in my lap.

SGM Kelly said that he needed a good sergeant like me, with combat experience, to honcho an empty convoy into Saigon and Bien Hoa and pick up badly needed supplies for the division. If I accepted the mission, SMG Kelly promised that when I returned, he'd make sure I got a chopper ride to Dau Tieng to see my dog.

Those were exactly the words I wanted to hear. With no hesitation, I volunteered. To be able to see my dog again outweighed the risks of the mission. Despite my previous experience with army promises, I had a good feeling that the SGM wouldn't fuck me over on this deal.

What I missed most about Clipper was his loving companionship and how he got excited when I called his name. I wanted to roll around in the dirt with him one more time. I longed to have him sit next to me and lean against my leg when he was tired. I missed the simple pleasure of having Clipper at my side. It was torment not to be able to see my dog.

After I accepted the mission, SGM Kelly leaned close to my face, looked me in the eye, smiled, and told me that I'd separated myself from all the boys in Vietnam. I figured that was a compliment from a man who'd earned three Combat Infantry Badges, but to me, the incentive simply outweighed the risk of a trip outside base camp. Plus, I didn't have to walk, so I wouldn't be violating my medical profile restrictions. I decided I'd better not tell my doctor about the mission, or he might find a way to keep me from going and ruin my chances to see Clipper and my other K-9 brothers.

My orders were to leave at first light. The convoy would be fueled, engines running, and waiting at the staging area on the roadside near the PX. That night, some new pals I'd met —Freddie and a soldier I'll call "Red"— paid me a visit. Both worked for SGM Kelly in the PX. Red was supposed to ride shotgun in one of the convoy trucks. I soon learned that Red also had another reason for wanting to go to Saigon; he said he needed to see his Vietnamese dentist about a tooth problem.

I liked both Red and Freddie, but Freddie wasn't scheduled to ride shotgun, so he stayed behind. The trip was scheduled as a three-day mission: one day to get there, one to load up, and one to get back. After a long bullshit session with those guys, I turned in for the evening.

The next morning, I rode in a jeep at the head of the convoy, which was escorted by military police riding in several other equipped jeeps. If we needed them, gunships, artillery, and infantry troops were within immediate communication and striking distance of our route to Saigon. My jeep came with a driver, a machine gunner, a mounted M-60 machine gun, several thousand rounds of ammunition, two radios, and a radio operator who could communicate with SGM Kelly and the air-strike support. I was responsible for coordinating all tactical decisions with the experienced convoy-escort MPs who were in charge. I felt more comfortable knowing I'd be working with military police who had experience working outside the perimeter of a base camp. I considered the MPs highly respectable and capable infantrymen.

SGM Kelly issued me the Signal Operating Instructions (SOI) — a tiny booklet with the word "Secret" printed on each page. The SOI, which contained all the call signs and frequencies for getting military support, was attached to a chain that I wore inside my shirt. I was responsible for this highly classified military document; if in imminent danger of capture by the enemy, destroying that book was my highest priority.

The daylong convoy trip to Saigon put us on a road that went through the middle of the fiercest fighting in our war zone. Cu Chi was near Hobo Woods, where the Vietcong were heavily concentrated. Charlie fought like hell to keep Hobo Woods to himself, and many Americans and some of the 38th scout-dog teams had lost their lives in that dreadful place.

Highway 13 from Cu Chi to Saigon was damaged but clear for our seventy-mile trip. Mechanized and armored tank squadrons and infantrymen on foot had secured the most dangerous sections of the road, which was a vital link in our supply lines and had to stay open during all daylight hours. For obvious reasons, during the Tet counteroffensives, no convoys traveled outside base camp at night.

By the time the convoy of empty flatbed trailers attached to diesel tractors was assembled and prepared to roll, I was ready to go. I didn't have enough time to check over everything carefully, but what the hell—I'd learned to live without ever having enough time. I relied on the drivers to ensure that their vehicles were serviceable enough to make the three-day journey.

I put my M-16 and backpack behind my seat. Each truck had one man riding shotgun inside the canvas-covered cab. One MP jeep rode ahead of me; another brought up the rear. I was assigned the second vehicle behind the lead jeep. I walked down the line of ten flatbed trucks, their smokestacks filling the air with the stink of diesel exhaust. Not knowing what kind of road conditions we'd encounter, we planned to keep the column moving as close together as possible.

Everyone was ready. I hopped into my jeep and waited for the MPs to signal "Start rolling." The machine gunner handed me a set of goggles, saying I'd need them to keep the dust out of my eyes. Red rode shotgun in the first truck behind my jeep. My radio squawked with call signs for radio checks. After we were assured that everyone was on the net and the right frequency, it was time to go. One by one, we rolled out of the gate and into no-man's land.

I remembered that President Roosevelt said, "The only thing we have to fear is fear itself." Well, I was definitely feeling fear at first, but my stomach soon settled down as the slow and bumpy ride continued.

Several miles into that trip, I saw a few burned-out military trucks tipped over on the edge of the road, apparently pushed there by bulldozers. Helicopters followed overhead, and infantry troops were positioned alongside near the tree lines at various points along the route.

It looked as if the Americans had broken Charlie's back when he'd tried his maximum offensive a few weeks earlier. I figured that he was probably licking his wounds and regrouping, so we had timed this run well. So far, I felt okay about the mission.

Several hours and twenty miles into the trip, the convoy hadn't been attacked; not a shot had been fired and all the trucks were accounted for. We were going at a snail's pace, but our progress was steady, and it looked like we'd get into Saigon before dark.

Every bridge we needed to cross had been damaged, but the engineers had made paths around them that we could use. During some stretches, thick jungle closed in on the road. If Charlie was going to hit us, that was where we'd be most vulnerable. Maybe Charlie had already seen us and decided not to attack, thinking the convoy was empty—or maybe that was our lucky day.

Sections of the road were dry and dusty. The goggles came in handy as dust caked in the sweat on my face. It was a long, hot ride, but I still had plenty of water and snack foods. The radios stayed on but remained silent, except for giving us an occasional situation report.

At last, the convoy approached the outskirts of Saigon and headed for a secure staging area within the Cholon District. There, we were scheduled to park in a fenced and guarded compound and spend the night in a hotel across the street. The next morning the convoy was to roll from the city of Saigon and into the Ben Hoa beer-and-soda yard.

As we entered Saigon's Cholon District, I could see that some fighting had occurred there. Direct hits from tank and artillery rounds had made gaping holes in some of the buildings, and war debris littered the roadsides. Several civilian cars were burned and overturned on the shoulders of the road. Martial law had been declared, roadblocks were set up all over the place, and very few pedestrians walked the streets. The MP jeep ahead of mine was doing a good job of navigating the area. So far, we'd kept all the trucks intact and hadn't had to stop along the way for emergencies or maintenance problems.

At about six o'clock in the evening, the convoy reached a large parking lot surrounded by a ten-foot-high triple barbed-wire fence. South Vietnamese Army troops, wearing burgundy berets, opened the gate to let us through. All of the trucks and jeeps fit inside with plenty of room to spare. The South Vietnamese military would handle vehicle security, and our hotel expenses had already been paid. We had only to check in and get our rooms for the night.

Descending from our vehicles, carrying our gear and weapons, we headed for the hotel. I wanted one of those burgundy berets for a souvenir, so I approached a Vietnamese guard and offered a trade. He couldn't speak English, so I took a dollar out of my pocket and used hand gestures to bargain for his head gear. The soldier smiled, took the buck, and gave me his beret. I didn't realize it would be so easy; I'd been prepared to give more if he demanded it.

I stashed the beret, and Red and I walked to the hotel, carrying our M-16s, bandoleers of fully loaded magazines, lightly packed backpacks, and .45 caliber pistols. The trucks and jeeps were now under the full protection of the South Vietnamese Army.

The hotel's Mama San greeted us and assigned us to rooms. She recognized my stripes and said she had a special room for me. The hotel was three stories high and not fancy by any stretch of the imagination. My room had only a single metal frame bed and a beat-up dresser with a small dirty mirror. The window afforded me a view of our vehicles parked across the street. I noticed that a few Vietnamese troops were guarding them and patrolling the street. Curfew was in effect for everyone but the military.

Later that night, Red came to my room to talk. I knew from previous conversations that he had attended an American linguistic school somewhere in the States. Red spoke excellent Vietnamese and had been an interpreter for military intelligence in Saigon before being transferred to Cu Chi several months earlier. Red had less than thirty days before he'd be going home. When he became a short-timer, he'd talked his way into a rear-area job in the PX where we had met.

Red told me that he'd broken a tooth two days earlier and that it was infected. When he heard about the convoy run to Saigon, he volunteered to ride shotgun because he refused to see an army doctor or dentist. Instead, he insisted on seeing his Vietnamese dentist in Saigon. Because he could speak fluent Vietnamese and had been well established in Saigon before coming to Cu Chi, he had a lot of friends there. He didn't have approval from any military medical personnel to have a dentist in Saigon, but I could see that Red intended to pursue his dental preference in Saigon and that he was kind of asking my permission to go.

Red told me so many stories about Saigon that I trusted him to know how to get around the city, but I felt the need to remind him that we were restricted to the hotel for the night, that the city was under martial law and he was out of his fucking mind to leave the safety of the guarded hotel.

Red argued that there was nothing to worry about. His dentist worked only a few blocks from the hotel. He said he had to at least get some painkillers, and would be back before I could miss him. With those words, Red left my room and headed downstairs to the lobby. After he left, I paced back and forth for a few seconds. If he left that crappy little hotel and something happened, it would be my ass in trouble. *Aw, shit,* I thought. *I can't let him go by himself and I can't keep his fucking bonehead ass here, either.*

I grabbed my rifle and bandoleer of ammunition and followed after Red. I caught him on the street as he was about to climb into a black, covered, horse-drawn rickshaw.

"Red!" I yelled.

Red turned around, grinned ear to ear, waved, and told me to hurry. I caught up with him and climbed into the rickshaw, which was driven by a smiling Vietnamese. Red gave him directions to the dentist's office in Vietnamese. I looked at him, shook my head, and told him that I couldn't let him go alone, so off we went like a couple of war-zone tourists.

The driver headed toward the first Vietnamese-manned road-block where soldiers holding machine guns stood behind waist-high sandbag walls. When we arrived at the roadblock, Red spoke Vietnamese to the guards, who immediately smiled and let us through.

"Shit, Red, your dentist isn't down the street from our hotel, is he? Do you know where the fuck you're going?"

Sure, I do. We're almost there," he assured me with a big grin.

We turned down some side streets with no pedestrians on them and eventually pulled over in front of a row of small buildings. Several Vietnamese citizens were milling around the buildings, and I noticed that there were no military personnel in sight.

I checked my watch and saw that it was a little after seven. I advised Red that if his dentist wasn't there, we were heading back to the hotel before it got dark. Red said nothing as he stepped out of the rickshaw, walked to the entrance of a building, and knocked on the door. A Vietnamese woman opened it, smiled, and greeted Red as if he were a long-lost friend. They talked in Vietnamese and laughed when Red showed her his tooth.

I was getting nervous sitting outside in the rickshaw. Red finally came back to tell me that his doctor had left, but would be back at six a.m. He also said that we had plenty of time for him to get his tooth fixed and get back to lead the convoy by nine in the morning.

"Trust me," Red said. "The beer-and-soda yard at Ben Hoa is less than an hour away."

Why did I let myself get into this shit? I asked myself.

Red told me that the building was a hotel and a dental office. After I climbed out of the rickshaw, the well-dressed Vietnamese woman, who spoke broken English, greeted me with a smile as she bowed and motioned me inside. I didn't smile back, but gave Red a dirty look. I told him to call our hotel and let a member of our convoy team know where we were and when we'd be back. Using the Vietnamese woman's phone, Red made the call and spoke in Vietnamese to someone back at our hotel.

Then, he looked at me and said, "John, we're set. They expect us back by nine o'clock tomorrow morning. Hey, buddy, I'll take care of you. Isn't this a nicer place to sleep than that rat hole we were in?"

"Uh-huh, this is great!" I agreed, "but we're the only two people here, and there's safety in numbers — especially Americans numbers."

Red was right about one thing, though: the inside of this hotel was upscale compared to where we'd been assigned to spend the night. Aside from the Vietnamese woman and her family, no one else was staying there, which I thought a little too strange. Also, the dentist's office was locked. I wondered how Red would get the painkillers he said he needed, unless he planned to break in.

The Vietnamese woman asked if we were hungry. She said that the recent fighting in the streets had chased away her customers. She gave us bowls of steamed rice with chunks of meat mixed in.

"Hey, Red, this is pretty good," I said. "It's the first hot meal we've had. The meat tastes a little like beef. Ask her what kind it is."

Red looked at me and said, "It's dog! That's a delicacy in the Vietnamese culture."

I spat out a mouthful on the table. "Man, I can't eat this shit if it's dog. Why the hell didn't you tell me that before? You know I'm a dog handler, you asshole! What the fuck is wrong with you?"

Red smiled and said, "I think it tastes great!"

After he finished eating, Red decided that he wanted to visit a female friend he used to stay with when he lived in Saigon. He told me that she was a beautiful Vietnamese/French girl with round eyes. I immediately opposed the idea of his leaving the hotel, especially to see a woman. Red was really pushing his luck with me, but before I knew it, a small black car pulled up in front of the hotel. Red already had a plan, which he was now putting into action. He told me to bring my weapons and get into the car for a short ride. We were going to pick up the woman and we'd be back in a half hour.

I wasn't thrilled about a car ride in the dark of night. Red, on the other hand, was totally relaxed, as if there were no martial law or war going on in Vietnam. When he walked to the car, I couldn't see staying behind by myself, so I followed. Splitting up now would be an even worse idea.

I didn't like it that Red had put me in a totally reactive mode since our arrival in Saigon. His utter disregard for all the danger signs around us was driving me nuts. Although we hadn't heard any shooting since we'd entered Saigon, we had no way of knowing what could happen.

We sat in the back seat of the little black car, Red spoke Vietnamese to the driver, and off we went. Heading down a dark, quiet side road several blocks from the hotel/dental office, the driver turned left onto another side street, which looked more like an alleyway. Red looked nervous and spoke to the driver in a louder than normal tone. The driver turned his lights off and kept driving slowly down the alleyway while he talked with Red. Up ahead, several black-clothed figures suddenly appeared out of the darkness and slowly approached the front of the car. It looked like they were armed with rifles. Quickly jumping into the front seat, Red pointed his .45 at the driver's temple and spoke fast in Vietnamese. The car screeched to a sudden stop.

The armed men continued moving in our direction, their weapons at the ready. From a distance, I assumed that they weren't friendly, so I chambered a round into my M-16 and quickly rolled down the window. I stuck the barrel out and awkwardly pointed it in the direction of the approaching figures. Red screamed in Vietnamese at the driver. All of a sudden, Red's pistol went off. I flinched and ducked, ears ringing like crazy. I looked up to see what had happened; Red hadn't hit the driver, but he'd blown out the driver's side window.

The driver slammed the car into reverse and turned the headlights back on. The men started shooting at us. Several bullets hit the front of the car. I returned fire with my M-16. The car's jerking made my aim terrible, but I squeezed off round after round.

Finally, we backed out of the alleyway. The car screeched on the pavement as the driver spun the wheel to straighten it out. Red was still pointing the barrel of the .45 at the driver's temple. We sped down the street and made a sharp turn onto a different road. I didn't know where the hell we were. My heart thumped hard, but I was relieved that we weren't being chased or fired at anymore.

Red's face dripped sweat and his eyes bulged out of their sockets—he looked like an enraged madman. He kept talking to the driver, who answered him in a terrified voice. To my surprise, the man suddenly stopped the car. I was scared. All I could think was *We need to get the hell out of here!* The city of Saigon at night was an unfamiliar battleground. We had to make it back to our hotel as soon as possible. The Tet Offensive had brought the war to every nook and cranny throughout Vietnam; we weren't safe anywhere.

Red shouted, "John! Get the fuck out!"

I didn't hesitate or ask questions. Once I was outside the car, I nervously looked up and down the street, but saw only darkness. Red scooted over to the door. I pointed my weapon through the windshield at the driver, who froze, both hands on the steering wheel. Red frantically shouted at him in Vietnamese, then came flying out the door and told me to follow him and not look back.

My heart was in my throat as I ran after Red. He turned the corner and ran across the street. To my amazement, we were only a block from the dental office/hotel. The streets were bare and totally dark. Red suddenly stopped, turned, and banged a clenched fist on the hotel door, which opened to let us inside. By that time, we were completely out of breath.

The nicely dressed Vietnamese woman who managed the hotel looked bewildered as she and Red chattered in Vietnamese. After they finished, Red told me the woman wouldn't be letting anyone else into the hotel that evening. Of course, she'd said more than that. Red wasn't telling me the whole story, but it was late and I was upset and not interested in asking questions.

One thing was certain: my right knee was killing me. I hoped it wouldn't swell up after I rested it. I didn't want to have to see the doctor with my knee swollen and have him tell me that he was putting a cast on it, or worse, scheduling me for surgery.

We locked the door, barricaded ourselves inside the room, and took turns pulling guard duty until the sun came up. Throughout the night, I heard vehicle noises and voices on the street outside. I was sweating that some enemy might have spotted us and knew where we were. I was scared to death and felt trapped.

Neither Red nor I caught a wink of sleep that night. At first light, I heard a man's voice downstairs. Red quickly sat up and smiled. He told me the male voice was his Vietnamese dentist. I looked at my watch and saw that the dentist had arrived promptly at six o'clock. Red moved the barricade, unlocked the door, and went downstairs. I was still stunned from the events of the night before. I stayed behind the dresser, my M-16 at the ready. From downstairs, I heard laughter and friendly voices. I cautiously made my way to the bottom of the carpeted stairwell. Red was already sitting in the dentist's chair, getting his tooth examined.

When the dentist finished, Red got up from the chair, pocketed some pills, and paid the man. All I wanted to do was to get the fuck out of there and safely back to the hotel where we were supposed to be staying. As we left, I saw few people on the street outside. Red flagged a rickshaw and we headed to our hotel. As we approached the first manned roadblock, I got really nervous. Red instructed me not to say anything, but to look tough and hold my weapon where the Vietnamese could see it. I did as instructed and, to my surprise, the soldiers lifted the arm of the roadblock and let us pass. We crossed three more roadblocks without incident before reaching the hotel.

We made it back before nine in the morning. Neither of us talked about our near-fatal encounter with the enemy. Red disappeared somewhere. I grabbed a can of spaghetti and meatballs from my pack and gulped it down as if I hadn't eaten in a week. After eating, I washed my face and shaved. Through the window, I saw our troops milling around the parked trucks inside the fenced yard. Grabbing my gear, I walked out of the hotel to my jeep. Red was already sitting inside the first truck behind my jeep. He waved at me with that grin his face.

I was fuming, thinking *How can that fucker smile at me after putting us through all that shit? The bastard's got a death wish, and I can only blame myself for becoming part of it.*

I walked past each vehicle and checked inside for a head count of drivers and shotguns. Every man was accounted for and ready to go. After a radio check, the MP jeep slowly led us into the street. The convoy wound its way through the narrow streets of Saigon and headed to the Ben Hoa beer-and-soda yard.

I noticed that Red had been right about one thing: Bien Hoa was only an hour from the hotel. And what an incredible sight it was to see so many stacked pallets of beer and soda. Vietnamese civilians operated forklifts, lifting pallet after pallet onto the flatbed trucks. They tied down the pallets with hand-held metal banding machines, while the Americans watched and directed the loading procedure. It took about five hours to fully load the trucks. Then the convoy maneuvered back through the streets of Saigon without incident, pulling into the staging area at Cholon before six o'clock that evening. We stayed at the same hotel across the street for our last night in Saigon. The second leg of the trip was over.

Back in the same hotel room, Red and I had a long talk over a few beers. We discussed the details of the incident that we'd barely survived the night before. According to Red, the Vietnamese driver had been a North Vietnamese Officer posing as a cab driver, and was trained to capture unsuspecting Americans. A serious look on his face, Red blurted out, "If it wasn't for my background in military intelligence and the fact that I speak Vietnamese, we'd both be prisoners of war right now."

I quickly responded in anger, "You're full of shit! You almost got us both captured or killed."

I wasn't too happy with myself, because I could have prevented the whole situation. I'd made two bad decisions: first, I let Red leave the hotel; second, I foolishly went with him. How stupid could you get to take such risks with only one lousy month left to serve in Vietnam!

I told Red that we were both out of our fucking minds and that I wanted to forget about the entire episode. Red didn't say another word. The next morning, we fired up the engines and headed down the road for the long trip back. I could hardly wait for the mission to end.

When we arrived back at Cu Chi, SGM Kelly was standing on the roadside, watching his convoy pull up to the PX. After I reported to him that all the men and trucks were accounted for and all the goods were intact, SGM smiled at me for the first time since we'd met.

"Job well done, Buck Sergeant! Give me that SOI and I'll have those trucks unloaded. Did anything happen on that mission that I should know about?"

"No, Sergeant Major, nothing but the usual bullshit!"

I intended to remind Sergeant Major Kelly of his promise to let me go see Clipper in Dau Tieng, and after that trip, my plan was to never leave base camp until it was time for me to catch a ride on a commercial jetliner back to the United States.

Chapter Twenty

GOODBYE CLIPPER

SGM Kelly kept his end of the bargain and personally coordinated space for me on a re-supply chopper to Dau Tieng. I packed a bunch of goodies for my dog-handler friends.

When I arrived, I had about a ten-minute walk from the airstrip to the K-9 compound. Thinking of seeing Clipper again, the painful limp in my step seemed unimportant. I first stopped at the kennel and met Dan Scott, who was standing at the entrance, shirtless as usual. We shook hands and I gave him a bear hug. It had been a long time since we'd seen each other, and Dan knew I couldn't leave Vietnam without coming back to say goodbye.

It felt like Christmas when I handed him a brand-new Zippo lighter with a pack of flints and a can of lighter fluid. I showed him a copy of my orders to leave Vietnam, and he was really excited for me. He asked how my gimpy knee was healing and what Cu Chi was like. After a short bullshit session, I decided to spend some time with Clipper. Dan and I planned to party in the K-9 Klub later that night.

I headed to the kennel, but Clipper wasn't in his run. I should have known that he'd be out under the shade of his tree during the day. As I walked through the kennel, it was great to see and smell all the other scout dogs and hear them bark like mad for attention.

I walked to the rubber trees to find Clipper. In the distance, I spotted him lying on the ground and taking a nap. I quietly whispered his name. Clipper's ears popped up and he canted his head. Looking in my direction, he rose to his feet, stretched out his legs and back, and turned his head slightly to the left and then to the right. I could tell that he was trying to figure out who had called him.

I walked closer without saying another word. When Clipper recognized me, he went crazy. He charged toward me until his leash fully extended and stopped him in his tracks. I rushed over to him and he jumped up and put his forepaws on my chest. Wagging his tail joyfully, he licked all over my face and, in his immense excitement, he piddled on my leg and boots. It felt great being with him again. I hugged his soft furry body tightly.

What an exhilarating moment! Words can't begin to describe the emotions that poured out of me. That dog was my best friend and we were together again at last.

I clipped Clipper's choke chain to the leather leash and took him for a walk to calm us both down. I gave Clipper no commands. He moved automatically to my left side and walked at a slow pace, constantly staring up at me with love and happiness in his eyes. He remembered exactly what my walking pace was and didn't once pull ahead or cross my path. After a while, I slowly worked him through some basic commands and scouting positions. It was as if we'd never been separated.

How am I ever going to leave this dog after seeing him again? I wondered. Clipper thought I was back to stay; he couldn't know that I'd only be visiting with him for a short time. We spent the entire afternoon together under the shade of the rubber trees.

Later that night, I joined the rest of the scout-dog handlers in the K-9 Klub. Some new guys had arrived since my departure. It was March 1968, and all my old friends from the original 44th had returned to the States. Their twelve-month tours had passed and I never got the chance to say goodbye. Dan Scott was also due for rotation in March, so he was now a short-timer like me. After we said our good-byes, I grabbed an empty cot in my old hooch for one last night's sleep in Dau Tieng.

I got up early the next morning to say my last goodbye to a dog who didn't deserve the fate in store for him. I walked into the kennel to see Clipper. When I opened his run, he ran off to wait under his tree until I caught up and hooked his collar to the twenty-five-foot leash. I filled his water bucket with fresh water and cleaned his run. Then, I sat with him under the shade of his tree and stroked his head and back, recalling all the combat missions we'd teamed up on, the many times Clipper had alerted me to danger, and the countless lives he'd saved. It was hard to believe I was going to have to leave him behind. He was a real American hero, but he'd never get to go home and receive the hero's welcome he deserved.

Obviously unable to speak for himself, Clipper was at the mercy of people who had recruited him for military life, teamed him with a handler, trained him for war, and shipped him off to Vietnam. As Clipper's handler, I felt I was the only one who had truly developed an allegiance to him. Now, because our government had classified Clipper as expendable equipment, I had to leave him behind. I felt as if I were abandoning a brother who was condemned to the dangerous job of walking point for the rest of the war.

How can my country burden me with this lifelong memory?

Clipper deserved to live the rest of his life in a peaceful environment away from that war. I wanted him to be given the same respect and dignity I expected for myself. He had earned it.

Dogs who served during WWII and Korea were given discharge papers and repatriated with their devoted handlers or original owners after the war. That was not to be for the valiant war dogs of the Vietnam War. For their service, heroism, bravery under fire and, risking their lives to save others, the surviving dogs were given to the South Vietnamese Army or disposed of by other means. They lie buried in war-dog graveyards that are all but forgotten.

Since I'd met him, it had always been my dream to bring Clipper home. He would have made a great pet. Clipper had already served in Vietnam for fifteen months, and I wasn't sure how many more missions he would survive. I feared that Clipper's death would be violent, especially after the Tet Offensive had ignited the war into such a frenzy. I could only hope that when Clipper finally did fall, he'd die quickly and painlessly. As I sat under that tree with him leaning against my leg, I knew that I'd never see him again in this life. The tragedy of it haunted me like a nightmare.

I noticed that the sign I'd placed above Clipper's tree ten months before was still there. War is good business – Invest your dog. That sign disgusted me now. I ripped it down and broke it into tiny pieces.

At last, the time had come for me to let go. I tried to hold back my tears. I didn't know how to say goodbye to my best friend, so I looked into his big brown eyes and gave him one last loving farewell bear hug. Then, I turned and walked away, awash in the sad, bitter truth that Vietnam would become my dog's final resting place.

Clipper stood erect, ears pointed high, like the champion he was. I felt him watching me until, never looking back, I vanished down the dirt road leading away from the 44th Scout Dog Platoon. I knew then that I truly had no more reason to stay in Vietnam, but every reason in the world to keep Clipper alive in my heart for the rest of my life.

Goodbye, Clipper
(Tattoo – 12X3) – March 1968.
(Author collection)

Chapter Twenty-one

LEAVING VIETNAM

In March 1968 I left Cu Chi for Saigon to hop on a commercial flight to the States. My departure couldn't have been scheduled at a worse time: I was fortunate not to have my exit orders rescinded because the Americans were in the middle of a fierce counteroffensive against the North Vietnamese Army near Cu Chi and Tay Ninh Province.

Before I left, Sergeant Major Kelly summoned me to his office. He promised me another stripe if I'd stay six more months. I politely declined his offer, saying, "No fuckin' way!"

I knew it was time for me to leave the war behind, go home to Littleton, Colorado, and have a big party with my family and friends. Two years was enough to spend fighting in Southeast Asia.

I made it out of Cu Chi base camp in the back of a troop truck, part of a heavily armed convoy escorted by tanks and helicopter gunships. The road to Saigon was still littered with burned-out vehicles pushed to the roadside. Along the way, infantry troops were positioned off the road to protect the convoy from attack and keep the road open. Without incident, the convoy reached the city limits of Saigon, where the devastation had reached a new level since my last convoy ride. The Tet counteroffensive operations had more deeply scarred an already beleaguered and battered city.

Saigon remained under martial law. Homeless pedestrians walked the roadways and filled crowded busses. Armed military police and South Vietnamese Army troops barricaded and manned the city's major intersections.

The convoy stopped along the road next to Camp Alpha, the U.S. Army Replacement Center where I'd first entered Vietnam. I climbed out of the truck, grabbed my duffel bag, and handed my M-16 and bandoleer of ammunition to a sergeant who'd been riding shotgun. As I entered the gates of Camp Alpha, I handed a copy of my orders to a soldier who stood at the gate with a clipboard in hand. Each step was bringing me closer to returning to the world outside Vietnam.

I stayed in Camp Alpha for several days to out-process. My name was placed on a manifest, and I was assigned a group number. When I heard my group number called, I reported to a numbered building where we all were strip-searched. The military police looked for and confiscated any pistols, grenades, knives, and other items that wouldn't be allowed onboard a commercial jetliner.

I hadn't tried to bring any of those kinds of souvenirs out of Vietnam. Clipper was all I had wanted to take home with me.

After the search, I boarded a bus to Tan Son Nhut airfield. During the ride, I sat on a bench seat next to the window and thought about my Vietnam experience, Clipper, and the friends I was leaving behind. Before I realized it, the ride ended and I was standing on the runway. Military guards in jeeps surrounded a commercial jetliner. In single file, we walked to the plane, where a military attendant with a manifest checked off our names as we climbed aboard. I found an empty seat next to a window.

When everyone was onboard, the doors closed and the aircraft slowly moved down the runway. As soon as it lifted off, a resounding cheer filled the plane. I settled back into the soft seat and looked out the window, watching the airfield and the city of Saigon grow smaller as the plane climbed. After several minutes, only the South China Sea was visible below.

Our next stop would be San Francisco, where we'd set foot once again on American soil.

Despite the ongoing counteroffensives, the timing and process of getting everyone out of Vietnam had been impeccable. Recent battles must have lit a spark under their butts; they wasted no time getting us out. In a matter of only twenty-four hours I was out of harm's way and leaving Vietnam forever. I only wished they'd apply this same sense of urgency to rescuing our four-legged brothers.

During the long flight, cute, round-eyed American stewardesses smiled as they waited on the passengers. They served coffee, tea, soda, snacks, and hot meals, but no alcohol.

I had a lot of time on that flight to think about going home. I couldn't wait to be part of the American culture I'd left behind two years earlier.

How will the new cars look? Will clothes be different? I'll see a lot of American girls again—will they like me? Who'll be my first date when I get home? Will my friends have changed from how I remember them?

My only fear was that I'd heard some of the new guys who'd recently come to Vietnam say that people back at home were starting to reject the war. I didn't remember reading anything about this in my letters from family and friends. Everyone was always wishing me well and saying how they couldn't wait to see me. I didn't understand how people who hadn't been there could think they knew anything about Vietnam.

I thought about some of the first things I'd do when I returned. I knew I wanted to get my very first brand-new car. I'd heard that the '68 Dodge Charger 440 RT had a 300 horsepower engine and ram-air, and could clock a quarter mile in thirteen seconds. I had to have that car. My plan was to find a date one night, drive up to a lookout point in the Colorado Rockies, and peer down on the city of Denver.

I still had my tiny red address book listing the names and addresses of family and friends with whom I'd corresponded while in Vietnam. I hoped they hadn't moved or changed their phone numbers, because I wanted to call and see them all again. I couldn't wait to live halfway around the world from the sounds of explosions, machine guns, helicopters, fighter jets, armored vehicles, infantry talk, and the permanent stink of fish.

As the wheels touched down at San Francisco International, another chorus of cheering reverberated through the cabin. When the bottoms of my shoes touched the runway pavement, I was so grateful to be home that I bent down and kissed the ground.

Military policemen greeted us and escorted us to several military buses parked on the runway. They took us past U.S. Customs and directly to Oakland Army Base where we were confined to a warehouse that was a holding area for in-processing, reassigning, and discharging U.S. Army personnel. There were no marching bands or welcome-home parades. We were, however, treated to steak dinners in the warehouse mess hall.

I was on American soil at last; that was all that mattered to me. During out-processing, I was paid in American greenbacks. I reached into my pocket and felt a coin. I pulled it out and saw that it was a South Vietnamese silver-plated five-dong coin dated 1968. I decided to hold on to it as a keepsake, a permanent reminder of the year I returned home from Vietnam.

Within eight hours of arriving in Oakland, I was released on furlough. The personnel sergeant told me that I'd soon be receiving a stateside unit of assignment in the mail at my home of record, Littleton, Colorado. And that was it—I was free to leave Oakland Army Base.

Taxis lined up outside the gate to take us wherever we wanted to go. Several of us shared a ride to San Francisco International to continue our journeys home. When the cab pulled up in front of the airport, I hooked up with another infantryman, George Johnson, whom I'd met during out-processing at Camp Alpha. He was going home to New York.

George and I had a hard time believing that in just a day and a half we were out of the jungles of Vietnam and on the streets of San Francisco. We agreed that things were happening a little too fast, so we decided not to book a flight home right away. We wanted to go into San Francisco, clear our heads a bit, and get used to American soil, so we put our baggage in lockers inside the terminal and took off for downtown.

On this day, March 15, 1968, we proudly walked the sidewalks of downtown San Francisco, wearing our Class-A khaki uniforms,

Combat Infantry Badges, and Vietnam combat ribbons. The next day would be my twenty-first birthday. It felt so peaceful in downtown San Francisco.

George wanted to buy us our first beers in America, so we stopped at a downtown bar and sat down to enjoy the scenery. I began to notice that we were the only soldiers in the place. It wasn't crowded and the bartender was friendly to us. I ordered a bottle of Coors, but they didn't have any. I figured I'd have to wait till I got to Denver to get a cold Coors. We ended up ordering bottles of Pabst Blue Ribbon.

Suddenly, our uniforms became targets for some angry Americans who were protesting against the Vietnam War. One of the patrons blurted out, "Hey, baby killers, did you enjoy burning down villages?"

I was outraged by the man's taunt. I gnashed my teeth, holding back my anger. Having gone through what I had in Vietnam taught me how to control my emotions in a heated situation. I realized that getting into a bar fight would mean police and jail time.

I felt perplexed because I didn't understand why this man was so fired up against soldiers who had served in Vietnam. I wondered if the people who'd been writing to me while I was over there had held back the truth about how they really felt about the war. I started to feel apprehensive about other unexpected attitudes that might be waiting for me when I arrived home.

George raised up from his barstool, but I put my hand on his shoulder and told him that fighting this guy wouldn't be worth the consequences. George agreed and we ignored the remarks. A few other men sitting in the joint started to let us know that we weren't welcome there. This surprised and confused us; we didn't know what to think or say. The longer we stayed in the bar, the more uncomfortable and upset we became. We decided to keep our mouths shut and just get the hell of there. George paid the tab and we walked out without finishing our beers.

George suggested it would be a good idea to get out of our damn uniforms. We found the closest men's clothing store, bought civilian clothes and shoes, changed in the dressing room, and walked away carrying our uniforms in paper bags. Only our military haircuts still distinguished us from the rest of the American male public. God, how we wished we had long hair so we could blend into the crowd. I felt totally depressed and self-conscious, trying not to appear so military. My dream of coming home and feeling welcome had been shattered in just one afternoon.

I'd be back in Colorado on furlough for forty-five days. The plans and dreams I'd had flying home on the plane were already crumbling. I no longer felt enthusiastic about buying a car, having a big party, or hanging out in public places with my friends. I'd spent almost two years in military service and now, back in the States, I felt like an outsider. Soon the army would send me orders to report to another military duty station. It surprised me to realize that, given the attitudes of my fellow citizens, I now felt safer and more comfortable among military people like me, who understood one another, than around civilians.

After getting home, I wanted to believe at first that the incident in San Francisco had been an isolated one, but it wasn't. I soon learned that many people my age around the country were protesting the Vietnam War. From this point on, even in my hometown, I fought a war of words with people who had no idea what we'd been through over there. Occasionally, I got pushed around and wound up in a fistfight. The TV news covered the war every day. Protesters were everywhere, flower-power was in, draft-dodging was acceptable, and "Hell, no, we won't go!" was the chant of the day.

After the initial shock of homecoming, I worked hard to re-acclimate myself to the American way of life and to appreciate the fact that we all had freedom of speech. Eventually, I overcame my fear of having some protester bust my head open.

I endured many nightmares about my war experiences and often awoke up from them unable to go back to sleep. I'd stay up, staring into the darkness of my room, worried about my inability to adjust to a normal life. The emotions I was confronting at home reminded me of the enemy I'd faced so many times in the Vietnam jungles.

The tables had turned in a direction I hadn't expected. I felt that the people who I thought were supporting me while I was fighting in Vietnam now saw me as their enemy. In my own backyard, I was fighting a miniature Vietnam conflict.

It'll be a cold day in hell, I thought, *before I let anyone drive me out of my country or deprive me of the freedom I bled for and will continue to defend until the day I breathe no more.*

Stormy

U.S. MARINE CORPS
VIETNAM SCOUT DOG

Ron Aiello, U.S. Marine Corps, Vietnam veteran scout-dog handler, served in South Vietnam from 1966–1967. He was stationed in an area just south of the demilitarized zone (DMZ) that separated North Vietnam from South Vietnam. Aiello was discharged from the Marine Corps in July 1968, raised a family, and became a very successful businessman.

In the year 2000, Ron founded the U.S. War Dogs Association, Inc. He and a team of other veteran war-dog handlers and supporting members raised public funds to place a War Dog Memorial, sculptured in bronze, on the grounds of the New Jersey Vietnam Veterans Memorial & Education Center in Holmdel, New Jersey.

Ron is also credited with leading the way in helping Sergeant First Class Russell Joyce, U.S. Army Special Forces, get Fluffy (Iraqi German shepherd) out of Iraq and into the United States for adoption by Sergeant Joyce and his family in North Carolina.

After joining the Marine Corps, Aiello teamed up with Stormy, a friendly young female German shepherd scout dog, in December 1966. After graduating from a twelve-week scout-dog training school at Fort Benning, Georgia, the pair shipped off to South Vietnam aboard a military C-130 cargo plane along with several other marine scout-dog teams.

While serving with the U.S. Marines in South Vietnam, Ron and Stormy worked a number of search-and-destroy patrols, day and night, during their thirteen-month tour together. There are many combat missions Ron says he'd rather forget, but one mission sticks in his head in vivid detail, like it happened yesterday.

U.S. Marine Scout Dog, Stormy, and her loving handler, Ron Aiello – 1967. (Photo courtesy of Ron Aiello)

Ron and Stormy had just returned to base camp for a well-earned rest from a daylight patrol not far from their base camp. After a short rest, Ron was ordered to report to the company commander for a new mission briefing. He was to fly out of camp within the hour to join a sister company of a marine battalion that desperately needed another scout-dog team to assist them in flushing out pockets of enemy resistance in a remote jungle area.

Ron hustled to pack his gear, oil his weapon, and check the condition of his ammunition clips. He buckled on Stormy's brown leather body harness and connected a six-foot leather leash to a metal ring fastened on top. They walked to the flight line to a waiting chopper. Just before boarding, Ron strapped a muzzle over Stormy's head and mouth because most chopper pilots and door gunners felt more secure when the marine dogs were muzzled.

After a ten-minute flight, the chopper started its descent into a flat landing zone of short grass surrounded by thick jungle. Just as another chopper dropped its load and lifted off the ground, Ron spotted a scout-dog team running for cover.

When their chopper landed, Ron and Stormy jumped out and quickly headed for cover. Ron reported to the command post for a mission briefing and was joined by his friend, Dave Gradeless, and Dave's scout dog Devil.

Marine intelligence had reported evidence of a group of heavily armed North Vietnamese Army regulars operating in the mission area. The scout-dog teams were assigned to scout for the lead platoon the next morning. That platoon had the job of sweeping through the area in an attempt to flush the enemy into a trap. The remainder of the marines would be working ahead of them in an effort to set up a blocking position to trap and engage any NVA troops flushed in their direction.

At six o'clock the next morning, Ron and Stormy and Dave and Devil joined the lead platoon. Ron attached Stormy's harness and leash and removed her choke chain. Stormy was fresh, frisky, and ready to work as they moved to the point-man position in front of the platoon. Following close behind was his assigned bodyguard.

The platoon commander spread the marines out in a tactical sweeping formation. Dave and Devil were about fifty-yards away on Ron's left flank. Once everyone was in position, Ron made eye contact with Dave and gave him a head nod to signal that he was ready. Dave nodded back and Ron gave Stormy the command to search. Stormy moved out to the end of her leash and the mission was on. Two scout-dog teams separated by fifty-yards led a heavily armed veteran platoon of U.S. Marines on a sweep deep in enemy territory.

After moving ahead about a hundred yards, Stormy stopped and alerted at 11 o'clock. Ron knelt on one knee, weapon at the ready. He scanned the hedgerow in the direction of the alert on his left flank. Dave and Devil had also stopped and were looking in the same direction. Both signaled the marines following closely behind to pass the alert to the platoon commander. Word quickly came back for the scout-dog teams to continue moving into the direction of the alert.

As the teams cautiously moved into the hedgerow, they discovered an old trench with a wall of tall grass behind it. The overgrown trench was thought to be a French defensive position from the time the French army had occupied Vietnam.

The site was in a remote area and well hidden from the probing eyes of the alert marines, but not from the keen senses of well-trained dogs. Checking out the location, they found fresh mashing and cutting of the vegetation, indicating that it had been quickly vacated. Ron's assessment was that the enemy was using this site as an outpost, and, realizing that the dogs had alerted on them and the marines had changed direction and started moving in to investigate, they'd immediately departed. This meant that the enemy knew the marines would be hunting them. Ron hugged and praised Stormy for her alert. Now the question was how large an enemy force was hiding out there.

The marines continued to move carefully in the direction they thought the enemy was traveling. Ron and Dave's bodyguards traveled close behind for additional security, because Ron and Dave had to keep their eyes on their dogs' body language so they wouldn't miss an alert.

After about an hour of slow, cautious movement, Devil gave a strong alert, his head and ears erect and pointing straight ahead. Dave quickly got down on a knee, pulled Devil down next to him, and simultaneously hand signaled the trailing marines to halt.

At that very moment, a khaki-uniformed enemy soldier holding an AK-47 rifle jumped up from the brush right in front of Devil and started running away across the field of bushes and knee-high grass. Dave's bodyguard quickly took aim, fired, and killed the soldier with one shot through the head. The man's AK-47 was confiscated and, after his body was searched, he was left where he lay.

Stormy immediately alerted to Ron's right flank as a machete-wielding female enemy soldier leaped up from her hiding position, screaming as she charged directly at Ron and Stormy. Ron froze, his eyes fixed on her charge, then quickly drew his .45 caliber pistol and fired, hitting her in the arm. The arm splintered and jerked violently from the bullet's impact, but it didn't stop her raging attack. Stormy charged aggressively to the end of her leash, lunged, and hit the soldier hard on the side of her body, sending the machete flying out of her hand. An instant later, a bodyguard stormed around Ron's right side and hammered the woman with the butt of his M14 rifle. The impact of both hits knocked her off her feet; she hit the ground hard, out cold. She was disarmed, searched, tied up, blindfolded, treated for her wounds by the platoon medic, and held as a prisoner of war.

It was late morning when things settled down. Ron was still emotionally and physically shaken by the incident, and Stormy was agitated and hot to the touch. Ron found some shade under a large bush, sat down, and poured some water into his helmet for Stormy. He hugged and praised her for the heroic actions that saved his life. Ron also thanked his bodyguard for his quick reaction after Stormy knocked the attacker away from Ron.

The incident was over and it was time to move out and continue the mission of flushing out the enemy. Stormy was in her search mode for a few minutes, then stopped in her tracks and stared straight down at the ground, sniffing. Ron's first thought was that she might be scenting hidden land mines or booby traps.

Glancing over at Dave and Devil, Ron saw that they too were staring at the ground in front of them. At that point, Ron thought they were definitely headed into a minefield. Without moving an inch farther, Ron passed the word back. The platoon commander moved up to Ron's position to learn what the alert was all about.

Ron pointed out that both Stormy and Devil were sniffing the ground, which indicated the possibility of hidden land mines or booby traps. To investigate, they carefully cleared the grass from a small patch of ground where Stormy's scent alert appeared strongest. What they found was neither a land mine nor a booby trap, but a small hole. It appeared to be an air hole, which meant they were standing atop some kind of underground hiding place or tunnel complex. The platoon commander gave the order to carefully probe the surrounding area for a hidden tunnel entrance.

Ron and Dave praised their dogs for the scent alerts and continued the search for several more hours, finding more air holes that covered a broad area of ground. At about 3 p.m. their search led them to the top of a bushy ridge where both Stormy and Devil alerted to their left flank. Ron signaled the platoon behind. The marines stopped probing for tunnel entrances and passed the word that both handlers had picked up strong alerts from their dogs.

Ron carefully scanned the area and spotted a narrow trail running alongside the ridge line in the direction of Stormy's alert. A fire team of marines was dispatched to check it out. When they returned, they reported seeing nothing unusual. The fire-team leader asked if one of the dog teams would join them for a second search—not standard operating procedure for dog deployment. Once an alert was given, the dog team was to move back into the main element of the platoon for protection, not go off on small probing patrols outside their protection. Since Stormy had done such a great job that day, Ron felt confident and volunteered to go, but reminded the marines that they'd better provide quick support if he got into a fix.

Ron moved out, fire team following close behind. They walked up the narrow trail, wound their way over the top of the ridge, and started down the other side. Halfway down, Stormy stopped and alerted directly into the side of the ridge, which was covered in thick vegetation. Ron asked a marine rifleman to check out the spot where Stormy was alerting.

As everyone stood, weapons at the ready, the marine rifleman cleared a way through the vegetation, carefully checking for a booby trap. He discovered a tunnel entrance. Ron was so excited that he hugged and praised Stormy for having worked so hard all day. Locating the tunnel entrance was a great moment for everyone. The small band of marines thanked Stormy by patting her on the back and shaking her paw.

When the entrances and exits to the tunnels had been found,

platoon engineer destroyed them using blasting caps inserted into high-explosive C-4 charges.

It was late afternoon when the word was passed that the mission was over and the platoon was to return to base camp. When Ron and Dave and their dogs arrived there, everyone seemed to be waiting for them. Marines were patting them on the back, giving them thumbs-up signs, and telling them what a hell of a job they'd done.

Not knowing what the big fuss was about, Ron and Dave looked at each other and shrugged their shoulders. Then they learned that their dogs' alerts throughout the mission had actually caused a group of enemy soldiers to retreat right into the hands of the marine blocking force. When the enemy realized that they had no way of escaping, they surrendered without engaging in a firefight. Not a shot was fired during the roundup and capture.

Ron and Stormy and Dave and Devil were officially credited as the primary reasons for the capture of the enemy soldiers. Personally thanking them for a job well done, the platoon commander rewarded them by offering the top floor of his headquarters, an old French-style brick house, as their new living quarters.

The problem was that the only way up to the second floor was by way of a ladder. The commander wasn't sure whether the dogs could climb it. Ron and Dave looked at each other and started to laugh. Then Ron gave Stormy the command "Hup, girl!" Both dogs climbed the ladder to the second floor without a problem. The platoon commander had no idea how well those two marine canines were trained; he watched in amazement, shaking his head and smiling.

That was the final mission for Dave Gradeless. He left Vietnam and was discharged from the U.S. Marine Corps. Dave has since passed away. Devil died in Vietnam. As Ron says, "They're together again in God's care."

Fluffy

RESCUED IRAQI GERMAN SHEPHERD

At 8:30 A.M. on Mother's Day, May 11, 2003, Ron Aiello got a phone call from Sergeant First Class Russell Joyce, U.S. Army Special Forces. Sergeant Joyce was desperate as he spoke to Ron about having to get his German shepherd, Fluffy, out of Iraq. The U.S. Air Force had just stopped him from boarding Fluffy onto a military aircraft headed to the United States.

Sergeant Joyce was very worried about Fluffy's health and safety if Joyce was forced to abandon him in Iraq. The window of opportunity before the sergeant was ordered to leave Iraq was narrowing, so time was critical.

Sergeant Joyce had recruited a male German shepherd from a friendly Iraqi to serve as a sentry for his U.S. Army Special Forces team, operating in dangerous northern Iraqi territory. The nameless dog had a scarred snout, was missing a few teeth, was scrawny from not eating well, and was very aggressive. Out of the blue, Sergeant Joyce decided that the dog would be named Fluffy, and over time the name stuck with the rest of his unit.

As Fluffy got used to being around the American soldiers' smell and language and food, he started getting comfortable with Sergeant Joyce handling him and giving him fresh food and water daily. Joyce had never worked with military working dogs, nor did he know the basic commands used to manage and work them. Having no leash, harness, water bucket, or grooming brush and comb, he used rope for a collar and leash. As far as commands, the sergeant just called the dog and spoke whatever words came to mind. That was how they bonded and became inseparable. Fluffy even got a health check and vaccinations from a U.S. Army veterinarian.

Over time, Fluffy's health improved and he started packing a few more pounds onto his scrawny frame. Fluffy was turning out to be quite the sentry at night; he responded aggressively to anything that made a sound or moved into his area, even at great distances. Fluffy benefited the unit with reliable early warnings of potential danger. The soldiers relied on him more and more as they moved about the Iraqi terrain scouting for danger, hidden enemy equipment, and troop concentrations and movements.

During that Mother's Day phone conversation, Sergeant Joyce asked Ron to help him get Fluffy out of Iraq and into the States. What Ron heard in the sergeant's voice was something he'd heard many times from Vietnam war-dog handlers over the years. It was that heartfelt bond of love and affection that Sergeant Joyce had for Fluffy that got to Ron.

Ron had felt these same emotional ties when, many years ago, he'd had to leave Stormy behind in Vietnam. Ron believed that he owed it to Stormy and the rest of those Vietnam canines to get involved and help get Fluffy into the States. He told Sergeant Joyce that he'd do all he could to find a way. After the phone call, Ron received an email from Sergeant Joyce confirming the details they had discussed.

Ron immediately dropped everything he was doing and waded right in. He phoned and emailed everyone he thought could help get the word out about the Fluffy's plight. Then he decided to go right to the top, and composed a personal letter to Secretary of Defense Donald H. Rumsfeld, explaining Sergeant Joyce's dilemma and what Fluffy had done to save American lives in Iraq. In his letter, Ron noted how the American government had abandoned and euthanized thousands of surviving military canine war heroes instead of bringing them home after the Vietnam War. He went on to say that America had a chance, right now, to save one dog, named Fluffy, from being deserted and from the certain death that would follow if Rumsfeld didn't soon do something to help the American soldier get the dog out of Iraq and into the United States.

Ron couldn't sleep that Sunday night, so he stayed up writing and rewriting his letter to Rumsfeld. When the morning light pierced his window on Monday, May 12, Ron put the final draft in an envelope, drove to the post office, and dropped it in a mailbox.

On Thursday, May 15, Ron received a call from a Pentagon official named Mr. Stump, who said that he'd been instructed to contact Ron to discuss what the Pentagon could do to help. Ron gave Mr. Stump all the facts and contact information he had, including the fact that Sergeant Joyce had official orders from his commanding officer and a military veterinarian authorizing him to escort Fluffy to America. Ron told Stump that the air force air controller on duty at the time had ignored the official documents and stopped Fluffy from boarding the military plane to the States because he was not an official military working dog of the United States.

From May 15, 2003 until the time Fluffy arrived in the States on May 31, 2003, Ron was in daily contact with officials at the Pentagon and the U.S. military in Iraq.

On May 28, TSgt Steven Smith telephoned Ron from Iraq and told him that Major Pompano, U.S. Air Force, was assigned to escort Fluffy aboard a military plane headed to the United States. TSgt Smith also stated that Fluffy's flight would have departed earlier had it not been for some enemy rockets attacking the airfield just before takeoff.

TSgt Smith was the air force kennel master for the military working dogs operating in Iraq at the time. He had met Ron Aiello when he was kennel master at McGuire Air Force Base in New Jersey, near Ron's home in Burlington. He and Ron became friends and corresponded while TSgt Smith was serving in Iraq. When Sergeant Joyce sought a military veterinarian for Fluffy's medical needs, he met TSgt Smith, who took a look at Fluffy and gave Joyce some pointers on training him and caring for his health, including providing him a military-issue leather leash, collar, muzzle, and some nutritious dog food.

When Sergeant Joyce was prevented from boarding Fluffy on the plane, he immediately contacted TSgt Smith and pleaded with him to take care of Fluffy at the U.S. military canine kennel while he sorted things out. Because Fluffy wasn't an official U.S. military working dog, TSgt Smith could hold him for only a short time.

Smith gave Joyce the address and phone number of Ron Aiello as someone who might be able to help him. That was the link between Sergeant Joyce and Ron Aiello and the phone call that started Fluffy's stateside processing on Mother's Day 2003.

The following are actual email extracts from Ron Aiello's personal files:

5/31/03: Fluffy has arrived and they are on their way to Fort Bragg.

From: Ron Aiello

Sent: May 31, 2003, 8:21 P.M.

Subject: Another Update on Fluffy

I have been notified that SFC Russell Joyce has Fluffy with him and the two are on their way back to Ft. Bragg.

5/31/03 Fluffy is on plane heading to AFB in SC.

From: Ron Aiello

Sent: Sat May 31, 2003, 4:28 P.M.

Subject: New Update

Everything has changed. SFC Russell Joyce is at this time waiting at Charleston AFB, SC, for Fluffy's plane to land, which should be in thirty minutes. Fluffy is almost here.

5/28/03: Good News—Fluffy is on his way to the USA.

From: Ron Aiello

Sent: May 28, 2003, 3:24 .M.

Subject: Fluffy Update

Great News: Fluffy is on his way to the USA. He left this morning on a flight out of Iraq with Major Pompano, his official military escort. He should be arriving in the USA on Saturday, May 31, 2003.

5/24/03: Update

Sent: May 24, 2003

From: Ron Aiello, president

Fluffy Update:

Fluffy will be coming to the United States through the Military Adoption Program (H.R. 5314). The first step will be for Fluffy to be put into the military system at Lackland AFB, Texas, as an Honorary Military War Dog. Then arrangements will be made to have Fluffy put on a military transport with an escort. Once Fluffy arrives in the United States he will be retired through the U.S. Military Adoption Program. Once retired, he will be adopted by Sgt 1st Class Russell Joyce and his family. The above sequence of events will start following the Memorial Day weekend.

*Russell Joyce, U.S. Army Sergeant First Class, Special Forces, holding
Fluffy's leash, and Ron Aiello, Vietnam Veteran Marine Scout Dog
Handler, at Vietnam Veterans Memorial in Washington D.C. – 2003.
(Photo courtesy of Ron Aiello)*

Ron says, "I fulfilled my objective when I got directly involved in helping get Fluffy out of Iraq. I did it to honor the memory of my Stormy and the several thousand other war-dog heroes abandoned in South Vietnam after the war."

I had the opportunity to meet and spend time with Sergeant Joyce and Fluffy while Joyce was visiting relatives in Alexandria, Virginia. And I stay in close contact with my longtime friend Ron Aiello. Ron is very active in supporting America's military working dog teams in the fight against terrorism in Iraq, Afghanistan, and other parts of the world. He has personally shipped them many items of need (e.g., dog food, medical supplies, vests, booties, toys, and people food and coffee.). You can learn more about what Ron's doing to help by visiting his website: www.uswardogs.com.

Stubby

WORLD WAR I HERO DOG

*Article information obtained from the
Connecticut State Military Department.*

Stubby joined the 102nd Infantry, 26th (Yankee) Division, at Yale Field, New Haven, CT, in the spring of 1917. He was a bull terrier with a short tail from which he received his name. He was several weeks old at the time of his arrival. Private J. Robert Conroy was his only master. In July 1917, Stubby was smuggled aboard the S.S. Minnesota at New Port News, VA, and sailed to France. Stubby was at the war's front lines in the trenches on February 5, 1918 and participated in 17 WWI engagements.

Stubby's first battle injury was gas exposure. He was nursed to health in a field hospital, but his near death experience made him very sensitive to the smell of gas. A few weeks later the Germans launched an early morning gas attack. The men in Stubby's trench were sleeping. Stubby sniffed the air and then quickly ran through the trench barking and biting at the sleeping soldiers. Stubby's alert saved many soldiers from injury.

Stubby was an expert in locating wounded men in the "no man's land" between the trenches of the opposing armies. Stubby would listen for injured men shouting in English. He would then run to them and bark for the paramedics. One day, while on patrol in no-mans land, Stubby heard a noise coming from a small patch of brush. He went to investigate and found a German spy making a map of the allied trenches. The German soldier called Stubby to him but it didn't work. Stubby started barking. The German began to run and Stubby took off after him, biting at his legs causing him to trip and fall. Stubby attacked the German's arms and finally bit and held onto his rear-end. When the allied soldiers arrived on the scene they realized Stubby had captured a spy.

In a later battle, Stubby was wounded with shrapnel in his chest and right leg from a German grenade. He was rushed to a field hospital and stabilized after several operations. When Stubby was well enough he spent his time visiting the wounded soldiers and socializing with the nurses. After healing, Stubby rejoined the Yankee Division.

After the Armistice, Stubby met President Woodrow Wilson during his visit with the 102nd Infantry in France on Christmas Day 1918. Stubby became an American folk hero and participated in many parades, war bond rallies, and hospital visits. Stubby was rewarded for his service with many military service medals, badges, patches and a promotion to sergeant. He visited the White House in 1921 to meet President Harding and again in 1924 to meet President Coolage. In 1921, General John J. Pershing awarded a gold medal to Sgt. Stubby. Sgt. Stubby died on March 16, 1926. His remains are preserved at the Smithsonian Institution.

"Sgt Stubby—WWI U.S. War Dog Hero" by Terry Waldron, (2004)
www.terryjamesart.com

ROBERT W. HARTSOCK

The Medal of Honor is the highest military decoration for bravery that the United States of America can bestow upon a U.S. military service member.

U.S. Army Staff Sergeant Robert W. Hartsock, 44th Infantry Platoon Scout Dogs, 3rd Brigade, 25th Infantry Division, is the only war-dog handler awarded the Medal of Honor during the Vietnam War. Sergeant Hartsock was born on January 24, 1945 in Cumberland, Maryland. He entered the U.S. Army at Fairmont, West Virginia.

Staff Sergeant Hartsock was awarded the Medal of Honor posthumously for extraordinary heroism in the Hau Nghia Province, Republic of Vietnam, on February 23, 1969.

*Medal of Honor recipient — Staff Sergeant Robert Hartsock
and his partner, Duke, 44th Scout Dogs, Vietnam — 1969.*

CITATION

For conspicuous gallantry and intrepidity in action at the risk of his life above and beyond the call of duty. Staff Sergeant Hartsock distinguished himself in action while serving as section leader with the 44th Infantry Platoon Scout Dogs. When the Dau Tieng Base Camp came under a heavy enemy rocket and mortar attack, Staff Sergeant Hartsock and his platoon commander spotted an enemy sapper squad, which had infiltrated the camp undetected.

Realizing the enemy squad was heading for the brigade tactical operations center and nearby prisoner compound, they concealed themselves and, although heavily outnumbered, awaited the approach of the hostile soldiers. When the enemy was almost upon them, Staff Sergeant Hartsock and his platoon commander opened fire on the squad. As a wounded enemy soldier fell, he managed to detonate a satchel charge he was carrying.

Staff Sergeant Hartsock, with complete disregard for his life, threw himself on the charge and was gravely wounded. In spite of his wounds, Staff Sergeant Hartsock crawled about 5 meters to a ditch and provided heavy suppressive fire, completely pinning down the enemy and allowing his commander to seek shelter. Staff Sergeant Hartsock continued his deadly stream of fire until he succumbed to his wounds. Staff Sergeant Hartsock's extraordinary heroism and profound concern for the lives of his fellow soldiers were in keeping with the highest traditions of the military service and reflect great credit on him, his unit, and the United States Army.

WAR DOG ADOPTION LAW

Thanks to the late Dr. William W. Putney, WWII veterinarian and United States Marine war-dog platoon leader, who wrote about the heroism of his war dogs in his book *Always Faithful,* and U.S. Congressman Roscoe Bartlett of Maryland, for submitting the following bill of resolution to the House and Senate, which former president Bill Clinton signed into law on November 6, 2000. The bill allows civilians to adopt U.S. military working dogs after their retirement from active service. The adoption program has since placed many former military working dogs into loving homes across America.

Resolution H.R. 5314
Nov. 6, 2000
Public Law 106-446
106th Congress
An Act
To amend title 10, United States Code, to facilitate the adoption of retired military working dogs by law enforcement agencies, former handlers of these dogs, and other persons capable of caring for these dogs.

Be it enacted by the Senate and House of Representatives of the United States of America in Congress assembled,

Section 1.

Promotion of Adoption of Military Working Dogs

(1) Adoption of Military Working Dogs.—Chapter 153 of title 10, United States Code, is amended by adding at the end the following new section: Section. 2582. Military working dogs: transfer and adoption at end of useful working life.

(a) Availability for Adoption.—The Secretary of Defense may make a military working dog of the Department of Defense available for adoption by a person or entity referred to in subsection (c) at the end of the dog's useful working life or when the dog is otherwise excess to the needs of the Department, unless the dog has been determined to be unsuitable for adoption under subsection (b).

(b) Suitability for Adoption.—The decision whether a particular military working dog is suitable or unsuitable for adoption under this section shall be made by the commander of the last unit to which the dog is assigned before being declared excess. The unit commander shall consider the recommendations of the unit's veterinarian in making the decision regarding a dog's adoptability.

(c) Authorized Recipients.—Military working dogs may be adopted under this section by law enforcement agencies, former handlers of these dogs, and other persons capable of humanely caring for these dogs.

(d) Consideration.—The transfer of a military working dog under this section may be without charge to the recipient.

(e) Limitations on Liability for Transferred Dogs.— (1) Notwithstanding any other provision of law, the United States shall not be subject to any suit, claim, demand or action, liability, judgment, cost, or other fee arising out of any claim for personal injury or property damage (including death, illness, or loss of or damage to property or other economic loss) that results from, or is in any manner predicated upon, the act or omission of a former military working dog transferred under this section, including any training provided to the dog while a military working dog.

(2) Notwithstanding any other provision of law, the United States shall not be liable for any veterinary expense associated with a military working dog transferred under this section for a condition of the military working dog before transfer under this section, whether or not such condition is known at the time of transfer under this section.

(f) Annual Report.—The Secretary shall submit to Congress an annual report specifying the number of military working dogs adopted under this section during the preceding year, the number of these dogs currently awaiting adoption, and the number of these dogs euthanized during the preceding year. With respect to each euthanized military working dog, the report shall contain an explanation of the reasons why the dog was euthanized rather than retained for adoption under this section.".

(3) Clerical Amendment.—The table of sections at the beginning of such chapter is amended by adding at the end the following new item: 2582. Military working dogs: transfer and adoption at end of useful working life.

Approved November 6, 2000

Legislative History–H.R. 5314, Congressional Record, Vol. 146 (2000), Oct. 10, considered and passed House. Oct. 24, considered and passed Senate, amended. Oct. 26, House concurred in Senate amendment.

NATIONAL WAR DOG
TEAM MEMORIAL

I salute U.S. Congressman Walter B. Jones, North Carolina for championing the efforts of a group of Vietnam Veteran War Dog Handlers by submitting a congressional bill to the U.S. House of Representatives and the U.S. Senate to mandate a National War Dog Team Memorial in Washington, D.C. The memorial is designed to honor the service and sacrifices of all U.S. military working dog teams of all branches of the U.S. Armed Services and of all wars. A debt of gratitude goes to the entire staff of Congressman Jones, especially Joshua Bowlen, Legislative Director, for organizing the meetings, phone conferences and managing the congressional legislative process.

There are many reasons for establishing a National War Dog Team Memorial in Washington, D.C. The primary one is that our country's war dogs have earned the right to be recognized and honored at the highest level of our government for their service and sacrifices for our nation's freedom.

Over the course of our nation's military history, more than 100,000 dogs of many different breeds faithfully served America during WWI, WWII, Korea, Vietnam, and the Gulf War. Since the September 11, 2001 terrorist attack on America, the U.S. Department of Defense Military Working Dog Center at Lackland Air Force Base, San Antonio, Texas, is training and deploying more working dog teams in the war on terrorism in Afghanistan, Iraq, and other peacekeeping missions around the globe.

American families have always been there, donating thousands of their loving young dogs to help save American lives in warfare in distant lands. Numerous dogs have been rescued from the death rows of animal shelters nationwide and given a second chance to live and work.

There is no way the dogs could fully perform their jobs without the professional healthcare services provided by military veterinarians and vet techs. These expertly trained doctors and technicians treat the dogs with respect, patience, understanding, and love. They manage their diets, medicate their diseases, dress their cuts, bruises, and scrapes, mend their combat wounds, and nurse them to health; they also nurture their emotional stress, and give each dog a complete physical evaluation every six months. That's what I call excellent doggone healthcare at its finest!

There is overwhelming nationwide support for this memorial from many wonderful people, dog organizations, veteran organizations, troops of boy scouts and girl scouts, middle schools, high schools, colleges and universities, veterinarians, private businesses, and a broad spectrum of media (TV documentaries, TV news, newspapers, magazines, and the Internet).

Many artists were contacted and applied for the job of designing the memorial. Artist Renee Heading's rendering of the National

War Dog Team Memorial was selected. Renee's exceptional talent, awards for accomplishment, years of proven experience, understanding of the memorial concept, and humorous enthusiasm were a perfect fit with an eager committee of Vietnam veteran war dog handlers.

Proposed National War Dog Team Memorial to be constructed. Visit the website at: www.nationalwardogsmonument.org *for updates.*

The idea for a National War Dog Team Memorial in Washington, D.C., was initiated as part of an article, "Let Us Remember Our Forgotten Heroes," written for the April 1, 2001 issue of *PARADE* magazine by Pulitzer Prize-winning journalist Richard Ben Cramer. I was the newly elected president of the Vietnam Dog Handler Association (VDHA) when Cramer phoned and asked if I had any plans to establish a national memorial in Washington, D.C. during my tenure. "That is the dream of every veteran war-dog handler I've ever known," I replied.

Mr. Cramer gave me a few days to make a decision in order for him to meet his deadline for *PARADE*. It was a huge opportunity that I couldn't pass up: 33 million copies circulated across America, with a huge front-page photo of Stubby, WWI canine hero, and a full feature article on war dogs. Not having time to canvas the entire membership, I took advantage of that tiny golden window and made a command decision to launch the National War Dog Team Memorial project. I later met with Richard Ben Cramer in northern Virginia and thanked him for the great story he'd written and for his support of a national memorial.

The VDHA membership was caught by pleasant surprise when they got their copies of *PARADE* magazine in their Sunday newspapers and were congratulated by family, relatives, friends, and co-workers. The massive public response was 100 percent in favor of the memorial effort—way beyond our expectations.

The VDHA officers spent the next several months getting organized to support the project and replying to the thousands of letters, emails, and donations from people all across America. It was truly an overwhelming experience of joy for all.

Although I've been credited with being its founder, it was truly a team effort. The following Vietnam veteran war dog handlers deserve equal recognition for their time and commitment to seeing the National War Dog Team Memorial project though:

Board Members

www.nationalwardogsmonument.org

John C. Burnam, Chairman (Virginia)

Johnny Mayo, President (South Carolina)

Richard Deggans, Secretary (Texas)

Tony Vymazal, Treasurer (Pennsylvania)

Bill Wigginton, Board Member (Alabama)

Ron Sevier, Board Member (Louisiana)

Alan Driscoll, Board Member (Massachusetts)

Former Board Members

John Harvey, Chairman (Connecticut)

Dick King, President (Ohio)

Vance McCrumb, Secretary (Michigan)

Bob Hubbard, Board Member (North Carolina)

Robert Konarske, Board Member (West Virginia)

Jim Hart, Board Member (Washington)

Perry Money, Board Member (North Carolina)

Pete Peters, VDHA Secretary (South Carolina)

John Sciascia, VDHA President (California)

America, as a leading free-world nation, owes its war dogs this memorial, mandated by Congress, and erected in the nation's capitol of Washington, D.C., for the entire world to see and know that they are *not* America's forgotten heroes.

VIETNAM WAR-DOG HANDLERS KILLED IN ACTION

Approximately 10,000 war-dog handlers and 4,000 war dogs served during the ground war in South Vietnam. Though their number was quite small compared to the several million American and allied men and women who rotated in and out of that country from 1960–1975, the war-dog-team mission and record for saving lives was quite significant.

German shepherds became the dogs of choice for military scouting and sentry duty; Labrador retrievers were selected for tracking. Both breeds were well suited because of their intelligence, learning ability, accommodating dispositions, ability to work with multiple handlers, and adaptability to variable climates, terrain, and working environments.

Each dog's ear was branded with a four-character alpha-numeric service number for identification and accountability. Each dog had an official military medical, training, and service record established upon entry into military service. The records were maintained by the veterinarian or veterinarian technician assigned to support the war-dog unit.

Americans gained a grudging respect for the enemy; the North Vietnamese Army, the Vietcong (VC) or "Charlie" as we called these fierce and savvy Asian warriors. They constantly surprised us with their hit-and-run guerrilla tactics. During the Vietnam War, Charlie inflicted thousands of casualties on American and allied soldiers, and destroyed tons of war materials worth billions of dollars. The enemy was adept at hiding within local civilian population or in neatly camouflaged positions and remote jungle base camps, where he was exceptionally difficult to find or surprise.

Courageous, well-trained, disciplined war-dog teams were called on to counteract the enemy's tactical success. Their deployment in South Vietnam dramatically improved the infantry's ability to search, locate, and engage the enemy, and eradicate his ability to surprise, inflict casualties, and destroy equipment. Due to the extraordinary success of the war-dog teams walking point, tracking, and guarding, the enemy placed price tags on their heads and hunted them down with extreme prejudice.

The following are the various types of K-9 units that supported the army, air force, marines, and navy during the Vietnam War:

Scout Dogs: A handler and a German shepherd were a team that performed the mission of leading combat patrols and providing early silent warning of danger. A scout-dog team was deployed out front as "point man," the most vulnerable and dangerous position in a tactical formation moving through enemy territory. Scout dogs alerted on enemy movement, booby traps, land mines, base camps, underground tunnel complexes, and underground caches of weapons, food, and medical supplies. The U.S. Army had the highest number of scout-dog units deployed in South Vietnam; consequently, army scout-dogs teams suffered the highest number of casualties. Fort Benning and Fort Gordon, Georgia, were the primary training centers. Formal scout-dog training was twelve weeks. Upon graduation the entire class was formed into a numbered K-9 unit, fully equipped, and shipped to South Vietnam to support infantry ground operations. Veterinarians and veterinarian Technicians were assigned to support their medical needs.

Combat Tracker Teams (CTT): Labrador retrievers were used to track the enemy's scent and blood trails after contact had been broken. A CTT consisted of a dog and handler, cover man, visual tracker, and team leader. The dog handler concentrated on the dog for signs of danger. The Labrador's naturally acute ground-scent instinct could be relied upon to locate the target. The team was equipped with a radio for communication and support. CTTs were highly trained and effective in locating the enemy, as well as finding wounded and dead American soldiers, in all weather and terrain conditions. CTTs received most of their training at the British Jungle Warfare School (JWS) in Malaysia.

Sentry Dogs: German shepherds were very effective in defending aircraft, airfields, supply depots, ammunition dumps, defensive perimeters, and many other strategic military targets throughout South Vietnam. Sentry-dog teams were usually deployed as an American base camp's first line of defense, and they patrolled day and night. Sentry-dog teams received their initial training at Lackland Air Force Base, San Antonio, Texas. The air force deployed the greatest number of sentry-dog teams.

Patrol Dogs: A handler and his German shepherd were deployed to patrol and protect air bases. The patrol-dog team usually operated along the perimeter and often outside the wire, searching the surrounding area and villages. They were trained to track, search buildings, and attack if necessary. Often, they rode in jeeps with military law enforcement officers and assisted as required. Patrol-dog teams proved very effective in South Vietnam.

Mine & Booby-trap Dogs: A German shepherd and his handler were generally deployed with infantry and combat engineer units. They were trained to sniff out mines and booby traps planted in roads, and to search Vietnamese villages and other populated areas that were suspected hiding places for explosives, arms, ammunition, and other supplies. Their deployment successfully reduced casualties and the enemy's stock of hidden war materials.

Water Dogs: The navy successfully used German shepherds on patrol boats to alert on the breath scent of enemy underwater swimmers breathing through reeds, snorkels, and other underwater apparatuses. Operating throughout the American-patrolled waterways of South Vietnam, water dogs proved quite successful in saving lives and equipment as well as reducing the enemy's capacity to conduct underwater sabotage operations.

If a war-dog handler was killed or wounded, or was lucky enough to complete his twelve-month tour of duty in South Vietnam, his dog was reassigned to another handler. In what turned out to be a tragic decision, the U.S. Department of Defense designated war dogs as military surplus equipment. Their mission was to serve in South Vietnam until they died in combat, were overcome by disease, or became fell victim to other unfortunate circumstances. They weren't expected to die of old age. Many dogs served more than one handler and most survived the duration of the war. When a young handler had to say goodbye to his best friend, parting brought on deeply felt emotions and tears. How do you tell a dog that you're going home and he won't be going with you?

Official military war-dog records archived at Lackland Air Force Base, San Antonio, Texas, revealed that a few hundred war dogs made it through the quarantine program and redeployed for duty outside South Vietnam. No one knows how many war dogs, if any, were smuggled out of South Vietnam by determined handlers. The rest of the brave Vietnam war dogs were either put to sleep or given to the South Vietnamese Army (ARVN), which meant, given Vietnamese cultural practices, that the dogs might have been slaughtered for food.

Vietnam War-dog Handlers
Killed in Action

"In Memory of War Dog Handlers and War Dogs Killed in Action"
Oil on canvas by Julie Parker, 2003
Original painting–Author collection

List Courtesy of the Vietnam Dog Handler Association
www.vdhaonline.org

Name	Age	Unit	Home	Died	Vietnam Memorial Panel
Ahern, Robert	27	37th SPS – Air Force	Laconia, NH	03/30/1969	28W–89
Alcorn Jr., Dale	19	60th Mine/Booby Trap	Redondo Beach, CA	09/06/1969	18W–45
Amick, Richard	19	57th Scout Dogs	Nashville, TN	05/12/1969	25W–59
Anderson, William	21	66th Combat Tracker	Mt. Vernon, AL	11/06/1969	16W–36
Armstrong, Robert	20	Marine Scout Dogs	Fayetteville, TN	01/16/1969	34W–14
Atkins III, Joshua	19	Army Scout Dogs	Washington, DC	04/26/1967	18E–89
Baker, Donald	20	Marine Sentry Dog	Huntington Park, CA	09/06/1967	26E–5
Baker, Gary	21	Army Scout Dogs	Monroe City, MO	05/11/1970	11W–16
Baldoni, Lindsay	21	39th Scout Dogs	Detroit, MI	08/22/1967	25E–29
Banaszynski, Richard	22	59th Scout Dogs	Pulaski, WI	10/25/1968	40W–31
Barkley, Earl	21	Army Scout Dogs	Indian Head, PA	11/09/1971	02W–64
Beauregard, Richard	19	Army Scout Dogs	Woonsocket, RI	04/24/1971	03W–11
Beaver, James	20	50th Scout Dogs	Bradenton, FL	03/16/1968	44E–65
Beck, Terrence	18	Marine Scout Dog	Ft. Atkinson, WI	12/20/1967	32E–29
Beesley, Gary	21	43rd Scout Dogs	St. Louis, MO	06/22/1967	22E–036
Behrens, Peter	26	Marine Scout Dogs	Newburg, MO	12/04/1970	06W–105

Name	Age	Unit	Home	Died	Vietnam Memorial Panel
Belcher, Robert	22	Marine Scout Dogs	Winthrop, MA	04/11/1968	49E-19
Bell, Mark	19	Marine Scout Dogs	Redondo Beach, CA	06/09/1969	22W-117
Bennett, John	20	Army Scout Dogs	Columbus, OH	10/14/1969	17W-76
Berge, James	24	50th Scout Dogs	Portland, OR	01/23/1968	35E-13
Best, Billy	18	Marine Scout Dogs	Baltimore, MD	03/03/1969	30W-19
Beuke, Dennis	21	Combat Tracker Team-8	Chicago, IL	10/11/1967	27E-87
Bevich Jr., George	22	377th SPS– Air Force	Summit Hill, PA	12/04/1966	13E-9
Blaauw, James	21	Army Scout Dogs	Grayling, MI	03/22/1968	45E-54
Blair, Charles	20	64th Combat Tracker	Orlando, FL	05/14/1970	11W-38
Bost, Michael	20	42nd Scout Dogs	Grand Rapids, MI	05/14/1967	19E-115
Bowman, Stephen	18	Army Scout Dogs	Alta Loma, CA	06/02/1968	61W-10
Boyd, James	22	3rd SPS – Air Force	Winston Salem, NC	02/28/1968	41E-25
Boyer, James	20	Combat Tracker Team-2	St. Louis, MO	09/22/1967	26E-111
Bozier Jr., Willie	21	Army Scout Dogs	New York, NY	07/09/1970	08W-1
Brede, Robert	24	Combat Tracker Team-2	Alexandria, MN	11/16/1967	29E-104
Brophy, Martin	24	41st Scout Dogs	Buffalo, NY	05/05/1968	55E-4
Brown, Charles	21	40th Scout Dogs	South Amboy, NJ	03/09/1967	16E-43

Name	Age	Unit	Home	Died	Vietnam Memorial Panel
Browne, Walter	21	41st Scout Dogs	Haiku, HI	08/02/ 1969	20W-85
Buckingham, Keith	22	43rd Scout Dogs	Minneapolis, MN	02/25/ 1969	31W-44
Bullwinkel, Alden	20	61st Combat Tracker Team	Dunellen, NJ	09/11/ 1969	18W-66
Burdette Jr., Hilburn	19	Army Scout Dogs	Simpsonville, SC	07/12/ 1970	08W-11
Burk, Jimmy	21	43rd Scout Dogs	Littlefield, TX	11/30/ 1969	15W-9
Burlock Jr., Kenneth	23	Army Scout Dogs	Jacksonville, NC	09/17/ 1969	18W-100
Burnette Jr., Archie	20	Army Scout Dogs	Aberdeen	01/31/ 1968	35E-89
Cabarubio, James	20	Marine Scout Dogs	Odessa, TX	06/18/ 1969	22W-73
Cain, Douglas	23	43rd Scout Dogs	Sioux City, IA	07/14/ 1968	52W-27
Camp, Anthony	21	Marine Scout Dogs	Dallas, GA	06/04/ 1969	23W-62
Campbell, William	21	49th Scout Dogs	Silver Hill, MD	03/03/ 1967	16E-8
Carinci, Joseph	20	Marine Mine/ Booby Trap	Derby, CT	12/30/ 1970	05W-7
Carrillo, Melvin	19	48th Scout Dogs	Roswell, NM	03/03/ 1968	42E-48
Carter, Merle	20	Navy Sentry Dogs	Sapulpa, OK	10/22/ 1967	28E-49
Castle, Russell	34	40th Scout Dogs	Woodbridge, VA	07/02/ 1967	22E-097
Chisholm, Ronald	21	Marine Sentry Dog	Jacksonville, FL	05/11/ 1967	19E-89
Clark, Walter	20	Army Scout Dogs	Roseville, MI	10/29/ 1967	28E-95
Clokes, Robert	21	40th Scout Dogs	New York, NY	12/04/ 1968	37W-38

Name	Age	Unit	Home	Died	Vietnam Memorial Panel
Colford, Darrell	25	38th Scout Dogs	West Chicago, IL	11/08/1970	06W−45
Collier, Steven	19	Army Scout Dogs	Branford, CT	10/27/1968	40W−42
Conklin, Michael	22	Army Scout Dogs	Midland, MI	06/24/1970	09W−88
Conner, Jack	25	557th Combat Tracker	El Monte, CA	04/04/1970	12W−92
Conners Jr., Ralph	22	41st Scout Dogs	Washington D.C.	05/22/1969	24W−74
Connors, Jack	23	557th Combat Tracker	Filion, MI	08/21/1969	19W−85
Cox Jr., Edward	20	76th Combat Tracker	Shreveport, LA	02/15/1969	32W−36
Crawford, Bobby	22	43rd Scout Dogs	Buncombe, IL	01/10/1968	34E−16
Crawford, Gordon	24	Army Scout Dogs	Ft. Wayne, IN	02/01/1971	05W−71
Creaghead, Clarence	21	49th Scout Dogs	Bessemer, AL	05/22/1969	24W−74
Cumbie, William	19	Marine Scout Dogs	Jacksonville, FL	02/09/1969	33W−92
Currier Jr., Gordon	22	Veterinarian– Army	Independence, MO	01/31/1968	36E−4
Czarnota, Christopher	20	Army Scout Dogs	Perth Amboy, NJ	03/22/1971	04W−65
Davis, Abronl	20	Marine Scout Dogs	Youngstown, OH	01/11/1969	35W−69
Davis, Alan	21	48th Scout Dogs	Tulare, CA	03/21/1971	04W−63
Davis, Eligah	19	Marine Mine/ Booby Trap	Cecil, GA	04/05/1970	12W−96
Deitrick, George	19	41st Scout Dogs	Antioch, CA	06/23/1969	22W−118

Name	Age	Unit	Home	Died	Vietnam Memorial Panel
Dell, Kenneth	21	49th Scout Dogs	E. Candergrift, PA	11/05/1968	39W-21
Detrick, Gary	20	47th Scout Dogs	Wapakoneta, OH	04/13/1969	27W-72
Dillinder, Randy	19	34th Scout Dogs	Dearborn, MI	12/10/1967	31E-72
Doria, Richard	21	48th Scout Dogs	White Plains, NY	08/19/1969	19W-67
Doyle, John	19	59th Scout Dogs	Prospect, CT	08/25/1966	10E-37
Drobena, Michael	23	Marine Scout Dogs	Temple, TX	02/23/1969	32W-96
Drum, Thomas	21	62nd Combat Tracker	Johnson City, NY	03/04/1970	13W-81
Drysdale, Charles	19	Marine Scout Dogs	Birmingham, AL	01/26/1969	34W-83
Ducote Jr., Lonnie	22	34th Scout Dogs	Corpus Christi, TX	08/13/1967	24E-107
Duff, Phillip	20	Army Scout Dogs	Cornelia, GA	07/07/1972	01W-53
Duke, Douglas	23	Veterinarian-Army	Rush Springs, OK	12/20/1968	36W-49
Dunning, William	24	Veterinarian	Bridgeport, CT	06/22/1970	09W-78
Elliott, Robert	24	Marine Mine/Booby Trap	Woodbury, NJ	08/09/1970	08W-97
Erickson, Russell	24	59th Scout Dogs	Franklin Park, IL	07/24/1968	51W-49
Esterly, Lawrence	20	Marine Scout Dogs	Lisbon, OH	07/18/1969	20W-14
Eubanks, George	21	25th Scout Dogs	Barboursville, WV	12/07/1967	31E-57
Evans, Ronald	24	44th Scout Dogs	Morrow, OH	04/29/1971	03W-17
Farley, Marshall	20	44th Scout Dogs	Folsom, CA	09/19/1967	26E-92

Name	Age	Unit	Home	Died	Vietnam Memorial Panel
Ford, Bernard		35th SPS–Air Force	Oak Lawn, IL	07/05/1967	23E–10
Ford, Richard	22	35th Scout Dogs	Surf City, NJ	01/18/1970	14W–42
Fox, Gary	18	25th Scout Dogs	Pittsburgh, PA	04/30/1967	18E–121
Fraley, Eugene	28	Navy Seal Team Dogs	Lansing, MI	01/21/1968	35E–5
Fraser, William	20	Marine Scout Dog	Manchester, NH	12/28/1967	32E–86
Freeman, David	20	34th Scout Dogs	Putnam, CT	08/11/1969	19W–1
Freeman, Jeffrey	23	39th Scout Dogs	Lakewood, OH	04/08/1970	12W–107
Freppon, John	20	35th Scout Dogs	Cincinnatl, OH	02/02/1969	33W–38
Fritz, Gerald	20	56th SPS–Air Force	Junction, TX	05/13/1975	01W–125
Fuller, Gary	21	366th SPS–Air Force	The Plains, OH	02/27/1967	15E–105
Fuller, Stanley	21	76th Combat Tracker	Fullerton, CA	12/12/1968	36W–11
Gaspard Jr., Claude	21	33rd Scout Dogs	Short Hills, NJ	05/20/1968	60E–4
Giberson, Jerry	21	Army Scout Dogs	Donnellson, IA	06/20/1970	09W–72
Glenn, Livingston	28	57th Scout Dogs	Boston, GA	12/09/1967	31E–68
Goudelock, William	19	57th Scout Dogs	Meridian, CA	03/18/1968	45E–22
Green, Billy	22	Army Scout Dogs	Los Angeles, CA	06/24/1966	08E–85
Grieve, Michael	21	Army Scout Dogs	Hazel Park, MI	01/31/1968	36E–11
Griffin II, William	23	63rd Combat Tracker	Pontiac, MI	12/15/1970	06W–122

Name	Age	Unit	Home	Died	Vietnam Memorial Panel
Groves, William	20	Army Scout Dogs	Seattle, WA	11/30/1967	31E-12
Grundy, Dallas	23	Army Scout Dogs	San Jose, CA	11/05/1966	12E-28
Gyulveszi, Theodore	24	42nd Scout Dogs	Lincoln Park, MI	02/10/1969	32W-6
Hales, Raymon	27	58th Scout Dogs	Springville, UT	07/19/1969	20W-19
Harding, John	19	557th Combat Tracker	Benton, AR	10/08/1967	27E-72
Harris, Jessie	22	Veterinarian- Army	Peoria, IL	01/31/1968	36E-13
Hartsock, Robert	24	44th Scout Dogs	Cumberland, MD	02/23/1969	31W-3
Hartwick Jr., Floyd	20	Marine Scout Dog	St Charles, MO	07/15/1967	23E-75
Hatcher, David	21	63rd Combat Tracker	New York, NY	11/12/1970	06W-54
Henshaw, Patrick	21	Army Scout Dogs	Spokane, WA	12/19/1967	31E-23
Hernandez, Victor	24	57th Scout Dogs	Fullerton, CA	10/18/1968	41W-73
Hicks, Larry	22	Army Scout Dogs	St Ann, MO	09/24/1970	07W-87
Hilerio- Padilla, Luis	20	Army Scout Dogs	Yonkers, NY	11/13/1969	16W-69
Hilt, Richard	20	57th Scout Dogs	Minneapolis, MN	02/13/1969	32W-26
Holland, Wayne	21	Army Scout Dogs	Salemburg, NC	10/26/1968	40W-37
Holley, Glynn	20	Army Scout Dogs	Midland, TX	12/26/1969	15W-93
Holt, Herschel	23	Marine 1st Provisional	Nashville, TN	08/03/1966	09E-103

Name	Age	Unit	Home	Died	Vietnam Memorial Panel
Hoppough, Dennis	22	Marine Scout Dogs	Rochester, NY	07/16/1969	20W-9
Howard, James	20	44th Scout Dogs	Detroit, MI	11/09/1967	29E-59
Howard, Mark	21	Combat Tracker Team-2	St. Louis, MO	11/16/1967	30E-2
Huberty, William	21	44th Scout Dogs	St. Paul, MN	10/17/1966	11E-82
Hughes III, Edward	19	44th Scout Dogs	Garden Grove, CA	11/27/1967	30E-97
Hurksman, Wilhelm	20	43rd Scout Dogs	Rhinelander, WI	07/22/1968	51W-33
Ilaoa, Faleagafula	26	56th SPS-Air Force	San Francisco, CA	05/13/1975	01W-127
Ireland, Elmer	21	42nd Scout Dogs	Star, ID	07/01/1969	21W-42
Jenkins, Clayton	21	Marine Sentry Dogs	Pembine, WI	06/03/1969	23W-53
Jenkins, Steven	21	981st MP Dogs	Santa Ana, CA	01/15/1969	34W-8
Jenks, James	20	45th Scout Dogs	Concord, MI	03/02/1968	42E-33
Jesko, Stephen	20	Army Scout Dogs	Hereford, TX	10/16/1970	06W-3
Joecken, Richard	22	44th Scout Dogs	Columbus, OH	08/28/1969	18W-2
Johnson, Arnold	20	Combat Tracker Team-2	Rochelle, IL	11/16/1967	30E-3
Johnson, Carl	19	34th Scout Dogs	Wakefield, MI	06/22/1968	55W-19
Johnson, Freddie	26	1st Combat Tracker Team	Selma, AL	12/07/1966	12E-18
Johnson, Herbert	19	Army Scout Dogs	Poughkeepsie, NY	07/05/1968	53W-20

Name	Age	Unit	Home	Died	Vietnam Memorial Panel
Johnson, James	22	39th Scout Dogs	Jersey City, NJ	07/01/1969	21W-42
Johnson, Larry	19	Army Scout Dogs	Anaheim, CA	11/14/1968	39W-68
Karau, Ronald	21	Army Scout Dogs	Lewisville, NM	03/20/1971	04W-61
Kiefhaber, Andrew	20	65th Combat Tracker	New York, NY	02/23/1969	31W-7
Kimbrough, Golsby	20	35th Scout Dogs	Philadelphia, PA	07/06/1969	21W-70
King, Alexander	21	557th Combat Tracker	Woodbine, GA	01/20/1969	34W-42
Kobelin, John	24	40th Scout Dogs	Cheyenne, WY	03/06/1969	30W-56
Koon, George	20	Combat Tracker Team-2	Baltimore, MD	11/16/1967	30E-4
Kuefner, John	20	35th Scout Dogs	Duluth, MN	08/14/1969	19W-40
Kuehn, Lloyd	20	40th Scout Dogs	Stillwater, MN	03/09/1967	16E-46
Kunz, Anthony	21	Army Scout Dogs	Kerrville, TX	05/04/1967	19E-38
Lagodzinski, Roger	22	57th Scout Dogs	Buffalo, NY	05/19/1970	10W-65
Land, David	19	Marine Scout Dog	Panama City, FL	06/07/1967	21E-69
Lane, Richard	23	Army Scout Dogs	Fontana, CA	06/16/1968	56W-5
Lawton, Edward	19	75th Combat Tracker	Thermopolis, WV	09/27/1968	42W-30
Lebrun, Robert	21	Army Scout Dogs	Woonsocket, RI	03/22/1971	04W-68
Lee, Edward	20	44th Scout Dogs	Belmont, MA	05/13/1968	59E-25

Name	Age	Unit	Home	Died	Vietnam Memorial Panel
Levins, Frederick	23	76th Combat Tracker	Naples, FL	06/16/1970	09W-57
Lindholm, Dan	20	Army Scout Dogs	Lindsborg, KS	09/08/1968	44W-4
Lindsay, Stephen	23	Marine Scout Dogs	Shreveport, LA	01/24/1971	05W-63
Lipton, Joseph	18	Marine Scout Dog	Floral Park, NY	05/01/1967	19E-6
Lockhart, Harlan	23	35th Scout Dogs	Fredricktown, OH	11/09/1966	12E-48
Loftis, Joel	22	35th SPS– Air Force	La Marque, TX	06/07/1969	23W-104
London, Dennis	26	56th SPS– Air Force	Sparks, NV	05/13/1975	01W-127
Lovellette, Gary	23	45th Scout Dogs	Fergus Falls, MN	12/29/1969	15W-107
Lumsden, William	19	Combat Tracker Team-3	Compton, MD	05/21/1967	20E-77
Magruder, David	21	Army Scout Dogs	Utica, NY	05/16/1970	11W-52
Mahurin, Elmer	19	Combat Tracker Team-8	Goodman, MO	10/11/1967	27E-90
Mansfield, John	21	Army Scout Dogs	New York, NY	03/09/1967	16E-47
Marasco, Joseph	22	62nd Combat Tracker	Somers, NY	07/22/1969	20W-34
Marchant, Paul	22	Army Scout Dogs	Moline, IL	10/18/1969	17W-88
Markey Jr., James	23	63rd Combat Tracker	Warminster, PA	01/26/1971	05W-65
Marrufo Jr., Rodney	20	66th Combat Tracker	Stewarts Point, CA	05/23/1968	66E-11
Marshall, Clifford	21	43rd Scout Dogs	Richmond, KY	02/19/1971	05W-121

Name	Age	Unit	Home	Died	Vietnam Memorial Panel
Marshall, Mark	18	Marine Scout Dogs	South Euclid, OH	03/29/1969	28W-83
Martin, Kenneth	20	40th Scout Dogs	Kalamazoo, MI	03/05/1969	30W-47
Martinez, Juan	25	41st Scout Dogs	Pueblo, CO	05/05/1968	55E-22
Mason Jr., Benjamin	18	Marine Sentry Dog	Piscataway, NJ	09/04/1967	25E-104
Matel, Ronald	20	1st Combat Tracker Team	Duluth, MN	06/09/1969	22W-9
Mattson, Paul	23	59th Scout Dogs	Lake Bluff, IL	04/20/1968	51E-9
Maurer, Walter	20	Army Scout Dogs	Whittier, CA	11/01/1970	06W-33
May, Robert	20	34th Scout Dogs	Buffalo, NY	02/12/1968	39E-8
Mazzone, Joseph	23	Army Scout Dogs	Hicksville, NY	09/22/1968	43W-54
McCarty, Glenn	21	Army Scout Dogs	Texas City, TX	02/20/1971	05W-126
McFall, Gary	24	34th Scout Dogs	Northridge, CA	09/13/1968	44W-51
McGrath, Edward	20	43rd Scout Dogs	Crestview, FL	10/06/1967	27E-60
McIntosh, Donald	19	Army Scout Dogs	Hutchinson, KS	11/08/1970	06W-46
McLaughlin, James	23	Army Scout Dogs	Bangor, ME	04/16/1971	04W-129
Merschel, Lawrence	20	Army Scout Dogs	Wayne, PA	05/01/1968	53E-35
Meyer, Leo	20	61st Combat Tracker Team	Fond du Lac, WI	10/05/1968	41W-14
Michael, James	21	Army Scout Dogs	Gainesville, GA	02/13/1971	05W-101
Miller, Timmy	21	Marine Scout Dog	Stockton, KS	11/24/1968	38W-51

Name	Age	Unit	Home	Died	Vietnam Memorial Panel
Mills, Rodney	22	Army Scout Dogs	Alma, MI	05/05/1970	11W-104
Montano, William	19	Marine Scout Dogs	Deer Park, NY	11/19/1970	06W-71
Morrison, James	20	39th Scout Dogs	Grand Rapids, MI	02/02/1969	33W-42
Mugavin, Martin	20	48th Scout Dogs	Cincinnati, OH	02/23/1967	15E-80
Munch, Michael	20	57th Scout Dogs	Council Bluffs, IA	05/13/1969	25W-107
Munoz, Jose	19	1st Combat Tracker Team	Detroit, MI	12/07/1966	13E-19
Murray, Harry	20	1st Combat Tracker Team	Baltimore, MD	12/07/1966	13E-19
Myers, Richard	20	39th Scout Dogs	Glenmoore, PA	11/13/1967	29E-91
Newell, Tim	24	47th Scout Dogs	Des Moines, IA	09/09/1970	07W-49
Nicolini, Peter	21	44th Scout Dogs	Chicago, IL	05/16/1967	20E-9
Norris, Robert	18	42nd Scout Dogs	Towanda, PA	12/19/1969	15W-72
Nudenberg, David	24	63rd Combat Tracker	Caldwell, NJ	11/12/1970	06W-55
Nurzynski, Joseph	24	59th Scout Dogs	Buffalo, NY	05/12/1969	25W-79
Oaks, Robert	20	Army Scout Dogs	Lamesa, TX	11/11/1969	16W-59
Ohm, David	20	Army Scout Dogs	Alden, MN	07/20/1968	51W-20-
Olmstead, John	21	48th Scout Dogs	Warren, IL	07/15/1967	22E-077
Orsua, Charles	19	35th SPS-Air Force	Sunnyvale, CA	07/15/1969	20W-2
Palacio, Gilbert	21	34th Scout Dogs	San Antonio, TX	05/06/1969	25W-14

Name	Age	Unit	Home	Died	Vietnam Memorial Panel
Park, Irving	23	12th SPS – Air Force	Ft Wayne, IN	03/06/1970	13W–88
Parker Jr., Carter	23	Army Scout Dogs	Monroeville, AL	10/24/1970	06W–19
Parrish, Billy	32	Veterinarian	Tacoma, WA	05/23/1968	67E–1
Payne, Howard	24	59th Scout Dogs	Doraville, GA	04/27/1971	03W–15
Payne, Robert	24	Marine Scout Dog	Hampshire, IL	03/18/1968	45W–24
Payne, Terry	22	Army Scout Dogs	La Crosse, WI	08/05/1970	08W–85
Pearce, Marvin	19	47th Scout Dogs	Capitola, CA	08/25/1968	46W–19
Petersen, Harry	21	Army Scout Dogs	Salt Lake City, UT	11/09/1970	06W–48
Piasecki, John	22	Army Scout Dogs	Chicago, IL	11/29/1969	15W–7
Pierce, Oscar	23	40th Scout Dogs	Pauls Valley, OK	03/09/1967	16E–47
Plambeck Jr., Paul	22	39th Scout Dogs	Austin, TX	11/13/1969	16W–70
Plattner, Ernest	23	44th Scout Dogs	Marathon, NY	11/08/1968	39W–37
Poland Jr., Leon	20	Marine Scout Dog	West Paris, ME	03/26/1967	17E–54
Porter, Richard	21	Marine Mine/Booby Trap	Hanover, NH	01/24/1971	05W–64
Pretter, Thomas	20	38th Scout Dogs	New York, NY	06/08/1967	21E–76
Pulaski Jr., Peter	23	42nd Scout Dogs	Howard Beach, NY	01/04/1970	15W–126
Quinn, Thomas	21	45th Scout Dogs	Minneapolis, MN	04/04/1969	27W–12
Randolph, Michael	20	1st Combat Tracker Team	Cumberland, MD	03/29/1970	12W–58

Name	Age	Unit	Home	Died	Vietnam Memorial Panel
Rathbun, Gary	27	42nd Scout Dogs	Cosmos, MN	05/25/1967	
Ratliff, Billy	20	76th Combat Tracker	Pomeroyton, KY	09/24/1970	07W-87
Ray, William	21	58th Scout Dogs	De Mossville, KY	07/04/1970	09W-119
Rhodes, Robert	19	Marine Scout Dog	Scituate, MA	05/27/1970	10W-110
Rivera, James	20	62nd Combat Tracker	New York, NY	03/09/1968	43E-69
Roberts, Virgil	21	557th Combat Tracker	Aztec, NM	01/22/1969	34W-61
Robinson, Charles	21	49th Scout Dogs	Easthampton, MA	01/07/1969	35W-51
Rosas, Jose	27	Marine Scout Dog	Weslaco, TX	05/08/1967	19E-65
Roth, John	21	50th Scout Dogs	River Rouge, MI	03/09/1967	16E-48
Rowe, Michael	20	Army Scout	Statesboro, GA	02/19/1969	32W-63
Sandberg, Charles	30	44th Scout Dogs	Philadelphia	05/13/1968	60E-2
Schachner, David	20	40th Scout Dogs	Charlotte, NC	05/14/1969	24W-11
Schmid, Robert	23	44th Scout Dogs	Hartsdale, NY	08/16/1966	10E-13
Schossow, Dennis	21	Marine Mine/ Booby Trap	Sheldon, ND	01/22/1971	05W-61
Schwab, Richard	21	57th Scout Dogs	Medford, OR	09/06/1970	07W-42
Schyska, Leroy	18	46th Scout Dogs	Moline, IL	12/06/1967	31E-54
Scott, Dave	21	Army Scout Dogs	Junction City, KS	01/24/1968	35E-27

Name	Age	Unit	Home	Died	Vietnam Memorial Panel
Segundo, Pete	22	Marine Scout Dogs	Oceano, CA	09/05/1969	18W-42
Selix, James	24	47th Scout Dogs	Colorado Springs, CO	10/30/1971	02W-56
Severson, Paul	23	Army Scout Dogs	Glenwood, IL	08/25/1968	46W-22
Sheldon, William	19	Navy Sentry Dogs	Chicago, IL	05/05/1968	55E-31
Shelton, Bobby	23	38th Scout Dogs	Flag Pond, TN	09/29/1967	27E31
Shepard, Raymond	24	Marine Scout Dogs	Chicago, IL	08/03/1966	09E-104
Sheppard, Ronald	22	49th Scout Dogs	Webster Groves, MO	09/20/1968	43W-50
Simpson, Edward	19	45th Scout Dogs	Collinsville, IL	05/11/1968	58E-26
Sims, William	21	60th Mine/Booby Trap	Compton, AR	07/16/1969	20W-8
Smith, Gary	21	39th Scout Dogs	Santa Ana, CA	02/27/1967	15E-109
Smith, Michael	19	59th Scout Dogs	Omaha, NE	04/28/1968	52E-44
Smith, Ronald	20	Veterinarian-Army	Dearborn, MI	03/03/1967	16E-14
Smith, Stephen	22	Army Scout Dogs	Convoy, OH	06/21/1970	09W-76
Smith, Winfred	22	Army Scout Dogs	Greenville, VA	06/08/1970	09W-30
Smoot, Robert	19	557th Combat Tracker	Sacramento, CA	01/05/1968	33E-54
Soto, Concepcion	20	25th Scout Dogs	New York, NY	05/06/1969	25W-15
Southwick, John	19	Marine Scout Dogs	Spokane, WA	10/19/1969	17W-91

Name	Age	Unit	Home	Died	Vietnam Memorial Panel
Spangler, Max	19	45th Scout Dogs	Dallas,TX	01/12/1968	34E-39
Spencer Jr., Daniel	23	Army Scout Dogs	Bend, OR	11/12/1968	39W-57
Steptoe, Raymond	20	35th Scout Dogs	Navasota, TX	08/15/1966	10E-11
Sturdy, Alan	22	41st Scout Dogs	Redwood City, CA	07/02/1967	22E-116
Sullivan, Donald	22	40TH Scout Dogs	Princeton, NC	01/29/1967	14E-96
Sullivan, Jeremiah	21	38th Scout Dogs	Ardmore, PA	10/23/1967	28E-55
Sunday, James	22	43rd Scout Dogs	Garfield Heights, OH	09/29/1967	27E-32
Sweat Jr., Herbert	20	34th Scout Dogs	Palatka, FL	02/21/1969	32W-74
Sweatt, Theodore	22	25th Scout Dogs	Terre Haute, IN	11/27/1968	30W 79
Tallman, George	21	Army Scout Dogs	Huntington Beach, CA	04/09/1967	18E-7
Taranto, Robert	21	57th Scout Dogs	New York, NY	11/29/1968	37W-8
Taylor, Mark	20	44th Scout Dogs	Chesterton, IN	06/02/1971	03W-62
Teresinski, Joseph	20	557th Combat Tracker	Oneida. WI	02/06/1971	05W-82
Thibodeaux, Michael	19	Army Scout Dogs	Crowley, LA	07/19/1970	08W-32
Tosh III, James	23	25th Scout Dogs	Mobile, AL	08/21/1969	19W-89
Triplett, James	22	Marine Scout Dogs	Orlando, FL	04/17/1969	27W-104
Truesdell, John	21	Army Scout Dogs	Enid, OK	03/20/1971	04W-62

Name	Age	Unit	Home	Died	Vietnam Memorial Panel
Van Gorder, William	20	57th Scout Dogs	Markham, IL	06/21/1968	55W-16
Vancosky, Michael	19	Marine Scout Dog	Scranton, PA	05/04/1970	11W-98
Vogelpohl, Rex	21	57th Scout Dogs	Butler, IN	01/11/1971	05W-41
Waddell, Larry	20	Army Scout Dogs	Richmond, OH	03/09/1967	16E-49
Ward, Danny	21	43rd Scout Dogs	Downey, CA	06/01/1968	61W-8
Ward, David	20	981st MP Dogs	Las Vegas, NV	07/04/1968	53W-14
Webb, Howard	24	42nd Scout Dogs	Rehoboth, DE	06/08/1967	21E-77
Whetham, Vernon	25	43rd Scout Dogs	Glasgow, MT	11/30/1967	31E-19
White, Garson	21	Marine Scout Dogs	Sontag, MS	02/13/1969	32W-30
White, John	21	57th Scout Dogs	Saraland, AL	01/22/1968	35E-12
Whitehead, Alfred	25	44th Scout Dogs	Harlan, KY	06/16/1968	56W-11
Whitten, Robert	21	Army Scout Dogs	Ft Myers, FL	05/08/1968	57E-12
Wickenberg, Erik	20	43rd Scout Dogs	Bertha, MN	07/06/1967	22E-024
Winningham, Richard	20	Army Scout Dogs	Battle Creek, MI	01/07/1969	35W-49
Wood, Robert	21	Marine Scout Dog	Ft. Benning, GA	04/09/1968	49E-7
Yeager, Michael	19	Marine Mine & Booby	Baltimore, MD	04/08/1970	12W-10
Yochum, Lawrence	19	59th Scout Dogs	Burney, CA	02/13/1970	13W-5
Young, Jon	22	43rd Scout Dogs	San Luis Obispo, CA	04/04/1968	48E-14

Vietnam War Dogs Killed in Action

*List Courtesy of the Vietnam Dog Handler Association
(www.vdhaonline.org)*

48th Infantry Platoon Scout Dogs (IPSD), U. S. Army, South Vietnam. The cemeteries were maintained as hallowed ground by the handlers. (Photo courtesy of Richard Claggett, Vietnam Veteran Scout Dog Handler. This was his unit's cemetery.

War Dog	Ear Tattoo	Died	Unit	U.S. Service
Alex	OK64	09/16/69	47th Scout Dogs	Army
Alf	KO88	11/23/70	48th Scout Dogs	Army
Amigo	043A	03/10/70	48th Scout Dogs	Army
Andy	5A48	01/09/70	50th Scout Dogs	Army
Arko	KO94	12/12/68	45th Scout Dogs	Army
Arras	KO72	01/12/68	45th Scout Dogs	Army
Arras	KO15	11/27/70	57th Scout Dogs	Army
Artus	KO12	12/11/70	42nd Scout Dogs	Army
Astor	KO92	11/10/70	39th Scout Dogs	Army
Axel	KO59	03/31/70	58th Scout Dogs	Army
Axel	84A6	01/29/71	39th Scout Dogs	Army
Bark	5A35	06/16/67	42nd Scout Dogs	Army
Baron	OX81	02/23/67	25th Scout Dogs	Army
Baron	53X9	04/07/69	39th Scout Dogs	Army
Bizz	16M6	03/21/69	47th Scout Dogs	Army
Black Jack	498M	09/23/71	48th Scout Dogs	Army
Blackie	3A33	12/07/67	25th Scout Dogs	Army
Blackie	03X7	03/21/69	49th Scout Dogs	Army
Blackie	38A3	09/09/70	47th Scout Dogs	Army
Blitz	X239	10/04/67	43rd Scout Dogs	Army
Bo-Bear	025M	11/12/68	58th Scout Dogs	Army
Bobo	7M25	07/24/69	40th Scout Dogs	Army
Bobo	66A5	12/26/70	43rd Scout Dogs	Army
Bootsy	9X64	09/19/67	48th Scout Dogs	Army
Bozo	9X40	09/12/67	377th SPS – SentryDog	Air Force
Brandy	323M	06/25/71	42nd Scout Dogs	Army
Britta	OX47	11/27/68	25th Scout Dogs	Army
Bruno	26X8	07/16/67	48th Scout Dogs	Army
Bruno	8M05	01/30/69	35th Scout Dogs	Army
Brutus	46M2	03/17/69	43rd Scout Dogs	Army

War Dog	Ear Tattoo	Died	Unit	U.S. Service
Buck	61X2	11/24/68	47th Scout Dogs	Army
Buck	7X74	06/02/70	Marine Scout Dogs	Marine Corps
Buck	UNK	09/01/71	58th Scout Dogs	Army
Buckshot	23X9	05/13/68	44th Scout Dogs	Army
Buddy	80X5	12/15/68	43rd Scout Dogs	Army
Buddy	6M61	09/02/70	59th Scout Dogs	Army
Buddy	898M	11/12/70	48th Scout Dogs	Army
Butch	6M36	11/08/70	38th Scout Dogs	Army
Caesar	3A55	05/19/68	38th Scout Dogs	Army
Caesar	5X56	03/04/68	39th Scout Dogs	Army
Caesar	07A2	04/10/70	50th Scout Dogs	Army
Cap	4K87	06/27/71	34th Scout Dogs	Army
Chase	98X6	08/20/68	57th Scout Dogs	Army
Chief	3M42	12/09/69	57th Scout Dogs	Army
Chooch	06M3	04/24/70	48th Scout Dogs	Army
Claus	K024	06/18/69	40th Scout Dogs	Army
Clipper	12X3	Unknown	44th Scout Dogs	Army
Colonel	1A96	03/01/71	981st MP–Sentry Dogs	Army
Commander	X482	04/26/69	41st Scout Dogs	Army
Cookie	41X5	09/28/68	50th Scout Dogs	Army
Country Joe	7K31	01/23/71	Mine&Booby Trap Dogs	Marines
Cracker	60X1	08/19/68	49th Scout Dogs	Army
Crazy Joe	X134	02/13/70	Marine Scout Dogs	Marine Corps
Crypto	8M63	02/23/69	45th Scout Dogs	Army
Cubby	612E	12/04/66	3rd SPS– Sentry Dog	Air Force
Danny	21M2	04/29/70	42nd Scout Dogs	Army
Deno	7M28	05/22/69	41st Scout Dogs	Army
Devil	Unknown	Unknown	Marine Scout Dogs	Marines
Diablo	X313	01/31/68	3rd SPS–Sentry Dogs	Air Force
Dix	M064	02/15/70	57th Scout Dogs	Army

War Dog	Ear Tattoo	Died	Unit	U.S. Service
Dug	112M	06/01/71	47th Scout Dogs	Army
Duke	9X60	01/15/67	41st Scout Dogs	Army
Duke	3A15	06/13/68	25th Scout Dogs	Army
Duke	5A23	04/07/68	35th Scout Dogs	Army
Duke	383M	12/06/69	57th Scout Dogs	Army
Duke	409M	02/23/69	49th Scout Dogs	Army
Duke	230M	03/24/70	57th Scout Dogs	Army
Duke	461A	06/03/70	48th Scout Dogs	Army
Duke	84A2	01/21/72	3rd SPS– Sentry Dogs	Air Force
Dusty	724M	07/28/70	37th Scout Dogs	Army
Dusty	62M6	04/27/71	58th Scout Dogs	Army
Dusty	23M8	10/17/71	48th Scout Dogs	Army
Dutchess	0565X	08/01/70	981st MP–Sentry Dogs	Army
Egor	751M	06/23/69	41st Scout Dogs	Army
Erich	3M92	01/18/70	35th Scout Dogs	Army
Erik	36X3	11/09/67	44th Scout Dogs	Army
Fant	K027	10/28/70	47th Scout Dogs	Army
Flare	X272	07/26/69	42nd Scout Dogs	Army
Frico	0H57	01/13/67	41st Scout Dogs	Army
Fritz	2M97	11/07/68	57th Scout Dogs	Army
Fritz	X740	10/18/68	57th Scout Dogs	Army
Fritz	4M69	10/15/69	47th Scout Dogs	Army
Fritz	999F	02/28/69	12th SPS–Sentry Dogs	Air Force
Fritz	M275	10/06/69	Marine Scout Dogs	Marine Corps
Fritzie	763F	01/26/69	35th SPS–Sentry Dogs	Air Force
Gar	789M	03/09/70	37th Scout Dogs	Army
Gretchen	3M32	11/18/68	44th Scout Dogs	Army
Gretchen	265A	090/3/70	39th Scout Dogs	Army
Gretchen	40X7	05/29/70	42nd Scout Dogs	Army
Gunder	1X07	08/13/67	34th Scout Dogs	Army

War Dog	Ear Tattoo	Died	Unit	U.S. Service
Hanno	0H03	02/16/67	33rd Scout Dogs	Army
Hasso	0K55	06/18/69	41st Scout Dogs	Army
Hector	X459	05/14/69	40th Scout Dogs	Army
Heidi	18A6	10/31/70	58th Scout Dogs	Army
Heidi	Unknown	09/01/70	Mine & Booby Trap Dogs	Marine Corps
Heidi	T031	11/12/70	63rd Combat Trackers	Army
Heidi	Unknown	02/19/71	43rd Scout Dogs	Army
Heidi	X017	04/23/71	57th Scout Dogs	Army
Hunde	M145	02/28/68	3rd SPS- Sentry Dogs	Air Force
Ikar	X682	07/02/69	40th Scout Dogs	Army
Jack	130M	10/18/68	57th Scout Dogs	Army
Jack	7X18	12/17/69	34th Scout Dogs	Army
Joe	6B54	06/15/70	45th Scout Dogs	Army
Kaizer	6M91	01/18/69	Combat Tracker Team- ?	Army
Kat	00M3	04/30/70	48th Scout Dogs	Army
Kazan	7X51	06/15/68	57th Scout Dogs	Army
Keenchie	14X7	12/10/67	34th Scout Dogs	Army
Kelley	14X7	12/10/67	34th Scout Dogs	Army
Kelly	Unknown	05/18/70	34th Scout Dogs	Army
King	0K87	07/01/68	43rd Scout Dogs	Army
King	334X	02/10/68	981st MP-Sentry Dogs	Army
King	49X0	07/04/68	57th Scout Dogs	Army
King	58X3	12/23/68	41st Scout Dogs	Army
King	66X5	01/10/68	43rd Scout Dogs	Army
King	8X87	09/13/68	34th Scout Dogs	Army
King	245M	03/20/69	33rd Scout Dogs	Army
King	81M5	08/14/69	37th Scout Dogs	Army
King	8M51	05/18/69	49th Scout Dogs	Army
King	9A18	11/13/69	39th Scout Dogs	Army

War Dog	Ear Tattoo	Died	Unit	U.S. Service
King	07M6	05/19/70	42nd Scout Dogs	Army
King	2A15	02/16/70	48th Scout Dogs	Army
King	7A65	02/13/70	59th Scout Dogs	Army
King	A642	01/13/70	8th SPS-Sentry Dogs	Air Force
King	X200	04/08/70	39th Scout Dogs	Army
King	72M4	06/28/71	47th Scout Dogs	Army
Krieger	65M8	06/02/71	42nd Scout Dogs	Army
Kurt	6A92	06/22/68	34th Scout Dogs	Army
Lance	82A6	01/26/71	42nd Scout Dogs	Army
Lightning	0M40	05/11/70	981st MP- Sentry Dogs	Army
Little Joe	223M	02/22/70	47th Scout Dogs	Army
Lobo	58M4	02/15/69	43rd Scout Dogs	Army
Lodo	729M	06/25/70	37th Scout Dogs	Army
Lucky	2X37	10/17/66	44th Scout Dogs	Army
Lucky	7K37	09/01/70	Mine & Booby Trap Dogs	Marine Corps
Ludwick	1X74	08/22/66	377th SPS- Sentry Dog	Air Force
Lux	0K29	08/19/68	43rd Scout Dogs	Army
Machen	2X99	03/31/68	39th Scout Dogs	Army
Max	8X18	06/04/70	42nd Scout Dogs	Army
Mesa	103M	08/24/69	49th Scout Dogs	Army
Mike	4X64	07/02/67	41st Scout Dogs	Army
Mike	760M	11/10/69	57th Scout Dogs	Army
Ming	X528	05/11/68	45th Scout Dogs	Army
Mister	3M13	06/01/70	58th Scout Dogs	Army
Money	32X3	01/24/69	50th Scout Dogs	Army
Notzey	X405	04/25/70	33rd Scout Dogs	Army
Paper	684M	06/26/69	42nd Scout Dogs	Army
Penny	9M96	10/05/70	34th Scout Dogs	Army
Pirate	8X71	12/02/68	34th Scout Dogs	Army
Prince	182X	12/09/65	3rd SPS- Sentry Dog	Air Force

War Dog	Ear Tattoo	Died	Unit	U.S. Service
Prince	30X7	03/02/67	48th Scout Dogs	Army
Prince	43X3	09/02/67	44th Scout Dogs	Army
Prince	703M	03/15/69	37th Scout Dogs	Army
Prince	271M	06/12/70	37th Scout Dogs	Army
Prince	288A	10/26/70	981st MP–Sentry Dogs	Army
Prince	74X1	01/30/71	47th Scout Dogs	Army
Prince	9A38	07/27/69	Marine Scout Dogs	Marine Corps
Princess	1M20	04/13/69	47th Scout Dogs	Army
Princess	45X9	02/02/69	39th Scout Dogs	Army
Princess	49A1	08/03/69	39th Scout Dogs	Army
Princess	764M	04/19/70	39th Scout Dogs	Army
Ranger	787M	03/16/69	37th Scout Dogs	Army
Reb	21X8	02/23/67	48th Scout Dogs	Army
Rebel	Unknown	12/04/66	377th SPS– Sentry Dog	Air Force
Rebel	X202	07/19/69	47th Scout Dogs	Army
Rebel	94A3	03/08/70	50th Scout Dogs	Army
Reggie	3A57	03/10/68	981st MP–Sentry Dogs	Army
Rennie	7K34	09/01/70	Mine & Booby Trap Dogs	Marine Corps
Renny	A548	01/11/68	35th SPS– Sentry Dogs	Air Force
Rex	8X60	05/25/67	33rd Scout Dogs	Army
Rex	OK11	02/07/68	43rd Scout Dogs	Army
Rex	4A85	05/04/68	40th Scout Dogs	Army
Rex	X306	02/07/68	43rd Scout Dogs	Army
Rex	5A77	02/22/69	35th SPS–Sentry Dogs	Air Force
Rex	83X4	03/06/70	48th Scout Dogs	Army
Rex	93M9	05/29/70	34th Scout Dogs	Army
Rinny	185E	07/04/68	212th MP– Sentry Dogs	Army
Rolf	KO86	06/17/70	42nd Scout Dogs	Army
Rommell	52X6	06/10/70	50th Scout Dogs	Army
Rover	M075	09/07/68	57th Scout Dogs	Army

War Dog	Ear Tattoo	Died	Unit	U.S. Service
Rover	475A	09/19/70	33rd Scout Dogs	Army
Royal	19X8	09/10/70	48th Scout Dogs	Army
Rusty	6A97	08/30/69	42nd Scout Dogs	Army
Sam	544M	05/06/70	57th Scout Dogs	Army
Sam	5A84	09/24/70	62nd Combat Tracker Team	Army
Sam	66A7	12/16/70	635th SPS – Sentry Dogs	Air Force
Sarge	292M	10/29/69	34th Scout Dogs	Army
Sarge	934M	01/12/71	57th Scout Dogs	Army
Sargent	6X81	11/27/67	44th Scout Dogs	Army
Satch	M–164	01/31/68	212th MP–Sentry Dogs	Army
Savage	M263	09/28/68	49th Scout Dogs	Army
Sgt. Bilko	8X00	10/25/68	Unknown	Army
Shack	9X28	01/28/69	Marine Scout Dogs	Marine Corps
Shadow	9X00	11/09/67	44th Scout Dogs	Army
Shadow	X622	05/27/70	Scout Dogs	Army
Shane	711M	02/18/69	Scout Dogs	Army
Sheba	7X54	08/27/71	48th Scout Dogs	Army
Shep	48X8	01/24/69	50th Scout Dogs	Army
Shep	69A3	01/29/70	47th Scout Dogs	Army
Sheps	8X63	01/13/67	41st Scout Dogs	Army
Silber	1M57	11/27/68	35th Scout Dogs	Army
Silver	X101	07/24/68	59th Scout Dogs	Army
Sissy	441A	01/26/71	43rd Scout Dogs	Army
Skipper	288M	07/25/70	50th Scout Dogs	Army
Smokey	1A82	09/18/66	25th Scout Dogs	Army
Smokey	X121	06/01/68	43rd Scout Dogs	Army
Smokey	36M0	05/13/69	57th Scout Dogs	Army
Smokey	X817	01/27/69	57th Scout Dogs	Army
Smokey	7M50	04/26/70	47th Scout Dogs	Army
Spade	3A43	12/17/68	Marine Sentry Dogs	Marine Corps

War Dog	Ear Tattoo	Died	Unit	U.S. Service
Spike	M004	03/01/71	981st MP–Sentry Dogs	Army
Storm	01M3	04/23/69	39th Scout Dogs	Army
Stormy	476M	Unknown	Marine Scout Dogs	Marines
Suesser	OK81	01/21/68	42nd Scout Dogs	Army
Taro	287M	08/30/71	59th Scout Dogs	Army
Tasso	OK40	05/26/70	25th Scout Dogs	Army
Tempo	50A7	12/02/70	48th Scout Dogs	Army
Teneg	T012	03/12/70	62nd Combat Tracker Team	Army
Thor	335A	06/03/70	42nd Scout Dogs	Army
Thor	326M	04/09/71	63rd Combat Tracker Team	Army
Thunder	4A45	05/15/68	42nd Scout Dogs	Army
Tiger	3A17	08/09/66	25th Scout Dogs	Army
Tiger	3M78	08/14/70	57th Scout Dogs	Army
Tim	19X2	09/11/68	44th Scout Dogs	Army
Timber	Unknown	Unknown	44th Scout Dogs	Army
Toby	Unknown	12/04/66	377th SPS– Sentry Dog	Air Force
Toby	T036	01/25/70	63rd Combat Tracker Team	Army
Troubles	1X16	12/30/67	25th Scout Dogs	Army
Tye	341M	09/29/70	42nd Scout Dogs	Army
Willie	6M11	07/27/68	47th Scout Dogs	Army
Wolf	150X	05/22/68	Marine Scout Dogs	Marine Corps
Wolf	OK43	01/07/69	49th Scout Dogs	Army
Wolf	7X03	02/26/71	33rd Scout Dogs	Army
Ziggy	2M78	04/10/69	41st Scout Dogs	Army

Military Acronyms

Acronym	Definition	Acronym	Definition
AK-47	Enemy military rifle	PFC	Private First Class (E-3)
APC	Armored personnel carrier	PSP	Perforated steel plating
CAR-15	American military rifle	Punji	Bamboo spear
CG	Commanding general	PX	Post Exchange
Charlie	Enemy	RA	Regular army volunteer
CIB	Combat Infantry Badge	REMF	Rear-echelon motherfucker
CO	Commanding officer	RPG	Enemy rocket-propelled grenade
C-Rations	Canned food	RTO	Radiotelephone operator
Dogman	Dog handler	RVN	Republic of Vietnam
FNG	Fucking new guy	S&D	Search & destroy
Gook	Enemy	S2	Military Intelligence
KIA	Killed in action	SGM	Sergeant Major (E-9)
LZ	Landing zone	SOI	Signal operating instructions
M-16	American military rifle	TET	Chinese lunar New Year
M-60	American machine gun	Top	First Sergeant (E-8)
M79	American grenade launcher	US	Draftee
MOS	Military occupational specialty	USWD	United States War Dogs, Inc. (www.uswardogs.com)
MP	Military police	VC	Vietcong
NWDM	National War Dog Team Memorial (www.nationalwardogsmonument.org)	VDHA	Vietnam Dog Handler Association (www.vdhaonline.org)
NCO	Noncommissioned officer	WIA	Wounded in action
NVA	North Vietnamese Army		
OCS	Officer Candidate School		
OD	Olive Drab		
P38	C-Ration Can Opener		